PITCHING UP IN STYLE!

Deborah Aubrey

Copyright © 2022 Deborah Aubrey

All rights reserved

The characters and events portrayed in this book are fictitious. Any similarity to real persons, living or dead, is coincidental and not intended by the author [JA23].

No part of this book may be reproduced, or stored in a retrieval system, or transmitted in any form or by any means, electronic, mechanical, photocopying, recording, or otherwise, without express written permission of the publisher.

ISBN-13: 9798359942409
ISBN-10: 1477123456

Cover design by: Art Painter
Library of Congress Control Number: 2018675309
Printed in the United States of America

DEDICATION

For Uncle Pete x

CHAPTER ONE

With his heart pounding fiercely in his chest, Tel knocked on the door of the CEO's office, his palms sweating, his innards quivering like electrified blancmange. He was about to ask Sophie's father for his daughter's hand in marriage. It seemed old-fashioned, but it also seemed like the right thing to do.

"What can I do for you today, Tel?" When John looked up from the papers on his desk he added, "Oh, from the look of abject terror on your face I think I can guess."

Tel stood in front of him, more nervous than he'd ever felt in his life. He gulped. His mouth was dry, his tongue sticking to the roof of his mouth. He clutched his hands together in front of him to stop them from shaking. "I … I would very much like your permission to ask Sophie to be my wife."

"Indeed." John put down his pen and indicated the chair opposite. Tel slowly and nervously sat down. "Do you think you're good enough for my daughter?" he asked.

"Frankly … no, I'm not. No one is."

"Good answer, and that knowledge will keep you on your toes, as Sophie's mother is always quick to point out. Marrying Camille is what made me the man I am today, because she believed in me, just as Sophie believes in you." John leaned back in his leather chair, steepling his fingers together under his chin. "I know you're ambitious, Tel, but be aware that marrying a partner at Forbes & Avery does not guarantee you a quick launch up the corporate ladder. Nepotism is not tolerated at this company, you'll have to earn it for yourself, as Sophie did, and you'll probably have to work twice as hard for it, as Sophie did. In fact, it may prove to be a disadvantage should you choose to work at another legal firm at any point in the future, since being the husband of a partner who is the CEO's daughter will not be viewed favourably."

"I understand, sir."

John stood up and came around his desk, saying, "You're a fine man, Tel, I admire your work ethic and I see the way you are with Sophie. I'm more than pleased to give you my blessing." Tel stood up, beaming with relief, as John held out a hand and shook his firmly. "I will warn you, though," he added, going back to his seat, "Hurt her in any way and I'll hurt you."

"I understand, sir."

John peered at him beneath his bushy eyebrows. "That's not an idle threat."

"No, sir."

"Sophie is very precious to us, our only daughter. Make her happy."

"I will, sir."

John smiled. "Good. I won't mention this to Camille, she'll either spontaneously combust with excitement or send out invites to each member of the royal family. Do you have anything special planned for the proposal?"

"I do."

"I look forward to hearing all about it. Good luck."

"Thank you, sir."

* * *

It was two weeks later when Tel jumped out of an airplane at 15,000 feet and made his first, failed, attempt to propose to Sophie as they plummeted to earth with men strapped to their backs. Thankfully, he survived and was able to make a second proposal surrounded by the campers they now called their friends, and, even more thankfully, she accepted.

An excited Sophie called her mother from the campsite the same day to give her the news. Camille became so high-pitched with excitement that Sophie thought only dogs could hear her. It was only when they returned home that they began to realise the enormity of what they had unleashed, when her mother arrived at the flat burdened with pamphlets, leaflets, and a scrapbook of wedding pictures she'd been collecting since Sophie was twelve years old. Sophie gawped at it in horror.

"The venue is the first thing we need to book," Camille said, spreading the paraphernalia across their dining room table. "Get in first and get the best." She turned to a page in the scrapbook that had 'Wedding Venues' printed in neat writing at the top. "I've already called Westminster Abbey."

"You've done *what?*" Sophie cried, "Westminster Abbey? Are you serious?"

"Organising a wedding is a very serious matter, darling. Sadly, they informed me that, unless we were members of the royal family or actually lived within its precinct, we were not eligible, and your father adamantly refuses to move house. So, I called Canongate Kirk in Edinburgh–"

"Edinburgh!"

"–where Princess Anne's daughter and that lovely Mike Tindall got married, but I'm not sure if it would be big enough–"

"Big enough!"

"–and your father said it was too far away anyway."

"I don't want to get married in Scotland!" Sophie cried.

"I scoured the internet and went and looked at Sumsuch House near Epson while you were away; beautiful place, perfect location, absolutely ideal for a big wedding."

"But we don't want–"

"I booked it for July next year, that should give us enough time to–"

"You booked it?" Sophie's eyebrows knitted together as she glared at her mother with wide, disbelieving eyes.

"Booked what?" Tel said, coming through from the kitchen. He lingered at the table for the briefest second, before noticing Sophie's face and going back – it sounded like women's talk and he didn't want to get sucked in.

"We haven't even *talked* about setting a date yet," Sophie snapped.

"July is a lovely time to get married, darling, and long engagements are so passé these days. You have to be quick about these things."

"I'm sorry, mum, but you'll have to unbook it."

"It's non-refundable."

"How much deposit did you put down?"

"Deposit? No, I paid the full amount. It's my contribution to the wedding, my little gift to you."

"Mum!"

"What?"

"You're taking over!" Sophie huffed and threw her arms up in the air. "I *knew* you'd do this, I *knew* you'd take control. It's *my* wedding, mum, *I* get to choose what I want for my *own wedding*."

"I'm just helping out, darling, wedding arrangements are so very tricky and time-sensitive. You're my only child, Sophie, allow me to indulge myself a little."

"I might not want to get married next July."

"When then? I can ring and rearrange."

"I don't know! We haven't thought that far ahead yet, we've only *just* got engaged!"

"Well, I want grandchildren before I'm too old to enjoy them."

"*Mum!*"

Tel came out of the kitchen and placed a glass of wine in each of their hands. Sophie angrily gulped at hers as her mother started talking about the minutiae of nuptial arrangements.

She never stopped.

"What do you think about tying the knot in twelve months' time?" Sophie whispered to Tel, after her mum had finally run out of steam and left.

He planted a kiss on her cute nose and whispered, "The

sooner the better, as far as I'm concerned."

She sighed. "Next July it is, then."

* * *

When Tel called his parents to tell them the good news, his dad – a local businessman of few words, who epitomised John Wayne's mantra, 'Talk low, talk slow, and don't talk too much' – said, "Do we have to … pay anything … towards it?"

"No, dad, it's usually the bride's family who pays, but we're financing it ourselves."

"Good. Well done. She's way out of … your league."

"Yes, thanks, dad."

His mother – to whom silence was an anathema and who firmly embraced the mantra, 'Talk high, talk fast, and talk as much as you can' – said quite a lot, quite quickly, ending 20 minutes later with, "I can get a staff discount at work for your reception buffet, they do some fabulous samosas on the delicatessen counter."

"Thanks, mum, but I think we'll probably have caterers."

"Oooh," she sang, "Get you with your caterers!"

"Lots of people use caterers, mum."

"Your nan is the fastest sandwich maker in Hackney, did you know that? People used to come from miles away for her fish paste and cucumber sarnies."

"We'll bear that in mind."

"I can get Beryl three doors down to make you a cake, if you'd like? She's very good, makes flowers out of icing, you'd think they were real."

"I think Sophie is picking the cake and everything. My job is just to nod or shake my head at her choices."

"They charge a lot though, don't they, these professional cake makers. There's a series about it on telly and, oh my God, you would not believe how much they charge for a vanilla sponge and a bit of fondant icing. Anyway, well done, my boy, I couldn't have chosen better for you m'self, she's a gorgeous girl and we love her to bits. I think you'll both be very happy."

"Thanks, mum."

* * *

Tel arranged a Zoom meeting with the camping gang a week later. None of them knew what it was about but they all suspected and felt very excited in a contained sort of way. They appeared on the screen in pairs – Brian and Faye, Mark and Olivia – except for Jim, who came in late saying that Beth was visiting her dad in London. He spent the first few minutes skimming through the face filters; pumpkin, alien, banana man, Viking helmet and beard.

"Pick one!" Brian bawled, "Before I have an epileptic fit!"

Jim finally settled on an underground potato – or buried fecal matter, they couldn't be sure – and smiled eerily at the screen.

"I think it's an improvement," Mark said.

"Shut your face," said the potato.

"Come on then, you two," Brian said, grinning beneath his beard, "Tell us what you wanted to tell us and put us out of our expectant misery."

Tel and Sophie looked at each other, then back at the screen. "We've set a date for the wedding," Sophie said with a huge smile.

They all cheered.

"Mid-July next year, so put it in your diaries."

"Us plebs don't have *diaries*," Faye laughed, "We have calendars."

"Oh, I have a diary," Olivia frowned.

"That's because you're not a pleb," Mark said, "You're a bit of posh totty."

The potato started singing about wanting to live like common people.

"Shut up, spud head."

"Will it be in London?" Faye asked.

"Just south of the city, at a place called Sumsuch House near Epsom."

They all made suitably impressed noises.

"The hotel rooms are a bit expensive though," Tel winced.

"How expensive?" Brian asked.

Tel told him and a shocked hole appeared in the middle of Brian's beard.

"But we thought..." Tel gave a big grin to camera. "...that it would be much more fun to ... bring the caravans!"

"There's a lovely campsite less than three miles away," Sophie added.

"Yay!" Olivia cried, "I love camping."

"Do you?" Mark said in mock surprise, "I'd never have guessed, what with you running a campsite and owning a motorhome and everything."

Olivia giggled.

"Some of our other guests would prefer the cheaper option too, so we've booked some static caravans and pitches in a secluded portion of the campsite for everyone."

"Excellent idea," Brian said.

"Oh, it's so exciting!" Faye cried, clapping her hands together. "I'll need a new dress, and a hat. Do the ladies still wear hats at weddings or is it more those little fascination things?"

"Wear whatever you want," said Sophie.

"I have a sombrero," the potato said.

"Yeah, wear a sombrero," Mark said, "You and everyone around you won't get to see the wedding but you'll be safe from sunstroke."

"Really?"

"No, mash mush."

"We'll email you all the details."

* * *

Early July the following year
Wednesday – 17 days until the wedding

Tel was on the sofa, eating a bowl of cereal in front of early evening television, when Sophie burst through the door of their apartment. He could sense her pulsating stress pour into the lounge long before she appeared. She was carrying several bags and awkwardly holding her phone up to her ear.

"No, mum, we can't add any extra people to our guest list, we have more than enough already. Who are they, anyway?" She raised her eyebrows at Tel, miming a silent scream. "Who? Second cousins? Have I even met them? Then why do I want them at my wedding?"

Sophie dropped the bags on the floor and threw herself down on the sofa next to him, sighing heavily. "Mum, can you stop searching for long-lost relatives on that genealogy website, I don't want any more guests!" She slumped back, clearly exhausted following an after-work shopping spree. Tel leaned over and planted a kiss on her forehead. "Not first cousins either, mum! I have to go, Tel's … made dinner."

She hung up, snatched the bowl of cereal from his hands and started spooning it into her mouth. "Not eaten all bloody day," she munched. "Bloody starving!"

"Why haven't you eaten all day?"

"Too busy. Breakfast meeting only had Danish pastries and croissants, which of course I can't touch because I'm on a diet."

"You don't need to be on a diet, Soph, you're perfect as you–"

"I do if I want to fit into the dress."

"Why didn't you get a dress in your size?"

Sophie stopped chomping. "I'm not walking down the aisle in a size twelve dress!"

"But you are a size twelve."

"Aiming to be a size ten for the wedding photos, they'll look better." She paused, staring into the bowl. "There's no sugar in this, is there?"

"Crunchy Nut Cornflakes?" Tel shrugged. "No, it's all natural additives. I could make you something if you're really hungry, one of my specialities?"

"Beans on toast, cheese on toast, or egg on toast."

"Take your pick from the quite extensive menu."

"I'll pass, but thanks." She finished off the bowl and placed it on the coffee table. When she leaned back again Tel's arm was already in place to hug her close to him. "Tell me everything," he said.

"How much time do you have?"

"Lots."

"Okay, well mum rang after the breakfast meeting to try and persuade me to hire a harpist for the ceremony. A harpist! She said they're very 'in vogue' at the moment and I told her I didn't read Vogue, but she didn't get it, she's too hyped up to indulge in any type of humour. Then she said that two little bridesmaids didn't seem enough to spread rose petals down the aisle and wanted to know if I had other friends with children, perhaps another eight. I mean, rose petals? Ten bridesmaids? I had to hang up on her in the end, the urge to scream was strong."

He kissed the top of her head.

"And then dad came into my office asking which important clients I'd invited. I said none and he went on about the need to impress potential new ones. *Potential!* So they're not even our clients yet, he wants me to invite complete strangers to my big day! Then the finance meeting was interrupted by an 'urgent' call from *your* mum, who vaguely and inexplicably wondered if the buttonhole flowers might clash with the flowers at the ceremony, and said she could get new ones at a discount price from work. I said the lavender roses were perfectly fine, and then she went off on a tangent and started talking about the table displays at the wedding breakfast again, and did I want her to get a few dozen champagne flutes while they were on special offer, all while the finance directors sat impatiently waiting for me to finish." She took a deep breath. "I had to hang up on her too when the CFO started tapping his watch."

"Sorry."

"Not your fault, and she means well, wants to be involved, but I do keep telling everyone not to ring me at work and everyone keeps ringing me at work! Etta ordered a sandwich for me at lunch, I got called into a client meeting before I'd even caught sight of it in the fridge, and when I came back it was gone; some complete moron had taken it! I was *furious*. I actually ran out of my office and screamed, 'Who's eaten my bloody sandwich!' and Etta, the temp, very sweetly offered me a bite of her Big Mac and some French fries, and I was tempted, Tel, I was really tempted."

Tel slid his arm from behind her. "Red or white?"

"Not bothered as long as it's alcoholic and comes in that giant joke glass your brother got me last Christmas."

"It holds a whole bottle!"

"I know. *Bring it*!"

* * *

"Oh, are we going passed Merry Hell?" Faye suddenly asked, seeing the shopping centre appearing like an adult theme park on the horizon.

"'Passed' being the operative word," Brian said, gently pressing down on the accelerator pedal. He wished he'd taken a different route home, but this was the quickest way back from her mother's house in Quarry Bank. Trepidation ripped through his heart and his wallet as Faye said, "Can we just pop in for–?"

"No."

"But I just want to–"

"No."

"It'll only take–"

"No."

"Spoilsport."

"What can you possibly need from Merry Hell anyway?"

"A dress!"

"For?"

"Sophie's wedding, of course!"

"But you went shopping for a dress 'up town' *three times* last week, and twice last month. Flo said she'll never shop with you again, and your mate, Sarah, pretty much said the same only with more expletives thrown in for emphasis."

"I know, but I couldn't find one I liked, they were all a bit … frumpy. I told you this!"

Brian shook his head. He had no recollection of any conversation about dresses. He might have zoned out.

"They'll have much more choice in Merry Hell, maybe give M&S another try."

Brian shuddered at the memory of many hours spent trailing after his wife in M&S, often losing her, sometimes giving up and slumping desolately on a chair outside the changing rooms in the hope that she'd eventually turn up.

"We don't have time," he said firmly.

"Why, what are we rushing home for?"

He scoured his brain for a suitable answer. "I don't want to miss…" What? Miss what? Was *Love Island* still on? What time did *Eastenders* start? He was clutching at straws, he'd never watched either and Faye knew it. Something on the sports channel then, snooker, or boxing maybe. "…a good sci-fi film that's on."

"What time does it start?"

"Nine o'clock," fell out of his mouth before he'd given it any thought, because that's what time films usually started.

"And it's now…" Faye glanced at her watch. "…5.45."

"It's too late to shop," he said.

"They're open till nine."

"Don't make me do it!" he cried, "I don't want to do it!"

"Turn right up here, Bri."

"No, I can't, the steering wheel's broken! If I slow down the car will explode."

"Turn right, Bri."

Brian started wailing like a giant baby as he turned right.

* * *

Beth came back from shopping and said, "I've bought you a suit, babes."

"What for?" Jim was standing in the middle of the living room killing zombies in his Quest headset.

"For the wedding."

"I have a suit, babes."

"You don't have a suit."

"Yes, I do, the one I wore to our wedding."

"That blue and grey striped satin monstrosity you've 'ad since you were fifteen years old?"

"That's the one."

"You don't have it, babes."

"It's in the wardrobe."

"It ain't been in the wardrobe since the day after our wedding."

"No, it's in there, babes."

"No, it ain't."

"Why isn't it?"

"Because I burnt it before we went on our 'oneymoon."

"You burnt my striped satin suit?"

"I did, and I enjoyed doing it an' all. There weren't much left of it after my dad tore it off yer body outside the church and insisted you wear me bruvver's suit instead."

"Yeah," Jim laughed, to the sound of gunfire and screaming. "Your brother weren't too happy about that, was he. I remember him sitting in the front row just wearing a shirt and a pair of Y-fronts. Your dad only ripped the sleeve though, babes."

"The sleeve while you were wearing it. Once he 'ad it off yer back 'e ripped it to shreds and stomped on it, saying, 'What type of bleedin' moron wears a bleedin' blue striped satin suit to 'is own wedding?'"

"Did he? I really liked that suit."

"It was 'orrible. I've bought you a better one. Look."

Jim double-tapped his Quest headset and looked at the grey, grainy image of Beth holding up something on a hanger.

"Take it off and 'ave a proper look, babes."

He pulled off the headset, looked, and said, "I am *not* wearing that."

***

"So, what do you think of this?"

'This' was dress number three. Dress number one had looked like a sack with shiny buttons, but Brian diplomatically said it didn't suit her. Dress number two he thought was a joke, but when he started laughing he discovered it wasn't a joke and that Faye really did consider wearing what looked like a 1950s mourning outfit to a wedding. Now, after fifty minutes of watching her searching endless rails and picking out garments, he sat resigned and limp outside the waiting room for Faye to showcase her finds. He was beyond bored and was slowly slipping into a self-induced coma.

He dragged his eyes up to view the pink, latex dress she'd somehow managed to squeeze herself into. It looked like a giant condom, and it squeaked when she moved. "Are you taking up pole dancing at a gentlemen's only club?"

"Are you saying you don't like it?"

A man, sitting on a chair opposite him outside the ladies changing room, sucked in air and whispered, "Careful, mate, it's a trap, they do it all the time."

Brian decided that honesty was the best policy because he couldn't muster the energy or the creative power to think of anything else to say. "You look like a shrink-wrapped sausage," he said, and the man opposite winced.

Faye stomped off, squeakily. She was gone for so long that he thought she might have left and he hadn't noticed. Then she came out in something long and white.

"You can't wear white at a wedding," he said.

"It's cream?"

"It's the bride's prerogative to wear white."

"It's 'alabaster'," she said, reading off the label, "And it has these embroidered flowers around the neckline."

"Which look like they died a long time ago."

"So," she huffed, hand on hip, "You don't like it then?"

"I do not."

"You're no help at all, Brian."

"I'm a *man*, I have my limitations."

Faye flounced off.

The man opposite leaned towards him and said, "Been here long?"

"Since the dawn of time."

"Three and a half hours I've been trapped in here. So many shops, so many choices. You lose the will to live after a while, don't you."

"Yes," Brian sighed. "I've learned that there's no point fighting the inevitable."

"You ever watched *Say Yes to the Dress* on TV?"

Brian raised a hairy eyebrow. "Do I look like someone who would watch something called *Say Yes to the Dress*?"

"Well no, you look more of a caber tossing type to me, but the dress programme is good for picking up hints and tips. I normally say yes to the third one; the first one is just a test to make sure you're paying attention, the second is something they've picked at random but aren't sure about, the third one is the one they *really* like, so always go for number three."

"I'm about to witness dress number five."

The man whistled in horror. "Whatever you think, just say yes."

Faye came out in a fitted tweed suit. "Shooting trip?" he asked.

* * *

"Parcel for you, Liv," Mark cried, closing the front door.

Olivia came running down the stairs. "Oh, lovely. It's Sophie and Tel's wedding present."

"What did you get them?" He followed her into the kitchen, where she used a carving knife to cut through the tape of a large box.

"What do you get the couple who literally have everything?" she said.

"A gift card?"

"Uber boring."

"A subscription to English Heritage?"

"Oh, I never thought of that."

"So, what have you got them?"

She took a box out of the box. At a quick glance the picture on the inner box looked like some sort of giant Alexa hub, or a remote-controlled spaceship.

"I gave it a tremendous amount of thought," Olivia said excitedly. "I flicked through catalogues and web pages, and finally decided to get them this."

"What is it?"

She opened the inner box and took out a large, oval, black thing that still looked like a giant Alexa hub or a remote-controlled spaceship. "A robotic vacuum cleaner!"

"Hey, that's pretty cool."

"Isn't it!"

He leaned over to kiss her. "You clever little sausage."

She kissed him back. "Tired little sausage."

"You're tired?"

Olivia put the black vacuum on the countertop and wrapped her arms around his neck. "*So* tired."

He glanced at the kitchen clock. It was 7pm.

"I have to say," he muffled through their kiss, "I'm feeling pretty exhausted myself."

"We should go to bed."

"We should."

She grabbed hold of his hand and they raced down the hallway and up the stairs.

"Is this normal?" Olivia giggled, as they tore off each other's clothes.

"Feels pretty normal to me."

"To still be like this after a year together, I mean."

"Honeymoon period, lasts about … seven or eight years,

fingers crossed."

"Oh goodie."

Afterwards, as they lay puffing in bed, staring up at the ceiling and smiling, Olivia said, "How on earth are we going to do that in the motorhome?"

"We've done it in there before."

"Yes, when the campsite was empty and before I found my 'voice'. We've only ever done it at the Woodsman, in the furthest bedroom from the guests, or at my house in Bath, where the neighbours send sweet little notes about the noise."

"Or at mine." He turned his head to look at her. "It's only two days, Liv."

"I won't last that long."

"We'll find a way."

"I could have it soundproofed?"

"Or," he said, turning towards her and rubbing her nose with his, "You could learn not to make so much noise."

"I can't help it, it's so nice. It's like that feeling you get when you lower yourself into a hot bath, times a million, with sparkles and fireworks and a choir singing in the background."

"Inflated ego, engaged," Mark said, puffing out his chest. "Maybe you could try to keep it down a little?"

"I'll have to practice."

"You will."

"Now?"

Afterwards, as they lay puffing in bed, staring up at the ceiling and smiling, Mark said, "I'd say you were louder that time."

"I definitely need more practice."

He laughed and held her hand under the covers. "Later," he gasped.

* * *

The mobile phone on the bedside table was ringing, dragging Sophie from a nightmare about toppling wedding cakes and broken champagne glasses.

"Who's ringing us in the middle of the night?" Tel muttered beside her.

Sophie snatched up her phone and looked blearily at the screen. "It's mum."

"It's three in the morning!" he cried, glancing at his own phone.

"I know! Do you think I don't know?"

"Don't answer it."

"It might be an emergency." She pressed the green button. "Hello, mum, is everything alright? It's three o'clock in the morning!"

"I know, but I can't sleep, I'm *so* excited!"

"About?"

"The wedding, of course."

"You're excited at three o'clock in the morning?"

"I'm excited 24/7."

"Does dad know this?"

"Gifts for guests," her mother said.

"I was rather under the impression that the guests brought us gifts."

"A little something to remember the day and to remind them of the date, that way you'll get anniversary gifts every year too. I was thinking of engraved keyrings, or perhaps a silver pendant for the ladies and, I don't know, rings for the men?"

Sophie cricked her neck to one side. "You're ringing me in the middle of the night to ask about guest gifts?"

"It's just occurred to me. I was dreaming about it."

"You were–?" Sophie let her hand with the phone fall to the duvet and sucked in air, then yanked it back up to her ear. "Mum, we do have a budget. We can't be splurging on unnecessary extravagances."

"This is just a little thing, a tiny little–"

"Mum, I don't want to have this conversation with you in the middle of the night or any other time. I'm hanging up now, don't call again unless there's blood or death involved."

She slammed her phone down onto the bedside table, hoping she hadn't tempted fate by using the 'death' word.

"Everything okay?" Tel asked.

Sophie shuffled back under the duvet. "My mother is clearly menopausal and has developed an unhealthy obsession with our wedding plans." She turned in bed to face him. "Can't we just elope? All these wedding preparations are driving me nuts. Well no, not the actual preparations, they're all sorted, mostly, it's the constant *interference* that's tipping me over the edge. Can't we just run away?"

"What, to Gretna Green?" He laughed, then stopped abruptly when she nodded her head on the pillow. "We can't just take off like that, Sophs."

"We *can*! If you value the remaining globules of my sanity you'll agree to it, before I start jabbering and dribbling."

"You do that anyway."

"I've started having palpitations every time my phone rings. When I catch myself in the mirror I wonder who that woman is who looks as if she's about to start screaming. If I have one more discussion about the colour of the chair covers I swear I'll–"

"We can't just run off, Sophs."

"Why not?"

"Scotland's a long way, and you said you didn't want to get married in Scotland."

"A pagan wedding then, we'll just slaughter a sheep, jump over a log, and say we're officially coupled."

"I'm not sure that's legally binding."

"I'll lobby government to get the law changed, I'm a lawyer, I can do that."

"Everything's almost sorted, isn't it?"

"Clearly not if my mother's calling me in the middle of the night to talk about trinkets. I just want it to stop!"

To Tel's horror, she suddenly burst into tears. He pulled her tight against him. "It's only two more weeks, Soph."

"Closer to three."

"Less than three weeks and it'll all be over."

"Not really how one is supposed to refer to one's own wedding, 'It'll soon be over,'" she sniffed. "I don't think I can survive another two weeks."

"What can I do to–?"

Her mobile started ringing again. She twisted in bed, snatched it up, and hissed, "Which is it, blood or death?"

"Bracelets!" her mother cried.

Sophie didn't trust herself to speak.

"I've just been flicking through the internet and came across the cutest keepsakes suitable for men and women, and I thought a leather bracelet with an engraved infinity–"

Sophie hung up. She turned off her phone, pulled off the back, took out her SIM card and hurled it across the room with a growl of rage. As she dragged the duvet up over her head she muttered, "I don't want to marry you anymore, Tel, it's too much hassle."

***

Thursday – 16 days until the wedding

Sophie was in her office, on her mobile. "Mum, everything is booked and paid for, the dress, the caterers, the flowers. The wedding is two weeks away and I'm not changing anything now, so can you *please* stop calling me, I'm *supposed* to be working!"

"Your father will understand if you slack off a bit. He shouldn't be giving you work anyway, he knows how time-consuming wedding arrangements can be."

"I have to fight against accusations of favouritism by working twice as hard as everyone else, mum, I can't 'slack off' whenever I feel like it, I have a job to do."

"You have a wedding to arrange, that's more important."

"I have to go, mum."

Sophie brought the phone down from her ear and tried to strangle it, shook it fiercely in both hands, and dropped both the phone and her head onto her desk. A tinny voice cried, "Are you still there, darling?"

She reached out and pressed the red button, then slowly turned her head and banged her forehead on the desk a couple of times.

"You okay?" said Etta, the temp, coming into the office with some files.

Sophie sat up. "Never get married!" she growled.

"Nobody's asked me yet."

"When they do, and they will, just say no, unless there's a written caveat attached to the proposal that clearly states a registry office, not a full-blown, out-of-proportion event that would put the Kardashians to shame."

"Duly noted." Etta put the files next to the pile of files already on her desk. "I've got Jacquie holding on the line for you."

Tel's mother. Sophie dropped her forehead onto the desk again with a loud thud. "Tell her we've eloped."

Etta laughed weakly and left, quietly closing the door behind her. Forty-five seconds later Sophie's mobile phone rang and, when she answered it, Jacquie screamed, "*What do you mean, you've eloped?*"

"We haven't eloped."

"Oh, thank God!"

"I'm just having a nervous breakdown."

"Pre-marital nerves are normal, love. Now, I've been thinking about music for the reception."

"We've booked a band."

"Are you sure a band is right for a wedding? What about a small symphony orchestra?"

"Is there such a thing as a *small* symphony orchestra?"

"Oh yes, it's called a *chamber* orchestra. Tel's cousin is in one, he plays the violin. There's only twenty-five of them, they're very good and, as luck would have it, they're available on the date!"

Noises were coming out of Sophie's mouth that she

couldn't recognise or identify; it was a cross between hysterical laughter and a howling wolf.

"Are you okay, love? You're not choking, are you?"

"Sophie!" Her dad came into the office carrying a piece of paper. "Your mother and I have decided to–"

"Is it about the wedding?" Sophie snapped.

"Yes, we were thinking–"

"Don't think. Don't suggest or recommend or question. Everything is booked and set in stone and there will be *no* last-minute 'break a leg' changes for good luck."

"*You're going to break your leg?*" Jacquie cried down the phone. "Is that a 'thing' now, to walk down the aisle in a cast?"

"It's just a figure of–"

"Don't do it, love, it will make things very awkward."

"Sophie," her dad said, "Why are you banging your head on the desk like that?"

"*Don't injure your beautiful face before the wedding!*" Jacquie squealed.

Sophie raised her head. She put Jacquie on speakerphone and said, very slowly and very clearly, "If anyone mentions this wedding *one more time* I'm calling the whole thing off and booking a registry office."

Jacquie gasped in horror. Her father inhaled to say something but Sophie threw up the palm of her hand. "Not … another … word."

Her father flustered with his sheet of paper for a moment and then left her office, leaving the door ajar. Jacquie said, "So what shall I tell Tel's cousin about the chamber orchestra?"

"Jacquie, I love you, thank you for your input, goodbye." She pressed the red button and sat back in her chair. "I'm going mad," she said out loud, "I am literally going round the bloody bend!"

"Cup of tea with a tiny splash of brandy in it?" Etta shouted from her desk outside.

"You're a star," Sophie called back. "Forget the tiny splash, just glug it in. And if you can find a fat marijuana joint somewhere that would be great."

* * *

"Are you drunk?"

"No," Sophie said, bouncing down the hallway as the phone in her outstretched hand continued to ring, "I'm relaxed and unstressed and its marvellous."

"What have you been drinking?"

"Tea."

"A special kind of tea, was it?" Grinning, he took hold of her arm and guided her to the sofa. "Did it have mushrooms floating in it?"

Her phone stopped ringing.

"Just tea," she beamed up at him, "Etta added something extra."

"Brandy, by the smell of your breath."

"Yes, that's it, brandy."

"I'll make us some coffee."

"Throw some brandy in it."

"We don't have any brandy."

"Some prosecco then. In fact, skip the coffee and just bring me wine."

"I think you've had enough."

Sophie's phone started ringing again – it had hardly stopped all day. She glanced at the screen. It was David, Tel's younger, very 'gay and proud' brother. "He clearly didn't get the memo," she said.

"What memo?"

"I sent a WhatsApp message to everyone this afternoon telling them not to contact me about the wedding under any circumstances or else I was going to arrange a secret wedding and not invite them."

"Oh, that one. I doubt David is much interested in the wedding per se, just the party afterwards."

"David," she said, answering the phone.

"Sophs, light of my life, angel in human form!" he

squealed. "I was just talking to Travis, and we were wondering if you're considering kilts at the wedding at all?"

"Not especially."

"Oh, that's very disappointing."

"Isn't it."

"We were thinking about wearing kilts."

"Any particular reason, since you're not Scottish and Travis is from Texas? Fashion statement, is it?"

"Travis thinks it will be more comfortable to have a free flow of air around the testicle area."

Sophie let a full second pass before she said, "Formal dress code, David."

"Are you sure?"

"Positive, unless my mad uncle turns up in a dinosaur costume, which is within the realms of possibility considering the Batman outfit he wore for Christmas lunch."

"So," he said sadly, "No kilts then?"

"Not unless you can provide a record of provenance for a Scottish background." She sat up, suddenly recalling Travis's various drag outfits and outlandish personalities, and quickly added, "I'd prefer it if Travis didn't turn up as his alter ego, Divine Diva, she is *such* a *cow*."

David turned his head away from his phone to shout, "She said no to bringing DD along."

An American drawl in the background cried, "Gosh darn it!"

"He's very disappointed."

"Yes, I can tell."

"How about Bianca Del Rio, can she come?"

Sophie frowned as she took a mug of coffee from Tel. She'd have preferred wine to top up her wonderfully numbing intoxication, she could already feel the tension returning to her throbbing temples. "Bianca's scathing wit is quite offensive, David."

"I know, she's utterly *fabulous*, isn't she?"

"A police raid at my brawling wedding reception isn't quite

what I had in mind. Can't he just come as himself?"

David huffed. "I don't think he knows who 'himself' is anymore."

"Please, take pity on a wedding-ravaged bride-to-be and just wear something suitably formal, for me? Please?"

"Party pooper," David huffed. "Okay, we'll be good, but only because we love you so much."

"Thank you."

Tel held out his hand for the phone and she passed it to him. As they started talking about a stag night, Sophie took her mug of coffee into the kitchen and emptied it down the sink. She pulled a wine glass from a cupboard, and then, suddenly, it felt like all of her internal organs dropped like rocks inside her and she was overcome with a huge sense of doom and complete exhaustion. She leaned heavily against the unit, dropping her head. The wine glass fell into the sink and broke. Behind her she heard Tel saying, "I'll call you back." When he rushed to her side she turned and fell against his chest, sobbing.

"I can't do it," she wailed, tears falling from her eyes. "I can't do this, Tel. It's totally out of control. It was supposed to be a quaint little wedding to celebrate and seal our love, but it feels more like an endurance test. I'm not even looking forward to it, I'm dreading it, to be honest, and I can't wait for it all to be over."

She slipped out of his arms and crumpled to the floor. He followed her down, held her tight as they leaned against the cupboard doors. Her phone rang. Tel was still holding it and saw her mother's name come up on the screen. He pressed the red button and tossed it up onto the countertop.

"What can I do to help?" he asked. "How can I take some of the pressure off?"

"You've been amazing," she said, peering up at him and wiping at her tears. "It's just ... *the mothers*! They're relentless! I wanted a simple wedding and they've turned the whole thing into a complete nightmare of *epic proportions*!" She struggled to catch her breath amongst the wretched sobbing. "Our guest list was 60 people and I thought that was too many, now it's 150 and half of them I don't even know! Mum picked the date and booked a sprawling mansion without even asking me! Your mother is obsessed with colour coordination, and mine is obsessed with nothing short of *total perfection*. I can't cope, Tel, it's not what I imagined it to be like at all. I feel like cancelling everything and running away. I'm sorry," she hitched, clutching at him, "I love you, but I can't go through with this."

He stroked her hair as he held her against his chest, letting her cry it out. He felt angry and helpless. "I'll tell the mothers to stop calling you."

"I've tried! They won't!"

"They will," he said, reaching up for the phone on the counter and tapping on the screen with his thumb. "As of now I'm diverting all your calls from the mothers to my phone. Don't answer them, I'll deal with it."

CHAPTER TWO

Stopping the mothers from getting in touch with Sophie was akin to King Canute trying to hold back the tide, and about as successful.

"I need to speak to Sophie," her mother kept saying, "It's *critically* important."

"Is it about the wedding?"

"It is."

"I'm afraid she's busy, Camille."

"Too busy to speak to her own mother about her own wedding?"

"I'll get her to call you when she has a moment."

She'd huff loudly and hang up.

Another time he was in a meeting when she called. "*Vitally* important," she cried down the phone.

"Is it about the wedding?"

"No, it's … her father, he's … ill."

"Ill?"

"Yes, very ill, I need to speak to her immediately."

Tel looked across the boardroom table at John, Sophie's father, who was glaring at him and impatiently waiting for him to end the call. "I'm sorry, Camille," he said, and John huffed loudly and rolled his eyes, "He seems perfectly fine to me."

John reached over and took the phone from him. "Stop calling!" he said, "People are trying to work!"

Camille took to calling in the middle of the night, hoping to catch Sophie off-guard. Even when Tel threw his phone into a bedside drawer he could still hear it vibrating. He tried turning off both phones before they went to bed, but they worried about emergencies and turned them back on again – Sophie's diverted, Tel's pulsating almost constantly in the drawer.

His mum sent endless texts with pictures of all the special offers they had on in the store, with messages reading, 'Do you want any of these?' Then she'd call and say, "I need to ask Sophie about the glasses/tablemats/cutlery/samosas."

"She's busy, mum."

"Always so busy!"

"I'll get her to call you back."

Her mum repeatedly turned up at the flat unannounced, claiming to 'just be passing', despite living on the other side of London. He generally said she was out, or having a lie down, or was nursing a terrible headache, and Camille would huff and storm off. *His* mum turned up at the door with boxes of glasses and tablemats and samples of samosas, and was politely but firmly sent away.

When the mothers realised that Tel wasn't going to back down and put them through on the phone or let them in the door, they turned to more underhand tactics.

Jacquie, having used her firmest 'mother's voice' on Tel, to no avail, went straight to the source and turned up outside Sophie's office. Etta came in and told Sophie she was there and Sophie, rather cruelly she thought later, said to send her away. But Jacquie didn't go away, she waited outside. Sophie didn't know this until she came out of her office and saw her sitting next to Etta's desk, Etta looking awkward and more than a little nervous.

"It's just about the flowers," Jacquie said, standing up, "I'm still not sure about the buttonholes and wondered–"

Sophie, caught off guard, stormed back into her office, slamming the door behind her. On the intercom she told Etta, "Tell her to go home and that I'm *extremely* busy for the next two weeks."

She peeked through the door later to check she was gone

before leaving her office, passing Tel in the corridor. "Contact attempt," she said.

"Your mother or mine?"

"Yours."

"On it."

Sophie's mother, denied entry to the building by the reception staff on the strict instructions of the CEO himself, started leaving notes at the foyer desk, which were sent up to Etta, who gave them to Sophie. The first one read, '*Sophie, do we really have to have–?*' She didn't read any more, she scrawled, '*Stop writing notes*' on the note and sent it back down to reception, who handed it to a waiting Camille, who left in a sulk.

A bouquet of flowers arrived. Sophie thought they were from Tel, until she read the attached card: '*I really have to talk to you about the harpist, call me the instant you get this. Love, mum x.*' She kept the flowers because they were pretty, but ditched the note without response.

A wrapped box appeared. Sophie shook it and recognised Thorntons chocolates when she heard them. She also recognised her mother's handwriting on the attached envelope. Without opening either, she tore the note off and threw it in the bin. She took the box out to Etta. "Chocolate fan?" she asked. Etta nodded and Sophie handed the box to her. Before she'd even closed her office door she heard the thudding stampede of staff racing up from the open-plan office. When she opened the door again a crowd were huddled around Etta's desk, the box of chocolates opened and already half gone.

"Whoever ate my sandwich in the fridge gets no chocolate," she declared, eyeing them all.

A rotund man at the back slumped his shoulders and shuffled off. "I thought it had been abandoned," he muttered.

"It had my name on a Post-it Note!"

Later, Tel rang and said, "I'm leaving in ten minutes if you want to share a taxi home?"

"I'm reading through depositions for next week's case."

"Bring them, we'll read them together over a nice bottle of wine."

"I concur," she said.

He came to her office and gave three firm knocks on her door. She came out and they both scoured the now empty office. Tel went ahead to the lift, checking around corners and humming the theme tune to *Mission Impossible*, before waving back at her and saying, "All clear." On the ground floor he checked the reception area, beckoned her forward, then checked the busy street outside before they left the building.

In a coffee shop across the road Jacquie stood up, half raising a hand to catch their attention. Spotting her, they quickly hailed a passing black cab, jumped in and roared off, straight into a traffic jam. Jacquie chased after them, tapping on the side window and holding up a plastic flower in a pot.

"For the tables?" she mouthed, "They're on special offer."

"Don't look at her," Tel said, turning his head away, "Pretend you don't see her."

"But I've already made eye contact."

"Eyes forward," he said.

The taxi pulled away, leaving Jacquie standing in the middle of the road clutching her plastic pot.

"This can't go on," Sophie said. "We're actively running away from our mothers."

"For good reason. My mum's called me *seven* times today and texted twenty-two pictures. Your mother's called nine, and texted from someone else's phone to say it was 'imperative' she speak with you. I don't know how you've coped with it for so long, I've only had to deal with it for a few days and I'm already a broken man."

"Slipping into long periods of catatonia helped me."

He gave her a hug. "We can do this, Sophs, we're nearly there, nearly there."

* * *

Friday – 8 days until the wedding

"What's all that stuff on Etta's desk?" Tel asked, as he walked past it into her office.

"Brochures, business cards, leaflets."

"For?"

"Special offers, harpists, a chamber orchestra your cousin's in, you name it, it's out there. The mothers have been sending them through the post, I've been absolutely inundated."

"I can sort that for you." He left her office, nodded at Etta, who flushed furiously, pulled out her waste bin and pushed the pile into it. "There, sorted. Just chuck 'em."

"There might actually be something important in there, like receipts or itineraries."

"Etta," he said, turning to her. She went puce and giggled like a teenager. "Go through Sophie's post and pull out anything that looks official. Bin the rest. Okay?" He gave her a smile and Etta looked like she was about to pass out from delight, like a fan at a concert who can't catch their breath.

Back in her office he pulled her close to him. "What time are you leaving for the hen party tonight?"

"I've brought a change of clothes and going straight from here." She quickly sniffed her armpits. "I should be okay. How about you?"

He sniffed his armpits. "I'm meeting the lads at that new bar down the road, and who knows where from there."

"Don't let them strip you naked and tie you to a lamppost or anything."

"I'll do my best."

"And no strippers, I specifically told Lucas no strippers." She laughed and rolled her eyes. "Even as I said it, I knew I was wasting my breath."

"I shall avert my eyes."

He kissed her nose and turned to leave. "Don't wait up for me," he said.

"Oh, I'll be home long after you, I have more stamina."

* * *

Saturday – 7 days until the wedding

"Tel?"

"Uh?"

"I'm too frightened to move, and there's fur in my mouth."

"Me too."

"What time is it?"

"Dunno."

Sophie risked opening one eye to glance at the window. There was bright sunlight around the edges of the blinds and she instantly regretted looking as pain shot through her retinas and straight into her throbbing brain. "I think it's late."

"Doesn't matter." He groaned. "I think I'm still drunk and this is just a fake calm before the storm."

Sophie gently rolled onto her back and stared up at the wavering ceiling. "All my internal organs just shifted. I think I'm going to be–" She shot up into a sitting position with her hand over her mouth. As the room spun around her, she leapt out of bed, crashing into the doorframe of the ensuite, and noisily hugged porcelain on her knees.

"Ugh," Tel grunted, "You're making me feel–"

He quickly crawled across the bed and joined her in the bathroom, noisily hugging the sink.

They quenched their raging thirst from the tap and crawled back to bed until the world stopped spinning.

"What time did I get in last night?" she eventually croaked.

"I don't know what time *I* got in."

"Was I here when you got back?"

"I don't know, it's all a blur."

"I don't remember you being here when I got home," she said. "Actually, I don't remember how I got home, the memories stop shortly after we got to the nightclub."

"I remember Roger dancing on a table with his trousers round his ankles."

"I've just had a flashback to Annie snogging a bouncer!"

"Shocker. I think the police were involved at some point,

I vaguely recall your dad persuading them to not arrest Lucas, who was *completely* hammered."

"No, it's coming back to me now," said Sophie, "Annie snogged the *barman* to get free drinks, it was your *mother* who was snogging the bouncer."

He turned his head on the pillow. "My mother was snogging the bouncer?"

"Or my mother, I'm not sure, but more likely yours."

"Are you saying my mother's a loose woman?"

"I'm saying she was drunk and my mother wasn't, and mine certainly doesn't snog bouncers."

"Sticks to the upper-middle classes, does she?"

"Shut up, you know what I mean."

He grinned. "David and Travis wore cocktail dresses and danced on top of the bar to Abba music."

"Normal night for them, then. Who did Travis come as?"

"Polly Darton, I think. Wore a massive wig and a pair of fake boobs, which fell out on the dancefloor and almost caused a riot, they were *very* realistic. Brought new meaning to the phrase, 'off her tits.' It was quite strange to hear a six foot four American with bulging muscles talk in such a high-pitched voice, he was really into it."

"I've told them to wear formal outfits to the wedding."

"They said they're wearing suits, seemed quite excited about it." He paused. "Did you say what type of suit?"

"A suit is a suit, isn't it?"

He sucked in air. "Oh Soph, you should have been more specific. Can you imagine those two, possibly the most flamboyant and outrageous gays in the whole of London, wearing *just* a suit, an ordinary, everyday suit? I wouldn't put it passed them to turn up in suits of armour, saying 'You said suits, Sophie, we're wearing suits!'"

"You're right, the word 'suit' is open to interpretation." She lifted an arm and grabbed her phone off the bedside table. "I'll call David."

"Don't bother, they're probably not even home yet."

There was silence, except for the pounding hum in their heads, and then Tel said, "How are you feeling?"

"A little better, I think."

"Can you stand up?"

"I'm not sure."

"Let's do it together. After three. One … two …"

Sophie rolled to the edge of the bed and stood up, unsteadily. Tel did the same, and they met up at the end of the bed. Holding hands, they made it into the kitchen, and daylight. They both squinted.

"Your eyes are bloodshot," Sophie said.

"I think my brain's been removed."

"Mine's detached and rolling around in a pool of alcohol. I'm never drinking again."

"Famous last words."

Sophie automatically dragged cereal bowls out of the cupboard, then stared down at them. "Should we risk eating breakfast?"

Tel glanced at the kitchen clock. "It's four o'clock."

"Morning or afternoon?"

He shrugged, then said, "There's only one cure for a hangover of this enormity, a fry-up from the café down the road."

"Oh don't, *don't*."

As she turned towards him something caught the corner of her eye. She focused on a big pink thing with a hole in the top that was leaning against the fridge. "Why is there a blow-up doll in our kitchen?"

He squinted at it. "I don't know."

"No recollection at all?"

"Never seen it before in my life."

"A likely story." She lifted a very large bra off the breakfast counter between finger and thumb. "No memory of how this got here, either?"

"None whatsoever."

"Your denial would never stand up in a court of law."

"Circumstantial evidence."

She tossed the bra into the bin, then walked down the length of the breakfast bar, surveying the scattering of various snacks, the remains of a McDonald's, a Chinese and a curry in takeaway tins, several half-empty glasses, five bottles of wine and several cans of lager. "Yours or mine?" she asked.

Tel shrugged again.

There were some random clothes on the floor, a splayed pack of cards, an orange bollard next to the television set, and a snoring lump under a blanket on the sofa. She pulled back the blanket and found a naked man dribbling onto her cushions.

Tel shuffled over to take a closer look. "I think it might be Lewis from the office, or possibly Gary. Gary? GARY!" The man grunted but didn't move. "Lewis? LEWIS!" The man opened one red, vibrating eye.

"It's Lewis from IT."

"Are you sure? Lewis is a strip of wind with a face, and this one looks like he's been blown up with a bicycle pump."

"Kill me," the man gasped. "Kill me now and put me out of my misery."

"Orange juice?" Sophie asked.

"Do you have one of those giant water bottles they have in the office? My mouth is like a camel's arse."

"Nice metaphor," Sophie said, waving her hand in front of her face as the stench of camel's arse reached her.

"Get dressed, get a drink, and get out," Tel said.

"Hospitality's shit, mate."

"Don't care, I'm in pain and I want to suffer in solitude."

The man turned and fell off the sofa with a heavy thud, knocking over the coffee table and several glasses sat upon it. He was completely naked. Sophie gasped, trying not to look at anything she wasn't supposed to look at. He slowly crawled on all fours to a scattered pile of clothes near the window. Sophie averted her eyes. The man used the palms of his hands against the wall like Spiderman to steady his ascent into a standing position, then bent to put on a pair of underpants. Sophie quickly left the room, yelling, "I'll never be able to get that image out of my head, *never!*"

"Hurry up, Lewis," Tel urged.

"My name's not Lewis."

"What is it, then?"

"Derek."

"Derek? I'm not sure I know a Derek. Which department do you work in?"

"What does it matter?" Sophie called from the kitchen.

"I'm in Sanitation," Derek said, wavering as he leaned against the wall and pulled on socks.

"We don't have a Sanitation department at Avery & Forbes."

"I don't work for Avery and … whatever you said."

"Where do you work?"

"Look, mate, I've just woken up, I have a stonking hangover, and I didn't expect to face the Spanish inquisition."

"Nobody expects the Spanish inquisition," Sophie shouted from the kitchen, attempting a laugh and cutting off halfway through because it hurt too much.

Derek unsteadily stepped into his trousers.

"Do I actually know you?" Tel asked.

"Dunno, do you? I don't know you. I just joined this big party at the nightclub and ended up here."

"He's a *stranger*?" Sophie shrieked, "You brought a naked *stranger* into our flat?"

"Pretty sure he didn't arrive that way," Tel said, crossing his fingers. "I'm sorting it, Sophs."

She came through from the kitchen with a glass of orange juice, handing it at arm's length to the semi-naked man.

"Thanks, Soph," he said, taking it and chugging it down.

"You know my name?"

She looked at Tel. He looked at her. They both looked at Derek.

"Yeah," he nodded, handing the glass back, "You're Sophie from the nightclub."

"*You* brought him home?" Tel cried. "You let a naked *stranger* sleep in our flat?"

Sophie shrugged, confused and memoryless.

"He could have killed us in our sleep!" Tel hissed.

"Might have been a blessing," she replied, rubbing her throbbing temples.

"Ain't the killing type, mate," Derek said, pulling a shirt over his beach ball stomach. "Got a bad back, and most murders involve some form of physicality."

"And you know this because?"

"Seen it all in Sanitation, pal." He pushed his feet into shoes and said, "Where's my wife?"

They found her naked in the bath.

"Was there an orgy?" Tel asked Sophie.

"I don't remember one. I think I'd remember an orgy. Wouldn't I?"

"Why else would two strangers be naked in our flat?"

"They were hot? They're nudists?"

Derek shook his wife's shoulder and she started to stir. "We sleep in the nude," he said over his shoulder.

"In other people's houses?"

"Yeah."

"Don't get invited to stay over much, I expect."

"No."

They both left the room as Derek helped his groaning wife out of the bath.

"Well, bye, Derek from Sanitation and his wife," Tel said, showing them the front door and watching them stagger out. "It was … bizarre having you."

The couple bounced off down the stairs, just as Camille was coming up with a pile of folders. There was a skirmish where they met in the middle, but Camille managed to break free, fanning her hand in front of her nose as she took the last few steps. Tel thought it was too late to shut the door and pretend he hadn't seen her, and she burst into their flat like an explosion of unrestrained enthusiasm.

"Sophs!" she cried, "I've had the most brilliant idea!"

"Not now, mum."

"Fireworks!"

"I'm too hungover for this, mum."

"A big display in the grounds of the house. I've called them and they've said they can arrange it. Now, I just need to know which types of fireworks you'd prefer, and, since this is the last weekend before the big day, we need to go through *everything* and triple-check the arrangements."

Sophie fell onto the sofa and was about to pull a cushion over her face when she remembered Derek, recently lying on it, naked and dribbling, and stormed into the bedroom instead, with her mother close on her heels talking about fireworks, the catering menu, the bridesmaid's dresses, the–

"TEL!" she cried, "MAKE IT STOP! YOU SAID YOU'D MAKE IT STOP!"

"Hi, son," said Jacquie, coming through the open front door with a box of yellow-stickered items, "Did you have a good night out?"

***

Monday – 5 days until the wedding

Tel sent a message to the WhatsApp campers' group: 'CODE RED EMERGENCY. Sophie in meltdown. Need your help. Video call in one hour. Imperative you attend.'

Tel sat in his office at his computer at the allotted time. Jim appeared on screen first, sitting next to a churning concrete mixer. He started talking but Tel couldn't hear him above the noise. "Could you move somewhere a bit quieter?" he asked.

"What?"

"Can you move somewhere a bit–?"

"What?"

"MOVE!" Tel yelled.

"Oh, okay," said Jim, "It's a small site but ..."

Tel watched him walking around a half-built house to the back, where a pneumatic drill was fighting a rocky garden. Tel dropped his heavy, stressed head into his hands as *da-da-da-da* pounded from his speakers. Jim walked into the house. You could still hear the concrete mixer and the pneumatic drill, but you could also, if you strained really hard, just about hear Jim's voice coming through too.

"Is that better?"

"Not much, but it'll do."

Brian arrived next, his phone wavering in front of him. A steel stockholders provided his backdrop, and he was wearing a hard hat in a nice shade of filthy yellow. Machines thumped and hummed as blades screamed through metal, and there was the constant clanging of bars hitting the ground and men yelling at each other.

"S'up, lad?" boomed Brian.

"Let's wait for the others."

Brian cupped an ear. "What was that?"

"I said let's wait for the–"

"I'll just go into the restroom, bit quieter in there."

It wasn't.

Faye and Olivia came on at the same time and squealed in delight at seeing each other. Faye wore a pale blue healthcare tunic and was sitting on a high-backed chair. Other auxiliaries and old people shuffled around behind her. Olivia was in a kitchen, standing at a counter next to a tagine pot, frying chicken in a pan and looking for all the world like Nigella Lawson with an overbite.

Mark popped up next, sitting in an office surrounded by flowers and vast amounts of cardboard packaging. "Ooh," he said, "What's for dinner, Liv?"

"Moroccan chicken."

"Lovely."

Beth appeared. A man was flamboyantly doing her hair. He leaned over her shoulder and wiggled his fingers at the camera.

"Hi, babes," Jim yelled.

"Alright, babes?" She gave a little wave. "Is it okay for me to be 'ere? I got the message but I didn't know whether you meant to include me."

"Of course," Tel said, "You're part of the gang."

"Oh, that's nice."

"So?" boomed Brian, "What's up, lad?"

"It's Sophie,"

"Is she okay?" Olivia and Faye gasped together.

"I'm desperate," Tel gasped, rubbing his forehead. "She's gone into meltdown and talking about cancelling everything. She says it's not me, it's *them*."

"Them?" Brian asked.

"The mothers, hers and mine, they're out of control and driving her nuts."

"What can we do?" Mark asked.

"I need to get her away from everything. I thought ... I thought a couple of days hanging out with you guys would do her the world of good. Can you come to the campsite early? Can you come tomorrow?"

"I'm okay with tomorrow," Beth said. "I'll bring my massage oils and candles, pamper 'er a bit, that'll sort her out."

"Thank you," said Tel.

"You good for tomorrow, Mark?" Olivia asked, still shifting chicken round a sizzling pan.

"Yeah, I'll leave Jason in charge of the nursery. Is the motorhome good to go?"

"I think so."

"I can get someone to cover my shifts for me here," said Faye. "What do you think, Bri?"

Brian rubbed at his beard and glanced around the empty restroom.

"I really need you most of all, Bri," Tel urged. "Please, can you do it?"

"I could run the foreman through the orders for the next couple of days," Brian said, almost to himself. "It should be okay."

"Excellent!" Tel sat back in his chair, sighing with relief. "I can't begin to tell you how grateful I am, you really are amazing, all of you. Thank you *so* much, I really, really appreciate this."

In his square box on screen Jim was waving to get their attention. "Just one problem," he shouted above the noise, the camera phone so close to his face you could see his nose hairs. "We don't have a caravan."

"Oh, don't worry about that, babes," Beth said, "We'll hire one."

"Thank you," Tel said with feeling.

"Here for you, lad," Brian bawled. "We'll be there tomorrow morning."

* * *

The car had barely stopped before she pulled on the handbrake. Grabbing her bag from the passenger seat, she jumped out and hurriedly unlocked the front door.

She went straight upstairs to the bathroom, taking the box out of her bag and pulling out the instructions. She read through it so fast she didn't take anything in. She read it slower, then read it through a third time as she followed the instructions.

She did the deed and set a four-minute timer on her phone.

Now she sat on the toilet seat, looking everywhere except at the sink on her right. She sighed heavily and glanced at her phone. Three minutes and 25 seconds to go. 24 seconds. 23. Surely seconds were supposed to pass quicker than that?

She wanted to stare at it. To distract herself, she stared at the cushion flooring beneath the fluffy rug, trying to remember where they'd bought it and what had made them choose that particular colour. Her eyes pulled right. She pulled back, looking up at the ceiling, at a crack above the bath and a spiderweb on the fluorescent light. She fluffed up her hair, fiddled with her earrings, glanced at her phone.

Two minutes and ten seconds to go.

She sighed, turning her head resignedly left, at the shower, at the tiles, at the door. Glanced at her phone again. Still two more minutes! She watched the timer count down each … individual … second, and wondered if time had actually stopped and she was stuck in this kind of time warp in the bathroom.

One minute, 40 seconds. How slow could time pass?

Very slow indeed, it seemed.

Don't look right, don't look right. She quickly looked right and snapped her head away again. She started humming and tapping on her legs. She forced herself to think about other things but couldn't think of anything.

Another glance at her phone – one minute, 35 seconds. It felt as if she'd been sat on this toilet seat for *hours*.

She stared into space – where time no longer existed – and thought about the consequences. They were terrifying, exciting, difficult to imagine. Her heart was pounding. Was she sad? Happy? She wasn't sure. She decided not to think about it until she knew for certain, she could be panicking over nothing. Panicking? Was that how she felt?

One minute, ten seconds to go.

She changed the toilet roll, even though it didn't need changing, pulled on the curtains at the window, dangerously close to the thing on the edge of the sink. She wasn't sure she liked the cushion flooring any more. Or the rug.

Or the curtains.

55 seconds. She took some calming breaths. They didn't work, she just felt lightheaded.

50 seconds. Her heart seemed to be beating really fast in her chest.

49 seconds. She *willed* it to go faster, for the time to pass *quicker*.

48 seconds.

She growled into the empty room. Think of something else, she told herself, a watched kettle never boils.

She couldn't think of a single thing, her brain had just stopped working.

"Need toilet roll next time I go shopping," she said out loud, putting a new roll on the holder and picking at the full roll she'd just taken off. What should they have for dinner? What should they have for dinner tomorrow? Should she get her nails done again so they were perfect for the wedding or would they be all right as they were? She stared at them, not seeing them, and glanced at her phone.

25 seconds. Her heartbeat quickened. She felt faint. She would have splashed cold water onto her face if it wasn't for the thing perched next to the sink – she didn't want to get it wet and she didn't want to look at it. Her stomach suddenly lurched. She felt queasy. Was she going to throw up? Quite possibly.

20 seconds.

She started hyperventilating.

15 seconds.

Oh. Oh.

Ten seconds.

She wasn't sure she wanted to know. If she ignored it, it might go away and she wouldn't have to think about it anymore.

Seven seconds.

Six seconds.

Five.

Four.

She slowly turned her head and picked up the plastic stick next to the sink. She looked at it and blinked. She stared at it, holding her breath.

It gave her the result in words, so there was no confusion, no uncertainty.

"Oh!" she said.

CHAPTER THREE

Tuesday – 4 days until the wedding

Brian and Faye arrived first, making their way to the far corner of the campsite and left onto a small spur off the main site that had four large, gravel pitches. To the right a double row of static caravans lined the rest of the driveway before it turned right again. All of it surrounded was by fields and encompassed by trees and a thicket of brambles. It was very pretty.

They set up quickly, hoisting the awning with minimum bickering and only one threat of physical violence when Faye hissed, "I'm going to strangle you if you don't stop shouting orders at me!"

"You can't get your hands round my neck, lass, it's too thick."

"I'll ... I'll use this rope," she snapped, shaking it at him.

"Once you figure out how to untie it, you mean? And it's a guy line, not a rope."

"Shut up."

"And if I don't tell you what to do," Brian smirked beneath his beard as he stretched out a pole, "How will you know what to do?"

"We've done this *loads* of times, I *know* what to do!"

"Okay, what do we do next then?"

"We put these up," she said, pointing vaguely at some poles on the ground.

"Put them where?"

"Up there. Somewhere." She huffed loudly. "Just stop

yelling at me."

Faye was just setting out the camping table when Olivia's motorhome pulled up.

"Watcha," Mark grinned out of the driver's window as he neatly reversed onto the pitch next to them. "Still got the vintage caravan, I see. How old is it now?"

"Age is just a number," Brian said, patting the caravan side fondly and hoping nothing would fall off, like the door.

"What number's that, then?"

Brian lifted his chin and said, "Thirty-three."

"Blimey. Does it still have gas lights fitted?"

"You dissing our caravan?" Faye asked, "It's not old and scruffy, it's 'shabby chic.'"

"I'll have you know that this caravan is a testament to the strength of modern glue and sheer willpower," Brian said.

"Ever think about getting a new one?"

"No."

"Too stingy?"

"Yes," Faye laughed.

Bristling, Brian said, "Are you turning into a camping snob, Mark? As I recall, yours is the scruffiest caravan in the Cotswolds."

"Not mine, a mate's," Mark countered.

"And this beast." Brian waved his hand down the length of the grey and rather splendid motorhome. "Yours, is it?"

"Well, er–"

"No, it's not, so wind your neck in, lad."

"Duly reprimanded. My apologies."

Mark jumped down from the driver's seat just as Olivia came running round from the passenger side. The women hugged. Brian grabbed Mark by both shoulders and pulled him tight against his chest, gently squeezing the air from his lungs. "Good to see you, Mark. Sorry it's been a while, lost some lads at work and we've been short-staffed."

"Lost?"

"Left, not died. We don't tend to get many deaths these

days, just the odd serious injury."

"Good to know."

Brian surveyed their four-pitch camping area, and said, "Maybe you should turn the beast around and put her in head first so our doors face each other? Jim and Tel can park opposite, it'll make a nice grouping."

Mark jumped back into the motorhome. By the time he'd manoeuvred and parked up again the others were already sitting on the grass area with mugs of coffee and a plate of biscuits on a plastic coffee table. He picked his up as he sat down.

"Oh, isn't this lovely," Olivia sighed, looking at the surrounding countryside.

"Not as nice as your campsite though," said Faye.

"You two good?" Mark asked. "No bickering or fighting or wedging yourself naked between sofas lately?"

Brian and Faye glanced at each other, smiling. "Yeah," Faye said, "We're good. Yourselves?"

"Never better," Mark said, squeezing Olivia's hand.

"We're still in the honeymoon period," she giggled.

"Perhaps you'd prefer to park on the far side of the campsite?" Brian suggested, "Save poor Liv's blushes in the mornings."

Olivia blushed.

"What time are Tel and Sophie getting here?"

Brian pulled out his phone and called Tel. "ETA? Okay, we're ready. No, just waiting for Jim and Beth. See you soon. They're on their way," he told them, hanging up, "About half an hour."

"Right, we'd better get things ready for their arrival," Faye said, getting up. "I'll get the blanket and the cushions."

"Blanket?" Brian said, "It's 90 degrees in the shade!"

"It's for putting on the weightless chair you're getting out of the car."

"I don't have any weightless chairs in the car."

Faye glared at him.

"I have some zero gravity chairs, will they do?"

"Don't be so pedantic, just get them. Liv is giving Sophie a foot massage."

"Oh," Mark groaned, "She gives the *best* foot massages."

"Calm yourself, lad."

"Beth is doing hands, shoulders and face," Faye added, hurrying into the caravan, "If that doesn't chill her out nothing will."

"Can I book a slot on this massage-fest?" Mark asked.

"Later," Olivia winked, jumping up into the motorhome.

"You've certainly brought her out of her shell," Brian laughed, as they heard the women rummaging around inside.

"*And* some. You could be right about parking on the other side of the campsite though. Liv wanted to have the van soundproofed. When I told her we could go without for a couple of days I thought her eyes were going to pop out of her face."

"Oversharing much?" Brian laughed.

"Can't help it, I've never felt so happy, I want to tell the world."

"Pleased for you, lad, for both of you, you deserve it."

Olivia jumped down with a small wicker basket of oils and gently swatted Mark on the back of the head with her free hand.

"What's that for?" he cried in mock horror.

"Oversharing," she said, glancing at Brian. "Faye, have you brought the cucumber?"

"Yes."

Brian and Mark stared at each other. Mark was the first one to cough and say, as casually as he could, "The cucumber?"

"Yes, for Sophie."

Brian said to Mark, "Not just any old cucumber but 'the' cucumber."

"For?" Mark asked.

"To put on her eyes with the face mask."

"Oh!" they both cried in unison.

Faye came out with a plate of thinly sliced cucumber covered in clingfilm. "Gravity chairs, Bri?"

He hauled himself up and was just opening the boot of his car when a motorhome came down the driveway towards them. They all watched to see if it turned into one of the many sideroads leading to other parts of the campsite, but it continued towards them until they could see Beth behind the wheel and Jim sitting next to her in the passenger seat. She pulled up and leaned out of the window. "Alrigh'?"

"That's a big one," Mark gasped.

"That's what Beth keeps saying," Jim yelled over.

Beth rolled her eyes and said, "Where do you want us?"

"Opposite Bri, but park it head first so we're all facing each other."

"Gotcha." She put the vast white motorhome into gear. With a little skid of gravel, she spun it in a tight semi-circle, pulled onto the pitch and slammed on the brakes. Faye and Olivia hurried over for hugs. The men shook hands.

"Thank goodness you're here," Faye said, "We were just getting ready for their arrival. They should be here in …" She glanced at her watch. "… about ten minutes!"

Faye launched into fluster mode, rushing to the back of their car and waving her hands at the chairs still inside the boot. Brian pulled them out and opened them up on the grass.

"Beth was just saying she hired the motorhome," Mark said.

"Had to slip him a ton to get it at such short notice," Beth added.

"A ton of what?" Olivia asked.

"A ton of money. 'Undred."

"Undred?"

"Not familiar with cockney slang, are ya, babes," Beth laughed, before clearly enunciating, "One hundred pounds."

"Oh!" Olivia giggled, embarrassed.

"Did you find it difficult to drive?" Mark asked.

"Do you find yours difficult to drive?"

"No, but–"

"But what?"

Mark dropped his head.

"I used to be a coach driver in London before me dad won the lottery."

"A coach driver?" Brian said, impressed.

"Yeah, got a proper licence and everything, so driving this was nuffink. Ain't letting him anywhere near it," she cackled, as Jim shoved his hands in his pockets and shrugged. "He ain't touching nuffink inside either after I saw what he did to the last one."

"The caravan of doom!" Faye laughed, throwing a fluffy purple blanket over the anti-gravity chair and adding a couple of cushions that Brian was sure he'd never seen before.

"Go get me box of lotions and potions, babes." Jim hurried off, with Beth shouting, "Don't break anyfink in there!"

Brian glanced at his watch. "They should be here soon."

"Operation Save Our Sophie!" Mark announced, "Battle Stations! Assume your positions!"

Faye came out of their caravan with a big table and unfolded it next to the blanketed chair. Beth unpacked her lotions and potions onto it, while Olivia went around the edge of the campsite picking wildflowers and putting them in a pint glass of water for the table. Faye ran off with a strange-shaped container, which she filled at the water tap in the corner and hauled back, placing it carefully behind the chair. Brian watched, enthralled, as she disappeared into the caravan again. He heard the sound of 'things under the sofa' being moved, and then she came hurrying out with a garden parasol held above her head that he'd definitely never seen before. She stuck it into the strange-shaped container and opened it up. It was enormous.

"New, is it?" Brian asked.

"No, we've had it ages."

"Have we?"

"Yes."

"Define *ages*."

She averted her eyes and said, "I don't want to."

"Okay, Mrs Prepared for Anything, what should I do?"

"Just look pretty," Mark grinned, and Brian immediately took on a very large, very hairy supermodel pose, which had them howling with laughter. He minced over to his chair, gracefully lowered himself onto it, and crossed his giant, hairy legs. He cocked his head and pouted.

"Well, if that doesn't cheer Sophie up I don't know what will."

Twenty minutes later they were slumped in chairs or lying on the grass, awaiting the big arrival. A car and caravan came towards them and they all sat up, but it turned right before reaching them and disappeared into another part of the campsite. They slumped back again.

"They should have been here ages ago," Olivia fretted. "They're only coming from Kensington. I hope they're alright. Do you think they're alright?"

"I'm sure they're fine," Faye said. "Maybe they had a flat tyre or took a wrong turn."

Brian rang Tel and put him on speakerphone.

"Where are you?"

"I don't know! Sat-nav suddenly stopped working, so now I'm just winging it. I'm on the A3, just coming up to … Tolworth. Where the hell is Tolworth?"

"It's near London, I think," Jim said helpfully.

"Get off and go down the A240," Mark directed, looking at Google Maps on his phone. "The campsite should be signposted from there."

"Did you hear that, Tel?"

"Heard it, doing it. Hang on, Sophie, we're nearly there." They could hear her in the background, whimpering slightly and sniffling. The women looked anxiously at each other. Beth stood up and checked the bottles on the table.

"You're only ten minutes away," Mark added.

Brian hung up and they sat and waited, constantly

glancing at their watches and down the driveway. Finally, they recognised Tel's Range Rover and caravan coming towards them and jumped up.

Tel didn't even try to park. He pulled up next to them, jumped out of the car, and ran around to the passenger side. When he opened the door they were horrified to see Sophie sitting there with red, puffy eyes, hair awry, holding a tissue to her nose.

"Mwuuuh," she whined, "Mwuuuh mnaaaaah."

"It's okay," Tel said, helping her out, "You're amongst friends now."

The women gathered her up and guided her to the chair, gently easing her into it and pulling it back until she was splayed out like a starfish. Faye adjusted the umbrella to shield her from the sun. Beth started shaking bottles. Olivia gently took off her trainers. They all muttered soothing words as Sophie wailed incoherently.

"You weren't joking when you said she's in a bad way," Mark said. "What happened?"

"It's a long story," Tel said, staring at her cradled amongst the women. "She stopped speaking coherently when she drop-kicked her phone during a client meeting yesterday. Her secretary took her home and some friends came round to comfort her, but she only started calming down when we were driving out of London, kept asking how long it would take to get to Gretna Green."

"Gretna Green?"

"Yes, she has it in her head we're going there to get married." He turned to look at them. "We've got four days to put her back together and make her wedding ready. Do you think we can do it?"

"We'll give it our best shot," Brian said.

"I need more than your best shot," Tel squeaked, clearly on the edge himself.

"We can do this," Mark said.

That's when Tel started crying. Mark quickly led him away

to the other side of the car, out of sight, while Brian turned to Beth and said, "Can we use your motorhome?"

"Of course. There's brandy in the drinks cabinet. Oi!" she cried, when Jim started following them, "Don't touch nuffink and don't break nuffink!"

The men bundled Tel inside and settled him on the sofa. "The mothers," Tel squeaked, his eyes wide and blank, "They wouldn't let up, and then there was a problem with the bridesmaids' dresses and that really …" A sob caught in his throat. Jim opened the drinks cabinet and took out a bottle of brandy, which he promptly dropped onto the carpeted floor. He froze, listening for Beth's voice, then exhaled. Brian picked up the bottle and glugged brandy into a glass, hurrying back with it. "Here," he said, handing it over, "Down it in one."

Tel did as he was told, then covered his face with his hands and began to cry in earnest. "I'm sorry," he squeaked, "I can't help it."

"Don't you worry about that," Brian told him, refilling his glass, "You just let it out. There's no judgment here."

"And then the … and the …" He gulped back the contents of his glass. "But the … and oh, the …"

"It's okay," Mark soothed, gripping his shoulder, "You're safe now, you're amongst friends."

"Just take some deep breaths," Brian said. "We're here to help."

"Thank you." Tel dropped his head into his hands and burst into fresh tears. "Thank you."

Behind them, Jim dropped a glass on the floor. It broke.

* * *

The men came out of the motorhome a while later and walked across the gravel driveway. Olivia rushed over. "How's Tel?" she asked.

"Sleeping."

"Sophie too. I think they're exhausted, poor things. I couldn't get much out of her. What did Tel say?"

"Nothing that made much sense, just something about the mothers and the bridesmaids' dresses."

"What should we do?" Faye asked. "We can't leave Sophie in the chair, and I doubt Beth wants Tel in her bed tonight."

"Oh, I dunno," Beth laughed. Then, seeing Jim's look of horror, shoved him on the shoulder, almost pushing him over, and said, "Just kidding, babes."

"We'll have to move them," Faye said, looking at Brian, who put a hand on his back and said, "My days of carrying maidens across the threshold are long gone, lass. I'll park up their caravan and we can take it from there."

Brian thought he had never reversed a caravan onto a pitch so quickly. It was slightly skewed, but that didn't matter, it was parked and ready. The men hurriedly unhooked it and lowered the stabilisers, while the women checked inside.

"They clearly left in a hurry," Faye said, "There's hardly anything in here."

She set about making up the bed with sheets she found in a cupboard. Olivia checked for provisions and, taking out the tins, said, "They only have a tin of lobster bisque soup, a tin of duck confit, and … Sunday lunch in a tin?"

"They don't cook," said Faye, still amazed and more than a little jealous. "It's not a problem, they can eat with us."

"No tea, coffee, sugar or milk."

"Good selection of wine though," Beth said, browsing the wine rack in the cupboard under the sink.

"No toiletries in the bathroom either."

"I've got a bottle of brandy they can have."

"For the bathroom?" Olivia said, confused.

"No, they can drink it until they stop stressing," Beth laughed, adding, "I suppose they could use it as a deodorant, brandy kills anything, doesn't it? Or is that whisky?"

They shuffled out, walking in a tight group. Brian hurried over to his seat and sat back to watch with his giant arms folded over his enormous chest. Mark and Jim quickly joined him as the women disappeared into their vans, while Sophie lay, gently snoring, with her arms draped over the edges of the anti-gravity chair and her bare, oiled feet splayed out.

"Who do you think has the most 'spare stuff'?" Mark laughed softly.

"It'll be Faye," sighed Brian, "I have nightmares about what she's got stashed in that caravan."

Beth reappeared with a bag-for-life filled with clinking bottles and topped with a box of glasses. "Tel's still asleep, but I got the important stuff," she said, quietly laughing as she carried it into Tel and Sophie's caravan.

Olivia jumped out of her motorhome, almost tripping down the steps as she balanced a box of tea, a jar of coffee, a bag of sugar and two cartons of milk in her arms.

They waited in anticipation of Faye's stash. She eventually came out carrying blankets, towels, a bulging toiletry bag clenched between her teeth, and a twelve pack of toilet rolls.

"Are those *all* our toilet rolls?" Brian gasped. "What if there's another curry catastrophe?"

"These are just the spare ones," she muffled.

"Where do you put all this stuff?"

"Oh, I find space, Bri, there's always space. Bring the TV over, will you?"

"*Our* TV, or a spare?"

Faye gave a muffled laugh but didn't answer as she staggered over to Tel and Sophie's caravan.

Brian adamantly tightened his arms across his chest. "Who needs a TV when they're camping?" he snorted.

"And yet you're so determined to keep hold of yours," Mark laughed.

"I've brought a John Wayne box set in case it rains."

"Liv's brought *Fifty Shades of Grey* and *Fifty Shades Darker* on Blu-ray," Mark said.

"You definitely want to move your caravan far, far away."

"It's fine, I've brought these." He reached into his jeans pocket and pulled out several tiny packets.

"Earplugs?" Jim said, "Faye's already given us a load."

"Has she?" said Brian, raising his hairy eyebrows.

"Yeah, said she buys them in bulk for the unfortunate campers who have to endure your snoring."

"I don't snore."

"Like gallons of water going down a drain," Mark laughed.

"Impending thunder," said Jim.

Brian huffed. They listened to the women stomping around inside Tel and Sophie's caravan.

Faye came rushing out. "They only have two cushions!" she gasped as she passed them.

"Only *two*!" Brian cried, holding the sides of his head, "The horror!"

Faye swatted him with a cushion as she rushed by again, which popped the other six out of her arms. As she picked them up Brian said, "Faye, we really must talk about your cushion obsession."

"I'm not obsessed, I like to be comfy."

When the caravan had been prepared, Beth and Olivia gently roused Sophie, who started muttering incoherently again, and slowly pulled her up out of the chair. With an arm over each shoulder, and with Faye lifting her bare, oiled feet over the gravel driveway, they took her into the caravan. Lowering her onto the bed, she rolled over and huddled up to a pillow, quietly mumbling to herself.

"Girl's completely knackered," Beth whispered.

"The poor thing," said Olivia.

"Wedding stress," Faye said, "I've heard it's a terrible thing."

"Did you have wedding stress before you got married?" Olivia asked.

"A bit. I had to use waterproof makeup I was crying so much, and I drank so much Prosecco I staggered down the aisle bouncing from one set of pews to the other. Brian said nobody noticed, but he was drunk on emergency shots of vodka and wouldn't have noticed a herd of elephants stampeding through the church."

"Jim turned up in a silk, blue striped suit at our wedding," Beth laughed. "My dad tore it off him and made him wear my brother's suit! My brother's just wearing pants, socks and shoes in all the photos."

"I had no say in mine," Olivia sighed, "Dad and Richard arranged everything, on a budget. The dress was horrible."

"Poor you," said Faye.

"The divorce was much better, my friends took me out to celebrate and I got a bit drunk."

"There's no such thing as a 'bit' drunk," Beth said.

"I was drunk enough to sing on a table in the wine bar and get kicked out, and I got the taxi to take us to Richard's flat on the way home. His car was parked outside. I pulled a branch from a tree and beat it. It was very cathartic."

"Very Basil Fawlty," said Beth.

"Very satisfying," Olivia grinned.

Brian, Mark and Jim dragged a semi-conscious Tel into the van. When they lay him on the bed next to Sophie they snuggled up to each other and instantly fell asleep.

"Ah," said Beth, "Don't they look lovely together."

"What's happened to them?" Olivia asked, as they quietly exited the caravan.

"I guess we'll find out soon enough," said Brian.

CHAPTER FOUR

Wednesday – 3 days until the wedding

They thought Tel and Sophie might sleep for a couple of hours, but they didn't stir throughout the rest of the day. The group sat around, chatting and catching up; the women comparing wedding outfits, the men casting surreptitious glances at their watches and Brian's coolbox.

"You ever thought of getting a newer caravan?" Mark casually asked Brian.

"Why?"

"Well, this one's … old."

"I'm old, are you saying I should be traded in for a newer model?"

"Interested!" Faye cried.

"There's nothing wrong with it," Brian said.

"Nothing at all," Faye agreed, "Apart from the bathroom sink and shower don't work, the battery doesn't charge, the oven doesn't work–"

"Oh, doesn't it?" Olivia asked, aghast at the thought of having no oven.

"It's never worked! The plug sockets are loose, the blinds ping open in the middle of the night, and the front windows only stay in due to copious amount of glue."

"Sticks like Sh– … excrement," Brian chuckled.

"Brian!"

"That's what it's called, Sticks Like Sh– … doo-doo. Poo glue!" he laughed. "But no, I have no plans to get another caravan."

Faye tutted and said, "When the van walls cave in–"

"Like Jim's did last year," Mark laughed.

"– and there's nothing left but a rusting chassis and a couple of dodgy tyres, *that's* when he'll think about a replacement."

"Tight much?" Jim laughed.

"Long pockets, short arms," Mark added.

"Oi!" Brian cried, "I won't have my Yorkshire heritage defamed in such a manner."

"Alright, t'lad, keep t'beard on."

"Dreadful."

"Be nice to have a shower though," Faye sighed dreamily.

"You can use ours anytime," Olivia offered.

"You see what you've started?" Brian said to Mark.

"We've got a fixed bed in ours," Olivia added.

"A godsend when you've had one too many drinks." He suddenly looked at Olivia. "*Ours?*"

"Of course, darling. What's mine is yours, up to a point."

"Doesn't it remind you of Dick?" Faye asked, looking at the motorhome.

Olivia shook her head. "Not anymore." She glanced at Mark. "We've made new memories."

They swapped a kiss, smiling at each other, and Brian made a retching noise.

"Do you see much of Dick these days?" Jim asked.

"Last I heard he moved to London with a job, but he sends the occasional text late at night when he's clearly had one too many. I just ignore them."

Jim turned to Beth. "Does ours have a fixed bed?"

"Dunno, I just threw some clothes and a box of food in there. I guess we'll find out later," she winked.

"I'm on a promise!" he cried, raising his arms in the air.

Faye looked at Brian, feeling a bit left out amongst all the fixed-bed love. He kissed her cheek and whispered, "Later, you lucky girl."

***

They had a barbecue to celebrate the arrival of five o'clock, hoping the smell of cooking might stir Tel and Sophie. It didn't.

"Do you think they're alright?" Olivia said, as they sat staring at the silent caravan, sipping drinks and picking meat from their teeth.

"I've checked on them a couple of times," Mark said, "They seem fine, just really, really tired."

"They must have had a terrible time."

"Sophie seemed almost traumatised."

"Poor them," said Olivia.

Several times one of them ran across the driveway to press their ear against the outside of the caravan, returning and saying, "Still asleep."

"Or dead," Jim laughed, which made Beth elbow him and Faye run across to peer through the window to check they were still breathing.

Finally, at nine o'clock, their caravan door swung open and a dishevelled and bleary-eyed Tel fell out.

"Whatcha, coma boy," Jim laughed as he ambled over.

Mark raided the coolbox, tossing Tel a can as he sat down. Faye pushed a tea towel into the top of his t-shirt as Olivia, wearing oven gloves, placed a plate of barbecue meat on the table in front of him. Between bites and gulps, he told them everything.

"I don't think she's slept a full night in weeks. She keeps sitting bolt upright in bed shouting 'Bridesmaids dresses!' or 'Did we order the cake?' She dreams about wedding preparations and cries in her sleep. I've never seen her so stressed, and she does the hardest legal cases we handle, but …" He rubbed a hand down his face. "… this has really taken its toll on us both."

"Nearly there now, lad. Almost over."

Tel sighed. "When she broke down in front of a client

yesterday I knew I had to do something, I had to get her away from it all. The mothers have been terrible, not intentionally, just ... irrationally."

"Understand," Brian said.

"It's just so good to get away and actually *sleep*," he laughed. "I knew if anyone could bring her back to the land of the normal it would be you guys."

"Normal?" Beth laughed.

Mark licked a finger and smoothed down an eyebrow. Jim raised a can of beer in acknowledgement and said, "Plebs to the rescue."

Beth leaned over and patted Tel's hand, saying, "Always 'appy to 'elp, babes."

Brian cracked open another can.

"Bri!" Faye cried.

"What?"

"Haven't you had enough?"

"Well, clearly not since I've just opened another one. You okay there, hugging your bottle of Prosecco to your chest?"

"I'm not hugging it, I'm ... protecting it from the sun."

Brian looked up at the darkening, cloudy sky and raised an eyebrow. Faye huffed.

"This is just what we needed," Tel said, cracking open a can of his own and leaning back in his chair with a long sigh of satisfaction, "Sanctuary."

Half an hour later, Sophie stepped down from the caravan and wandered over to them like an exhausted zombie, one eyelid half raised. She lifted a hand at the table, giving a little wave, grabbed a carton of orange juice and swigged down half the contents. Blowing an air kiss, she turned and plodded back to the caravan, shutting the door behind her.

"And that, ladies and gentlemen," Tel laughed, "Is my lovely wife-to-be. Thanks for the food, the drink and for being there. I'll see you all in the morning."

* * *

"Brian."

"Yes, love?"

"Are we near a railway? I can hear a train?"

"No, love, that's the sound of somebody pulling their bed out very, very slowly."

She was quiet for a moment, staring up at the darkened ceiling, made darker by an old damp patch above their bed.

"Brian?"

"Yes, love?"

"Can you hear squeaking?"

"Not unless I put my hearing aid in."

"Can you put your hearing aid in?"

"No."

"I can hear squeaking. I hope we don't have mice in here."

Huffing, Brian lifted himself up onto his elbow, tilted his head, and held his breath, listening. "It's someone's suspension," he said, lying down again.

"A squeaking suspension?"

"Yes, Faye. Somewhere out there is a caravan rocking backwards and forwards, or bouncing up and down, depending on personal preference."

"Rocking backwards and …? Oh!"

"Night, Faye."

"Night, Brian."

A blind suddenly pinged open, making Faye scream.

Thursday – 2 days until the wedding

The following morning, after a restless night getting used to Brian's snoring and the sounds of a couple nearby who'd clearly had too much to drink and battled their way into the small hours, Tel and Sophie finally emerged from their caravan. Faye rushed to put the kettle on and Olivia hurried to check the contents of her oven.

Sophie looked groggy and puffy-eyed, but at least she'd stopped crying.

"Over 'ere, love," Beth said, holding out a chair for her at the table.

Tel sat next to her. Mugs of coffee and plates of fried breakfast promptly appeared in front of them.

"You eat up," Olivia told them, "It'll do you the world of good."

"This is lovely," Tel said, tucking in.

"Delicious," Sophie added, "I'm *so* hungry."

"Well, you've been sleeping for about 20 hours, so I'm not surprised."

"And she's on a diet," Tel said, pushing a sausage into his mouth.

"A diet?" Faye said. "What for?"

"So she can fit into her wedding dress."

The women looked at her, amazed. Sophie was tall, enviably svelte and completely gorgeous, inside and out, but they didn't say anything more.

"She sounds better," Beth whispered to Faye, "I think she might be–"

"Is this Gretna?" Sophie suddenly asked, turning to Tel.

Tel looked at her and said, "No, we're just camping with our friends."

"But I wanted to go to Gretna."

"We're here instead."

"Where is 'here'?"

"Sophie," Brian said, leaning forward across the table, "We're going to have a nice, relaxing day, just chilling and–"

"We've got massages and facemasks planned," Faye said brightly.

"Total pamper day," cried Beth.

"We're going to totally spoil you," Olivia giggled, "What Sophie wants, Sophie gets."

"And there's a pub just down the road," Brian added, "We can have dinner there later."

Sophie put her knife and fork down. "Where am I?" she asked.

"Epsom," Tel said. "We're near Epsom."

Sophie's face crumbled. Tel dropped his knife and fork and reached out to hold her hands. "It's going to be okay, Sophie. The mothers don't know where we are. I thought you needed to get away from it all for a while. Our friends are here." He stretched a hand out towards them. Not knowing what else to do, they all broke into huge smiles and waved at her. "It's going to be okay, Sophs, trust me."

Sophie started to cry. Faye rushed over to hug her, closely followed by Olivia and Beth. The men joined in, forming one huge, hugging group at the table with Sophie sobbing in the middle.

"We've got you," Faye whispered gently, "We've all got you."

"We ain't letting go, babes."

"We'll get you back again, Sophs, we'll make it better, I promise."

And, slowly, as they sat and held her hands and stroked her hair and dried her eyes, she stopped crying.

* * *

After breakfast, Tel rang Fi, Sophie's best friend from uni. She'd promised to come down yesterday and help piece Sophie back together again, but hadn't turned up. The ringing tone went on and on without answer before finally switching to voicemail.

"Fi, it's Tel. Just wondering where you are. Hope you're okay. Give me a call."

Outside a large London hospital, Fiona sat slumped behind the wheel of her car in the staff car park. Her head was back, eyes closed, mouth open, arms hanging loosely at her sides. Inside her bag on the passenger seat her mobile phone vibrated silently. It stopped, then vibrated again, twice.

She was awakened shortly after by a heavy pounding on the car window next to her head, and an agitated nurse was mouthing something to her, pointing up at the sky and tapping the watch on her wrist. Semi-conscious, Fiona struggled to turn the ignition key and wind down the window.

"Oh, Doctor Braddock!" the nurse cried, "I'm so glad you're still here! We have an emergency coming in, RTA. ETA, five minutes!"

Behind the nurse came the sound of whirling blades and a helicopter flew directly above her head, preparing to land on the roof of the hospital.

Fiona undid the seatbelt she'd clicked into place before sleep had dragged her away, and opened the car door. Glancing at her own watch, she realised she'd had a whole 57 minutes of rest. Before that, she'd been awake for 35 hours straight.

The nurse's urgency urged her on and she raced through the doors of A&E. She checked her phone as she ran and tried to call Tel as they waited by the lifts for the patient to come down, but he didn't pick up. She left a voice message.

"Tel, I'm sorry, I tried to get away and failed. Give Sophie my love and tell her it's all going to be ..."

There was a ping as lift doors opened and the emergency staff sprang into action. Fi hung up.

Tel rang back a couple of hours later and it went to voicemail. Later that afternoon he tried again, starting to feel a bit concerned. Fi often turned up late or not at all, but this was an emergency and Fi was usually very good with emergencies, working as she did in the A&E department.

"Tel!" Fi cried, finally answering, "I'm so, *so* sorry, it's manic here, absolutely insane. Can you manage without me? Is Sophie okay? I'm–" He heard someone in the background shouting, "He's gone into cardiac arrest!"

"I have to go," she said, and he could hear her running, "I'll come down as soon as I can."

She was gone again before he'd managed to utter a word.

***

A car pulled up next to them late afternoon, a little red sports car with its roof down. They were all scattered on the grass, attending to Sophie and casually chatting to make everything seem as normal as possible. Nobody mentioned anything about weddings.

A petite woman wearing designer sunglasses and a headscarf over a swathe of natural red hair jumped out, a large handbag hanging from the crook of her arm. Whipping the scarf off, she tottered towards them in high heels, making a beeline for Sophie. She looked very high maintenance.

Sophie stood up, held out limp arms and started wailing again. "Annie!" she sobbed, as the woman hugged her tightly.

"I came as fast as I could, darling," Annie said, her voice so sharp and high-class it could shatter glass, "You can stop worrying now, I'm here."

She pulled off her sunglasses, exposing extraordinarily green eyes, and surveyed them all. She was quite beautiful.

They all looked at Tel. "University friend," he whispered, then waved his hand in a circle at the side of his head, "Mad as a box of frogs."

"Cup of tea?" Faye offered.

"Do you have Darjeeling?"

"I don't think so."

"Green tea? Herbal tea? Anything at all from Whittard's of Chelsea?"

"We've got … Yorkshire tea," Faye said.

"I wasn't aware that Yorkshire had its own tea plantations, but I suppose it will do."

Faye looked at Brian, who raised a hairy eyebrow. Annie sat down and wrapped an arm around Sophie's shoulders, saying, "You look terrible, darling! Did you try that face cream I told you about? Absolutely incredible, takes *yars* off your face." She touched her own cheek and ran her fingers down her neck. "I've got some in my bag, we'll see if it helps."

She pulled the giant handbag from the crook of her arm and plonked it on the table in front of them, searching through it.

"Is that a Birkin?" Beth gasped, reaching out to stroke it. Annie snatched it away from her probing fingers and looked at them one by one. "And you people are?" she asked, glancing around at the caravans and motorhomes. "Gypsies?"

"Annie!" Tel snapped, "These are our *friends*."

"Friends." She rolled the word round in her mouth like a boiled sweet. "Like, actual friends who live in caravans? How very woke."

"Don't mock it till you've tried it," Brian grinned.

"I've been glamping."

"This is glamping on wheels, all the conveniences of home but more mobile."

"Fascinating," she drawled.

"Be nice, Annie."

"I am!" She looked at Beth, who had just stood up, and said, "Are you Adele?"

Beth laughed. "Nah, I just look like her."

"Before she lost all that weight, obviously."

"Annie!"

"Yeah, when she was still *curvy*," Beth said with a rictus smile.

Losing interest, Annie turned back to Sophie, who was muttering incoherently and gesticulating. "Yah, yah," she said, "Totally understand, darling." She looked at the mug of tea Faye was bringing over and said, "I hope that's not for me, I only drink from bone china."

"*Annie!*"

The red-head sighed and took the mug from Faye without acknowledgement, sipped it, pulled a face, and put it down on the table, gently pushing it away with an acrylic fingernail. Faye took it away again.

Brian suddenly leapt out of his chair and headed for his beloved coolbox. "Cold can, anyone?"

The men grunted as Brian handed them out. Faye and Olivia broke open a couple of bottles of Prosecco, while Beth sipped at a can of ginger beer for an upset tummy. Annie stared at the glass she was handed as if trying to figure out what it was. She took a sip, shuddered, and said, "Poor man's champagne?"

"Poor men drink beer," Brian snapped. "Poor women drink *Prosecco*."

Without a word, Annie leaned over to take Mark's can from his hand. Wiping the top with the side of her thumb, she took a gulp. Mark glared at Brian, surprised. Brian indicated for Jim to fetch him another. "Give me the highlights," she said.

Sophie's gesticulations got bigger as an array of expressions flashed across her face, her staccato words not making much sense.

"It's the stress of the …" Tel mouthed the word 'wedding'. "Interfering …" He mouthed the word 'mothers'.

"Yah, yah, my mother was exactly the same at my first wedding," Annie said. "She'd quite lost interest by the third."

"Just a general sense of desperation and hopelessness," Tel finished.

"That usually comes *after* the wedding. Would you like a Valium, Sophie, darling, to calm you down a bit?"

"I don't think drugging her up is the answer," Tel said.

Annie tossed her hair over her shoulder. "How about a tiny diazepam?"

"I thought you'd come to offer support, not dish out prescription drugs. Whose are they, anyway, these medications you're dispensing so casually?"

"Mummy's. Took them from her stash before I left, she'll never notice. I must say, Tel," she said, sipping delicately on her can of beer, "You're being awfully bossy about what's best for Sophie and you're not even married yet. Red flag?"

Tel stiffened. "I just want her fully compos mentis when we say our vows, not totally off her face."

"Well, isn't that for Sophie to decide?"

Everyone looked at Sophie, who was startled by several sets of eyes staring at her. Her mouth moved silently as she fought to find the words, and then she said, "I'm just so … tired."

Annie sighed and said, "I think I left the sleeping pills in my other jacket."

"*Annie!*"

"*What?*"

"Just talk to her! You're her oldest friend, say something comforting."

Annie turned back to Sophie. "How are you feeling, darling?"

"Awful."

"And what would make you feel *not* awful."

"Getting m-m-married in Gretna Green."

"Oh, how very Jane Austen."

A smog and a smell wafted over the campsite as several campers lit barbecues. Brian's stomach rumbled.

"Food!" he yelled, "I'm absolutely famished."

Annie stood up, draining her can. She bent to help Sophie to her feet. "Where are we off to?" she asked, "Are there any good restaurants around here? I quite fancy something a bit haute cuisine-y myself."

"T'pub."

"T'pub?"

"The pub, Annie, don't be so snobby."

"I'm not, I just didn't understand what he said. Does he have a speech impediment?"

"No, lass, I'm from *Yorkshire!*"

There was a sudden heavy silence, and then Annie said, "I guess we all have our burdens to carry."

Mark leapt up as Brian's face darkened. "Lead the way, Bri."

Brian gave Annie a hard look, then stomped off, with Faye hurrying after him. Olivia and Beth went to help Sophie up but Annie waved them away, saying, "That's okay, I've got this. Come with me, darling, we're apparently going to some pub restaurant. Oh," she said, as they started crunching their way down the driveway, "Are we not going in a car?"

"It's just down the road," Mark said.

"But I'm wearing …" She looked down at her high-heeled feet. "… D&G."

They all stopped, turned, and looked down at her designer shoes, Faye trying to figure out what D&G was.

"Why are you wearing D&G?" Tel asked.

"Heels, on a campsite?" Jim laughed, "This'll be interesting."

"They're *Dolce and Gabbana*," Annie stressed, letting go of Sophie to point down at them with both hands.

"Again, why?"

"I thought smart and casual." She looked around at the caravans. "I didn't think I was coming to a gypsy site or I'd have worn my Gucci trainers."

"Campers!" Brian boomed, striding ahead, "We're *campers*!"

Annie shrugged. "Gypsies, campers, what's the difference?"

Brian quickened his pace and marched off. Tel wrapped his arm around Sophie, Mark's around Olivia, and they walked off en masse, leaving Annie to delicately pick her way across the grass and gravel.

"Excuse me!" she yelled after them, "How far is this *t'pub* and how am I supposed to walk there in these shoes."

"You'll figure it out," Brian bellowed.

Annie did figure it out. She spotted a couple getting into a car outside their caravan and delicately picked her way over to them. "Could you possibly give me a lift to the nearest pub?" she asked, already opening up the back door and getting in. The couple looked surprised to have a complete stranger in their car, but drove off, past the group, with Annie leaning out of the window shrieking, "What's the pub called?"

"The Crown Inn," yelled Brian, who had already perused the menu online.

"The Crown Pub," she shrieked at the driver, "And make it quick, I've been poisoned with tea and fizzy stuff and need something to take the taste away, yah?"

* * *

Brian and Tel were sat at a table inside the quaint, old-fashioned pub. The others were at the bar, getting the drinks in.

"I didn't like her at first," Tel was saying, "But once you understand she's from a long line of upper-class lunatics and married three unrelated lunatics – at least, I think they were unrelated, it's quite hard to tell with the aristocracy – she kind of grows on you. You two have a lot in common, actually."

"I doubt that," Brian grumbled.

"You're both blunt, say it as it is, and like a drink."

"There's blunt, and then there's being bloody rude."

"She just lacks a filter."

Brian humphed, unconvinced.

"Just put up with her for a bit, for Sophie's sake?"

Brian reluctantly dragged a thumb and forefinger across his tight lips. Tel smiled and patted him on the back.

Mark and Jim came over with pints of beer. At the bar, the women were fighting off each other's purses as they struggled to pay for a couple of bottles of wine, their bank cards clashing under the bar lights. Annie was screeching at a cowering barmaid, the pub chatter silenced at the sound of her loud, plummy voice.

"What, no Dom Perignon? What champagne do you have then? *None?* Incredible! I'll have two *large* gins and tonics in the biggest balloon glasses you have. *Balloon* glasses. What, you don't know what a balloon glass is?" Several bystanders started laughing. The barmaid looked terrified as she pulled two wine glasses out from beneath the bar. "Bigger than that!" Annie hissed.

"They're the b-biggest we've g-got."

"I guess they'll have to do then, won't they." The barmaid pushed the glass under the gin optic and started to hand it over. "More than that!" Annie shrieked. "Keep going until I tell you to stop." The barmaid pushed the glass under the optic again and kept going, staring back at Annie for confirmation as she filled the glass more than half way. "Same again," Annie snapped, "And a bottle of tonic water."

Annie picked up the glasses and bottle and leaned towards Faye, who was the closest to her. "Pay for these, will you, Franny." It was a statement, not a question.

Faye glanced down at her purse.

"No worries, *Franny*," Beth laughed, "I'll get these. Oh, and a ginger beer please, love."

Annie carried the drinks over to the table and stood unnervingly close to Jim until he gave up his chair and squeezed onto the padded bench with the men. She put one in front of Sophie. "Get that down your oesophagus, darling, it'll make you feel much better."

Tel, who'd been stung by Annie's suggestion that he was bossy earlier, said nothing as Sophie gingerly picked up the glass and took a tiny sip.

"Not like that," Annie cried, "Like this." She demonstrated taking a deep gulp and burped loudly.

Sophie took a small mouthful and coughed, spraying the table. "It's a bit strong!" she gasped.

Tel picked it up and sniffed it. "Is this just gin?"

"It has tonic in it."

"On a ratio of, what, 90/10?"

Annie shrugged. "Just drink it," she said to Sophie.

She did, and on her second gulp something strange happened. After the cough she smiled, which made them all smile. "I can't taste any tonic at all?" she said hoarsely.

"Oh?" Annie said, green eyes wide with innocence, "Did they forget to put any in yours, darling?"

"Isn't that a full bottle of tonic water right there in front of you, Annie?"

She looked at it. "Oh, so it is!" She trickled just the tiniest amount into her glass and did the same with Sophie's. Tel took the bottle from her and upended it into Sophie's glass the bottle was empty and the glass was full, eyeing Annie the whole time.

"Gin is good for you," she said.

"Mother's ruin," Faye laughed.

"It's full of antioxy-thingies that are good for the skin."

"Made from juniper berries," Olivia said.

"See! It's almost a fruit salad!"

Sophie started sucking on her drink, laughing at nothing, while Tel Googled how much gin you had to drink before alcoholic poisoning set in.

* * *

In the four and a half hours they spent at the pub that night, Annie managed to annoy, insult and/or offend several people, including the two barmaids, who she loudly referred to as Tweedledum and Tweedledumber when they didn't produce her drinks fast enough. One angry man yelled for Tel to 'keep his girlfriend in order' and Annie blew a raspberry in his face, saying, "I don't have a boyfriend."

"Why am I not surprised?"

"I'm a free spirit."

"You'll be free spiriting your way out the door if you don't keep your la-di-da gob shut."

Annie wandered back to the table with her drink. "I think I've just been insulted," she said. "It didn't make much sense but I'm almost certain it was an insult."

"Don't give it large if you can't take it," Jim laughed, but Annie just looked at him blankly.

Towards the end of the night Annie made a discovery. "Oh, this table's wobbly." She wobbled it. They all grabbed at their drinks. "Watch this," she said, "Stable-hand taught me this trick."

Annie pulled a designer water bottle out of her Birkin handbag, sitting on a chair beside her, and poured it into her now empty glass. With mounting horror, they watched as she deliberately pushed the glass off the table and onto the stone floor. As the glass broke and the water splashed, Annie screamed, "I wish to speak to the manager!" Everyone in the pub went silent. "Hello, critical accident over here, I hope you have enough insurance! Am I talking to myself? I *want* the *manager!*"

A man appeared at their table. "I am the manager. Is there a problem?"

"This table is wobbly," she said, wobbling it, "And my drink has just crashed to the floor. We'd like a free round as compensation for my suffering and injury."

"What about *our* suffering?" a customer cried out.

"My ears are still ringing," said someone else.

The manager looked at them all, clutching their drinks to their chest, and eyed the empty glasses spread out on the table. He bent low and sniffed the air. He bent lower and put a finger into the spreading liquid on the floor, bringing it up to his mouth and tasting it.

"I see," he said, pursing his lips. "You think you can bring your London scams here, do you?"

"I beg your pardon?" Annie gasped.

One of the barmaids rushed over with a dustpan and brush and a mop. The manager took them from her and thrust them towards Annie, whose eyes widened at the close proximity of cleaning equipment.

"Clean that up," said the manager, "Before someone slips on it."

"For which you will be liable," Annie countered, jutting out her chin.

"Clean it up now or I shall be forced to ask you to leave."

"I don't *do* cleaning."

Annie held his gaze. He held hers, still holding out the mop and bucket.

* * *

"I've got this niggling feeling we've forgotten something," Brian frowned, after they were kicked out of the pub and were now staggering down a narrow lane, hopefully towards the campsite.

"Key*sh*?" Faye asked, burping.

He tapped his pocket. "No."

"Phone? Wallet?" She tripped over nothing in the dark and grabbed onto Brian's giant arm. He barely felt it. "Money? Glass*h*es?"

Brian shook his head, regretting it when the lane they were walking down started spinning around him. He slowly turned his head to check the others were still following and heard Olivia giggling.

"Leave the woman alone, lad," he laughed.

"No!" Olivia shouted, "I like it!"

"What'*sh* he doing, Liv?" Faye yelled back, still holding onto Brian's arm to steady herself.

"I'm not telling you."

"She'*sh* not telling you," Mark teased. "Don't tell her, Liv."

"I won't."

"Sophie, Tel, still with us?"

When there was no answer Brian stopped walking and turned around. Sophie and Tel were way behind them, pushing each other into the middle of the lane and giggling so hysterically they could barely catch their breath or keep their balance. A little way in front of them, Jim and Beth snogged as they weaved their way down the lane.

"We've lost one," Brian boomed.

"Which one?" Mark asked, licking Olivia's face.

"The posh one."

"ANNIE!" Tel shouted, and her name echoed through the trees.

"Anyone els*he* think walking through woods*h* in the dark is a bit *sh*pooky?" Faye asked, gripping Brian's arm tighter as she nervously glanced around. "It's very *The Hills*h *Have Eyes*h."

"Give up the horror films, Faye."

"I can't. I won't."

Brian watched Tel pick something up from the side of the road and lob it through the air, into the undergrowth next to Faye. The scream she gave as she wrapped herself around

Brian was ear-splitting.

"Calm yourself, woman," he boomed, peeling her off, "We're safe, I'm wearing my anti-werewolf, garlic-infused, zombie-repellent aftershave." And then he yelled, "ANNIE!" which made Faye scream again.

"Did we leave her at the pub?" Sophie asked, pushing Tel and sniggering.

Tel pushed back and said, "I thought it was quiet."

"Should we go back?" Beth asked.

"It's miles!" Jim cried.

"We've been on the road for literally five minutes, babes."

Brian suddenly gasped. "I've just remembered what we forgot!"

"Annie?"

"No."

"What is*h* it, Bri?"

"We forgot to order any food! We haven't eaten!"

"Ah," Sophie said, "That'll be why I'm *s*ho drunk on just three drinks."

"It was six, Sophs, and they were very big drinks."

"No food to soak it up though."

"You'd need a giant bath sponge the size of a house to soak up that much alcohol."

"*S*hponge," Sophie drawled, licking her lips. "Victoria *s*hponge. Madeira. *Black forest gateau!*"

"Stop!" Brian cried, rubbing his belly, "I'm famished."

"Not like you to not eat, Bri."

"I know! I was mesmerised by the migraine zig-zags Annie's voice produced in my eyeballs." He burped and then said, "'Ey up, there's either headlights approaching or the glowing eyes of a forest demon."

"Or aliens," said Jim.

Faye screamed as a small car came speeding up the lane towards them, its headlights cutting through the darkness.

"Keep to the right!" Brian yelled. "Other way, Mark. Tel, stop pushing Sophie into the middle of the road! Jim, you're

75

about to be run over!"

"I'd die a happy man," Jim said, pressing another passionate kiss onto Beth's face.

Brian tutted. "All those who want to live, step right!"

"Your right or my right, Bri?"

The car stood on its horn and they all jumped onto the grassy verge. It pulled up next to them and the driver lowered the window. A man stared at them blankly as Annie leaned forward in the passenger seat and screeched, "Want a lift? This barman-type chap … what was your name again?"

"It's Barry," said the driver, "And I can't fit them *all* in, it's only a Renault Clio."

"We could put the big chap in the boot," Annie said.

"We could not!" Brian growled, "Campsite's only round the corner, we're fine."

"Sophie!" Annie shrieked, "Get in, Larry will take us back to the gypsy camp."

"It's Barry," said Barry.

"Whatever. Get in, Sophs, get in!"

Sophie staggered to the rear door and tried to find the handle. Tel had to open it for her and she fell flat on her face across the back seat, laughing. When she rolled over and fell into the footwell, Tel launched himself across the seat like a high diver, landing with his head on a bent elbow, saying, "Do you come here often?" down at Sophie, who was still laughing uncontrollably on the floor. The driver tutted, pushed the rear door shut and roared off.

"And then there were s*h*ix," slurred Jim.

"Sex?" Beth said.

"Yes please."

"They're snogging," Faye whispered, gently stroking Brian's arm.

Brian lifted her up onto his hip and let her smother his face in kisses as he walked stoically and unsteadily towards the campsite.

After they trudged and snogged their way passed all the

other caravans, they found a laughing Annie, a sleeping Sophie and a wavering Tel on the chairs outside their vans. Annie now had an open bottle of wine in her hand and was being very loud, high-pitched and animated. Sophie looked like a rag doll that had been thrown carelessly onto the chair, arms and legs akimbo. Tel was perched on the edge of his chair, gently rocking backwards and forwards, occasionally from side to side, his eyelids falling shut and then snapping open again.

"Yah, yah, couldn't get my horse over the bladdy jump," Annie was shrieking at the top of her voice to no one in particular, "She dropped her head and off I rolled, right into a bladdy ditch."

Tel was nodding vaguely, millimetres from sleep.

"Ah, the wanderers return!" she cried, spotting them.

Brian let Faye slide off his hip and she staggered to a chair, grinning inanely. Jim fell back onto the grass, pulling Beth down on top of him, both screaming with laughter. Mark and Olivia sneaked into their caravan, quietly shutting the door behind them.

Brian ambled towards a chair. "No Barry?" he asked Annie.

"Who?"

"The barman who gave you a lift?"

"Oh, him. No, he had to leave because that caravan over *there* …" she said, pointing an acrylic talon, "… was complaining about the noise."

"You're still making a noise!" a man cried from the caravan. "Some of us are trying to sleep, you know!"

"Lightweights!" Annie shouted back, "It's only bladdy …" She squinted at her watch in the dark, yo-yoing her wrist in front of her face. "Early!" she finished.

"It's almost midnight!" yelled the man.

"What is this, a prison camp? Heaven forbid anyone should have any *fun*!"

Brian leaned towards her and tapped her arm. Struggling to stop his chair from toppling over, he said, "If you could keep the shrieking down a decibel or two, that might help."

Annie huffed and swigged from her bottle. Brian was amazed at her seemingly endless capacity for alcohol, she seemed so tiny and delicate.

She focused her eyes on his face and said, "You're very hairy."

"I was a gorilla in a previous life."

"Really?" She pronounced in ray-lay.

"And my good wife here," he said, turning to Faye and finding her slumped uncomfortably unconscious, "Was an angel."

"An angel? Is she dead?"

"No, she's just asleep."

"Don't you have to be dead to become an angel?"

Brian's pickled brain couldn't process this, so he said, "Time for bed."

"Excuse me?"

"Not you, my wife. FAYE!"

Faye spasmed into semi-consciousness, crying "Leave me here!"

"And have your cold carcass snuggle up to mine in the middle of the night? No thank you. TEL!"

"Hmmm?"

"Time for bed!"

"I can still hear you!" yelled the man from the caravan.

"We're going!" Brian yelled back.

"About bloody time an' all!"

"Hey!" Annie shrieked, standing up and waving her almost empty bottle at the offending caravan, "We can stay up as long as we like and it's got *bugger all* to do with you!"

"It is if you're keeping everyone awake!"

"No one else is awake!"

"We are!" cried a voice from a caravan further down.

"And us!" yelled two other caravans.

"*Shut up!*" screamed someone else.

Annie shook her bottle fiercely at the first caravan and screeched, "Stop hiding behind your plastic windows and come out and face me like a man!"

The caravan door swung open and a completely naked man came down the steps, striding across the grass and the gravel towards her, his dangly bits swinging in the cool night air.

"Left your manhood behind, did you?" she cackled, glancing down.

They started arguing and furiously jabbing fingers at each other. Her voice cut through his like a knife and slashed a swathe over the campsite. Ignoring them, Brian dragged Faye out of her chair and into the caravan.

Realising they hadn't made up their non-fixed bed, he growled and leaned her against the sink unit. She wavered a little but stayed relatively upright. Brian fell to his knees to pull sheets, duvet and pillows out from under the sofa, then dragged out the bed slats, threw the sofa cushions around, threw a sheet, two pillows and a duvet on it and, puffing, guided Faye onto it. She groaned and rolled into the duvet like a Swiss roll. He decided not to undress her, nor fight for his fair share of the duvet.

Returning to the gesticulating fracas outside, he shook Sophie and Tel out of their chairs. They staggered obliviously passed the arguing couple and into their caravan. Brian gently prodded a foot into Jim, who was lying on the ground with Beth on top of him, both of them fast asleep. Jim woke with a start and gasped, "Can't breathe! Beth, get off me!"

"What, babes?"

"Get off me, can't breathe!"

"Oh, sorry, babes. Come on," she said, dragging herself up onto unsteady feet and reaching down for him, "Let's go to bed."

They toddled off. Brian briefly glanced at Annie and the naked man, still arguing furiously, and decided to leave them to it; he was drunk and tired and hungry. Pulling off his clothes and dropping them to the floor, he pulled on his dressing gown in lieu of his stolen duvet, clambered onto the bed next to Faye and went straight to sleep, his snoring drowning out the sound of the argument outside, his rumbling stomach, and the gentle squeaking of a nearby motorhome.

CHAPTER FIVE

Friday – the day before the wedding

"What time is it?" Sophie croaked, stirring and yawning.

Tel brought his watch up to his face, noticing that they were lying on top of the bed still wearing their clothes. His head throbbed. "Ten o'clock."

"Oh. What day is it?"

He hesitated. "It's Friday."

"Friday?" She was silent for a moment, before saying, "And we're getting married when?"

"Tomorrow, Sophs."

He winced as Sophie sat bolt upright in bed, sucking in air. He felt the panic oozing off her like a great tidal wave. He wasn't sure what she was going to do next, he just instinctively knew it wasn't going to be good.

* * *

"Uhmm?" said Faye. When there was no response she said it again. "Uhmm?"

"What?" grumbled Brian.

"Uhmm?"

"Uh?"

"Uhmm time?"

Brian was about to raise his pounding head to look at the clock on the wall when they heard it. A scream, long, loud and piercing.

They both shot upright in bed.

"Sophie!" gasped Faye.

* * *

"What on earth is that?" Olivia cried, peeling open her eyes as a shriek echoed across the otherwise quiet campsite.

Mark didn't answer. He quickly shuffled off the bed and pulled on his dressing gown.

Olivia did the same, following as he jumped out of the motorhome and hurried across the gravel driveway, both ignoring the pain throbbing in their skulls and beneath their bare feet.

* * *

Beth hurried out of her motorhome, pulling on a dressing gown as she raced back to Sophie and Tel's caravan. The door swung open before she got there and Sophie staggered down the steps crying, "No! I don't want to do it! I won't do it!"

Tel was right behind her, steadying her, trying to hug her, but she kept pushing him away. Her eyes were wide, her mouth a perfect circle as she howled, "No! No!"

Brian and Faye rushed over. Brian took Sophie in a firm, one-armed bear hug from the side and guided her to the chairs on the grass opposite, with Beth gently holding her other arm and Tel anxiously following.

Faye rushed to make tea.

"It's okay, Sophs," Tel said, as Brian lowered her into a chair. "It's going to be okay."

"It's not!" Sophie said, in surprisingly deep voice, "It's *not* going to be okay."

"Faye!" Brian yelled, "Where's that tea?"

"I'm hurriedly squeezing the teabags with my bare fingers!"

"Use two spoons!"

"Oh, I never thought of that."

Olivia threw herself down on the chair next to Sophie and took hold of her hand, muttering soothing words. Beth did the same on the other side. Tel stood there, staring at his wife-to-be, running his hands over his head.

"It's okay, lad, it's just last-minute nerves."

"It's not, Bri, it's more than that. I think she's changed her mind. I think, subconsciously, she doesn't want to marry me at all."

"Mark," Brian said quietly, and Mark tore his bloodshot eyes away from the cooing women and looked at him, nodded, and put his arm around Tel's shoulders, leading him to a chair on the far side of the table.

"What should we do?" Jim asked, coming to stand next to Brian.

"Not sure."

Jim looked up at him. "You don't know?"

"No."

"We're doomed," Jim said.

Faye came out with a mug of tea, hurrying over to Sophie and placing it in front of her.

"Any more going?" Jim asked.

"Get your own," Brian said, nodding his head back at the hired motorhome.

"I'll make toast," Olivia said, hurrying off, "And pancakes. Does anyone want pancakes?"

"Will you people *shut up!*" the naked man from the previous night cried from his caravan. A window opened and he yelled, "Kept us up till all hours of the night, then wake us at the crack of dawn!"

"It's ten o'clock!" Beth yelled, "'Ardly the crack of dawn, is it, mate!"

"It is when you've been kept up 'till gone midnight!"

"Midnight ain't late!"

"It is for–"

"I'd give it up, lad," Brian boomed across. "We have a crisis on our hands and there's nothing we can do about it."

The window slammed shut.

Faye came out with two more mugs of tea, passing one to Brian. He slurped noisily, Faye sipped frantically, dying of thirst after a night consuming far too much alcohol.

Olivia returned with a piled plate of toast dripping with butter. They were snatched up in seconds, except for Sophie, who sat wide-eyed and snivelling softly.

"Eat something, Sophs."

"I don't want anything! I'm not hungry! I don't want to get married and there is nothing you can do to make me!"

Tel kneeled down next to her chair and took her hand. "Come back to me, Sophs," he said softly, "I don't like seeing you like this."

Sophie burst into tears again. Beth rushed behind her to give her shoulders a massage. Sophie continued to cry loud, wretched sobs. Faye and Olivia held her hands with tears in their eyes. Tel started crying. Nobody really knew what to do.

"Ugh!" came a tiny voice.

Brian glanced over his shoulder.

"Ugh!"

Brian stepped back, towards the red sports car parked at a jaunty angle in front of Tel and Sophie's caravan. Mark and Jim followed his gaze into the open-topped car. Annie was lying on the back seat, stirring under a tartan picnic blanket.

"Liquid!" she croaked, "Bring me liquid, any liquid, preferably cold, with ice, and some paracetamol."

"Please," Brian said, enjoying her discomfort after all the discomfort she'd caused the previous night.

"What's she want?" Faye asked from the table. "Juice? I'll get some juice."

She struggled back out of the caravan with three orange cartons and a stack of plastic glasses. Everyone helped themselves, except for Sophie, who couldn't stop crying, and Beth, still furiously attacking her tense shoulders, and Tel, who was too upset to swallow. Jim helped himself, swigging straight from a carton. Mark tutted and poured a glass for himself and one for Olivia, who took it with a weak smile. Brian ambled over to the table, poured a drink, and ambled back to the car, where he sipped noisily as he stared up at the clear blue sky.

"Where's mine?" Annie croaked.

"On the table."

"Bring me some."

"No."

"I want a drink!"

"I want a new caravan. We don't always get what we want."

"I do."

"I'll bet, but not on this occasion, you'll have to get it yourself."

With a huff and an evil look, Annie clambered, remarkably immaculate, out of the car and stomped over to the table in bare feet.

"What's up, Sophs?" she asked, pouring and gulping.

"I'm not getting married tomorrow," Sophie said, and burst into a fresh bout of tears.

"Cheers to that," Annie said, raising her refilled glass.

"Annie!" Tel hissed. *"Do* something?"

"Do what?"

"I don't know, you know her best, make her stop crying."

"Sophs," Annie said, "Stop crying now, it's getting tedious."

"Annie!"

"I want to go home," Sophie snivelled.

There was a long pause while everyone stared at each other, and then Tel said, "Do you want me to cancel everything?"

"Yes."

"Are you sure?"

"Yes!"

"There you go," Annie said, holding the empty toast plate out to Faye, who took it and went off to make more toast, "Problem solved."

"It's not solved though, is it?" Tel snapped, jumping up. "We're supposed to be getting married *tomorrow*, quite short notice to cancel everything, don't you think?"

"But not impossible," Annie said. "I left my almost third husband at the altar and flew off to Jamaica until the furore died down."

"Is that your recommendation to Sophie, that she leave me standing at the altar?" Tel looked angry and upset and completely deflated.

"No," Annie said, "Not my *recommendation*, just a serving suggestion."

"Sophie," Brian said, and she looked up at him, they all did. "Grab your drink, love, and let's take a walk."

"You're only wearing a dressing gown, Bri. You can't go walking around in a dressing gown."

"I'll start a new camping trend."

"You'll set off a stampede of screaming women!"

"I can't help my natural animal magnetism."

Sophie stood up. Brian gently put an arm around her and they started walking off together.

"Don't bend over or raise your arms!" Faye called after him, "You'll be done for indecent exposure."

* * *

"Talk to me," Brian said softly.

He gave her time to wipe her eyes and breathe as they walked. When she said nothing, he asked, "Do you want to marry Tel?"

"I do, but ... not like this. This is *so* over the top!"

"Probably should have mentioned that before making all the arrangements."

"I didn't make all the arrangements, my mother did. This giant debacle was never my idea. I wanted small and intimate, my mother wanted the world to know that her little princess was getting married in the most ostentatious way possible, no expense spared, the more the merrier."

They walked on in silence for a while, Brian letting her gather her thoughts. He sipped his juice from the plastic glass. Their feet crunched on the driveway. He ignored the gawps from fellow campers as they passed, pulling his dressing gown around him and tightening the belt as best he could with one hand and his teeth.

"The wedding took on a life of its own and just snowballed out of control," Sophie eventually said. "Aided and abetted by the mothers. I felt helpless against them, and my panic grew every day until it became this huge thing inside me that sapped all my energy."

"Did you tell them to stop?"

"I did. They didn't. You can't stop an avalanche, you can't stop a hurricane in full force. That's what it felt like anyway, the unstoppable, unrelenting mothers, like a tidal wave sweeping you up and carrying you off. Well, me, carried me off, Tel couldn't do anything to stop it."

"Can I do anything?"

"There's nothing anyone can do, and it's too late now."

"It's never too late. For every problem there is a solution." He wondered if he'd read that somewhere.

"There isn't."

"What would make it better?"

"If we just forgot the whole thing."

They'd reached the end of the driveway, passed the static caravans. It veered off to the right, towards the main campsite. In front was a field. They leaned on the wooden fence surrounding it, Brian making sure he didn't lean too much or inadvertently lift up the dressing gown with his arms. They both stared off into the distant scenery.

"Sophie," he said, and she turned her head to look at him, "Do you want to cancel everything? It's short notice, but I'm sure everyone will understand."

She gave a cold laugh. "They won't."

"Tel will. He's worried about you. He only wants you to be happy."

She stared across the field. "My mum used her credit card to buy five hundred bottles of champagne, the expensive kind. Dad's going to be furious when he finds out."

"Don't drink it, send it back. It's not really your problem, is it?" He paused, then said, "What worries you the most?"

"There's too many people coming."

"Only speak to five at a time, ignore the rest."

She looked at him with the tiniest grin pulling at the side of her mouth. He smiled through his beard and raised his eyebrows.

"The mothers are going to drive me completely bonkers, mine especially."

"I'll have them locked in a cupboard immediately after the ceremony. What else?"

"Tel's mother bought cheap, plastic flowerpots for the table decorations."

"Outrageous!"

"And some really tacky tealight things. I'm not sure what they are. They look like a catastrophe happened in a ceramics factory and someone put eyes on blobs to make them look like distorted creatures from another dimension. Or sheep, they could be sheep."

"So? What's it matter?"

She shrugged.

He said, "Is this wedding about the spectacle or the emotion? Is it about table decorations or you and Tel celebrating the start of your married life together?"

She hesitated, then said, "I'm worried the dress might not fit."

"Sophie, you would look extraordinarily beautiful wearing a flour sack and wellies."

"Wellies, Bri?"

"First thing that came to mind."

She sighed. "Some of the relatives don't get on."

"Excellent! Free entertainment."

"A few can get pretty raucous after a drink."

"Just my type, but you're not responsible for their behaviour, Sophie."

She stared off again. "It might rain tomorrow," she said,

smiling, despite herself.

"Then I'll huff and I'll puff and I'll blow those rain clouds away."

She laughed then and he was glad.

"What do you want to do, Sophie? We're here for you, whatever you decide."

"I don't know." She dropped her head. "Tell me what to do, Bri. You always seem to know what to do for the best. What should I do?"

He felt the weight of responsibility bearing down on him. He sighed and said, "Seems like you have two options."

"What are the options."

"Grit your teeth and go through with it tomorrow, then it will all be over and you can concentrate on living happily ever after."

"Or?"

"Cancel everything and start again with a smaller, more intimate wedding."

"There's a third option," she said, looking away.

"Which is?"

"Not get married at all."

"Is that what Tel wants?"

"No, but he'll adjust."

"Will he?"

She looked at him then, not sure of anything anymore, but she trusted him, this huge, hairy Yorkshireman with the loud, deep voice. "Do you think he'd leave me?"

"Something that drastic would change things, wouldn't it. Imagine if Tel told you he didn't want to marry you, how would that make you feel?"

She was quiet. "Yes," she finally sighed, "I understand what you're saying."

They watched two buzzards circling in the blue sky above them.

"What do you want to do?" he asked again.

He waited, watching the buzzards.

"Grit my teeth, I guess."

He smiled behind his beard. "Don't think of the wedding as a whole, break it down into small, manageable parts; getting ready, walking down the aisle, dancing with your husband, all the good stuff."

"Dealing with the mothers," she said.

"Your mother wants the best for her only daughter, and maybe she wants to show off a bit too."

"A bit?"

"Tel's mother wants to be involved in whatever way she can. It's her big day too, her son is getting married and she's getting a new daughter-in-law. It must be quite daunting for her."

"She's lovely, actually."

"Just indulge them." He paused, watching her face. "It's going to be a very splendid day."

Sophie took a deep breath and let it out slowly. "Immediately after the ceremony?" she asked with a tiny smile.

"Straight into a cupboard."

"Locked?"

"Of course."

"Only talk to five people at a time?"

"Any more and I'll have them removed. I'm sure Faye has a shepherd's crook in the caravan somewhere that'll perfect for the job."

She laughed.

"We could take this bull with us to break up any fights," he said.

"What bull? I don't see a bull."

"Me neither, but this sign on the fence reads, 'Do not cross field unless you can do it in nine seconds or less. Bull can do it in ten.'"

Sophie threw her head back and laughed out loud. Her eyes were sparkling. When she stopped she was silent for a moment, and then she said, "It's funny, it feels like a heavy fog has started to lift."

"That'll be the anxiety and the terror going away."

"How do you know?" she asked.

"I've experienced my own fog of fear from time to time, mainly when the kids were teenagers." He blew out his cheeks. "You don't know what anxiety and terror is until you've experienced adolescents. If you can survive that you can survive anything."

"I bet you're a great dad."

"I do my best, we both do."

"Am I doing what's best, Bri?"

"How do you feel about going through with it?"

She scrunched up her face. "Relieved, actually. Mothers in cupboard, small groups, my soulmate beside me." She nodded. "I think I can cope, one overwrought, overblown scene at a time."

"Good girl."

"Thanks, Bri."

"You're more than welcome."

She stood on her toes to kiss his hairy cheek and, from a distance, they heard Faye yelling, "Don't do that, you don't know where he's been!"

"I'm glad we met you all," Sophie said. "I'm glad we met you."

"Come on, lass," he said, offering her his huge arm, "Let's go back before the wife starts screaming across the campsite again."

They turned and ambled back, Brian pulling his dressing gown down with his free hand, hoping the wind wouldn't catch the front and expose him to the world.

"You okay?" he asked.

Sophie smiled. "I am, actually."

"Good."

Tel stood up from his seat, looking pensive, as they wandered back into camp. Sophie let go of Brian's arm and went up to him, hugged him. He held her tight, glancing over her shoulder at Brian, his eyes asking, 'What happened?' He was so, so afraid she was going to say, 'It's over, the wedding's off.'

Brian winked, then threw himself down into a chair, emotionally exhausted. He was about to cross his legs, then stopped and drew his dressing gown around his manhood – it was still too early for the screams of horrified women.

Relieved that something had changed, apparently for the better, they all started chatting and laughing, Annie's piercing vowels cutting through all the others like a sword: "Is this real butter? I only eat organic butter, not that plastic margarine stuff."

"Is there any more toast?" Sophie asked, "I'm starving. Ooh, coffee. Yes please."

"It's instant," Annie sniffed.

"That's okay," she said, "Instant is fine. Friends are fine. The wedding is fine."

"Is it?" Tel gasped, clutching at her hand.

"Sorry, Tel," she said, and he thought, 'No, this is it, the end'. "I think I had a bit of a nervous breakdown, but I feel better now."

He forced himself to ask, "And the wedding?"

"Will be fine, I have it on good authority." She glanced over at Brian and smiled. He raised his mug of coffee at her and winked.

Tel turned in his seat to face him. "I don't know what you did, I don't know what you said, but I do know that you're a bloody star."

"He is," said Faye and Sophie together.

"Oh stop," Brian laughed, throwing out a hand, "You'll make me blush."

* * *

A car slowly crunched down the driveway towards them. It stopped, and a young, untidy woman with wild hair sprouting from a bun laboriously got out. "Sorry I'm late," she puffed.

"Fi!" Tel cried, engulfing her tiny frame in a huge hug, "I'm so glad you could make it."

Sophie jumped up to greet her and Annie joined in. "All girls together," they shrieked.

"I'm so sorry I couldn't make it yesterday," Fi said breathlessly, "A&E went into overdrive and I just couldn't get away."

"That's okay, you're here now. Come and sit down."

"Tea or coffee?" Faye asked, as they sat at the table.

"Toast?" Olivia added.

"Oh, I'd *love* some," Fi gasped, "I haven't eaten since … well, it was so long ago I can't remember."

"I'll have some more," Annie said, holding up her plate. "Do you have any decent marmalade to go with it?"

"I have marmalade," Olivia said.

"Thick or thin shred?"

"I'm not sure."

"She'll take any marmalade you have and be glad of it," Tel said, glaring at Annie, who said, "When in Rome, I guess."

"Oh, it's so lovely to see you," Sophie cried, grabbing hold of Fi's hands. "You look knackered though, you're not working too hard, are you?"

"I'm a doctor, all doctors live in a permanent state of exhaustion, but my last shift was only 35 hours." She blinked slowly, each time her eyes staying closed for a little longer. A lingering yawn claimed her mouth.

"I'm just glad you made it. Can you believe I'm getting married tomorrow?" They all gave a little shriek of joy. "I think," she added, glancing at Brian, "I'm actually looking forward to it." She looked at Tel, who smiled and took hold of her hand. "Everything's arranged, we just have to enjoy ourselves now."

"So exciting," Fi said, deadpan, as she rested her head back on the chair.

"I can't wait to see your dress," Faye said.

"Yes, well I might be carrying it on a hanger down the aisle if it doesn't fit. Must check the hotel kitchen has flour sacks available, just in case."

They all laughed, except for Fi, who had her eyes closed and her mouth open.

"Toast!" Olivia declared, putting a plate full on the table.

"I'd like to thank everyone for coming today," Mark announced, making them laugh again.

Olivia placed a jar of Waitrose marmalade in front of Annie, who inspected it and said, "It'll do."

"And?" Brian said.

"And what?"

"Thank you, Liv."

"Who's Liv?"

"The lovely lady who's just brought you toast and marmalade."

"Oh." Annie looked up at Liv, gave a huge smile and said, "Cheers."

"Did you bring everything you need for the wedding, Fi?" Sophie asked, helping herself to more toast. "Fi, did you–?" She turned and saw that Fiona was fast asleep in the chair.

"I think she's a necrophiliac," Annie said.

"Narcoleptic," Sophie corrected.

"Although she does have access to dead people," Tel said suspiciously.

"She's always asleep!" Annie cried.

"She has a very difficult job."

"She should get a proper one."

"Emergency doctor *is* a proper job."

"What do you do?" Beth asked Annie.

"Me?" Annie slathered marmalade on her toast. "I'm an entrepreneur."

"Oh, that sounds exciting," Faye said. "What does that mean, exactly?"

"It means," Tel said, "She flits from job to job, not sticking to anything, pretty much like her lifestyle."

"Tel!" Sophie scolded.

"I tell the truth, the whole truth, and nothing but the truth."

"I'm a free spirit," Annie said, chomping on her toast. "I do what I want, when I want."

"Are you well off then?" Faye couldn't resist asking.

"My family are."

"Tell them your full name, Annie," Tel grinned.

"Ugh, uber boring."

"Go on."

"Yes," urged Olivia, "Tell us."

Annie swallowed, rolled her eyes, and said, "Annabelle Tamara Beatrice St John Forsyth-Smythe."

There was silence, except for Beth gasping, "Blimey, that's a mouthful! Could your parents not make their minds up?"

"You forgot your title," said Tel, enjoying himself.

"You have a title?" Faye gasped.

"Only from my third marriage. I married a Lord, he was very dull and boring."

"Probably shouldn't have married him then," Tel laughed, then stopped suddenly, realising what he'd said and hoping he hadn't just cursed himself and the whole wedding.

There was more silence as everyone avoided Sophie's eye. She didn't seem to flinch at the mention of the M-word. Instead, she said, "Leave Annie alone, Tel, stop picking on her."

"It's alright," said Annie, "I know he loves me really."

"I do," Tel laughed, "Against my better judgement." He turned his head and said, "Uh-oh, looks like the relatives have arrived. Brace yourselves, people, it's going to be a bumpy ride."

A cavalcade of cars came down the main driveway and turned right, pulling up in front of the static caravans. Some people waved as they got out, others just looked confused.

"Statics are boring," Brian said, sighing. "There's no squabbling or fighting or spilling of blood as you set up camp, where's the fun in that?"

"And so it begins," Sophie said, raising her eyebrows at Tel, who kissed her cheek and said, "We can do this, together. Now, put on your biggest smile and prepare to embrace insanity."

Sophie did and, hand in hand, they wandered into the throng of emerging aunts, uncles, cousins and friends.

* * *

As soon as Tel and Sophie were out of sight the others dragged their chairs around Brian.

"Occurring?" he asked, a bit unnerved by the sudden attention.

"What did you say to Sophie?"

"You left with a woman on the edge and came back with a glowing bride-to-be."

"How did you do that?"

"What did you say?"

"Oh, you know, I just gave her options, coping tools, promises I doubt I'll be able to keep."

"Like?" Faye asked impatiently.

"Locking her mother in a cupboard."

"You never said that!"

"It just came out. She seemed to like the idea though."

"Good, good," said Jim, "What else?"

"That's it, really."

"Well, *I* could have done that," Annie sniffed.

"You haven't got the Brian touch," Mark laughed, sitting back in his chair and clicking his fingers. "Man's got *skills*."

"I am going to need a *little* help though." Brian leaned forward in his seat, as did they. "We need to try and keep the mothers away from Sophie as much as possible, today and tomorrow."

"How do we do that?" Jim asked.

"Distraction."

* * *

Tel and Sophie tried to give them a Who's Who when

they sauntered back, and they all nodded, but nobody would remember any names, there were just too many.

"Camille's cousin, Charlotte, is an absolute scream," Annie said, pointing at a large woman standing outside the first static caravan, who was vigorously swigging from a hip flask as if inviting someone to challenge her. "Complete lush but *so* funny."

"Says the woman who drank six glasses of pure gin last night."

"It was seven, actually, Sophie couldn't keep up."

"I'm amazed I drank six!"

"I guess it helped that Tel diluted yours with the bottles of tonic they hid in … I want to say *Adele*?" Annie said, looking at Beth.

"Beth," said Beth.

"Yah, bottles of tonic in Beth's fake leather handbag under the table."

Sophie squeezed Tel's hand and whispered, "Thanks."

"Always got your back."

"Oh," said Faye, "I kind of did the same. When the glass was half empty I topped it up with tonic water."

"So did I!" Olivia cried.

"So, basically I was just drinking tonic water?" Sophie gasped.

"Seems so."

"So what happened to all the gin I bought?" Annie asked.

"*I* bought," Beth said, "Not that I mind, babes, but you told the terrified bar staff to put it on 'the fat girl's tab.'"

"Did I?"

"Yes, you did."

"I don't remember that."

"You never do," said Tel.

"So where did all the gin go?" Annie asked again.

"Do you remember when we all switched from wine to gin and tonics?"

"No, but go on."

"We just had tonics and shared Sophie's glass of gin between us."

"We did," Olivia giggled.

"Not me," Beth said, "I don't like gin."

"There was a lot of subterfuge going on every time you two went to the loo," said Mark.

"Lots of clinking glasses under the table."

"Did I consume any alcohol at all?" Sophie asked.

"First one," Tel said, "After that, zilch."

"I did wonder about the lack of a hangover this morning."

"Before or after the screaming?"

They all laughed, including Sophie. And then she stopped and said, "Oh no."

For a millisecond Tel thought she was going back to the way she'd been before Brian had spoken to her, all stress and panic. They followed her gaze and saw a Mercedes Benz crawling down the short driveway towards them.

"Oh," said Tel.

"Another relative?" Faye asked.

"Worse," he said, "It's–"

"My mother."

CHAPTER SIX

"Sophie, darling!" Camille cried, clambering out of the car, "I wondered where you were! They said you hadn't booked into the hotel suite yet, so I guessed you'd be here."

"Hi, mum," Sophie said, kissing her cheek.

"Annie!" Camille shrieked, "Gorgeous girl, so lovely to see you, and Fi ... oh."

"She's just finished a ridiculously long shift in A&E."

"Will she stay awake long enough to watch you walk down the aisle, do you think?"

Sophie put up two sets of crossed fingers and said, "Here's hoping."

"I just need to talk to you about–"

"Mrs Forbes!" Mark cried, jumping up, "So nice to meet you at last! You two look like sisters."

"Flattering for my mum, quite insulting for me," Sophie said

"The relatives have arrived," Tel said, gently easing Camille away from her daughter. "Why don't you come and say hello?"

"Yes, but first I need a word with–"

"HEY, EVERYBODY!" Tel yelled, "CAMILLE'S HERE!"

Charlotte, the large woman, quickly hid her hip flask in the back pocket of her jeans and pushed a rigid smile onto her face as they approached. "Cammie!" she sneered.

"Char."

They hugged woodenly and kissed the air some distance away from their cheeks.

"And ..." Tel paused, pointing at a teenager slouched on a chair with his head buried in his mobile phone. He couldn't remember who it was, or if they'd even met before. He pretended to cough.

"Pete," Charlotte snapped, and Pete briefly looked up, nodded, and went back to his phone. "And Ike's here," she sighed, "He's in the caravan. I'd call him out but he's probably asleep."

"Long drive from Tadworth, was it? What is that, ten minutes away?"

"Phew," Sophie said, watching Tel leading her mother away, "That was a close call. I'll just have to fake my own death before she comes back."

"No need," Faye said, "It's all in hand."

Sophie raised her eyebrows, then looked at Brian, who winked.

"Should we wake Fi up?" Olivia asked, staring at the woman slumped untidily in a chair.

"No, leave her, she's going to need all the sleep she can get before the chaos starts, and I'm depending on her to get me through it in one piece."

"Oh?" Annie said pointedly.

"And you, of course."

"I'm at your beck and call, darling, no task too big or too small for my bestie."

"Could do with a drink, actually," Sophie said. "All that walking and talking has left me quite parched."

"There's juice on the table," Annie said.

"Could you get me some, please?"

"Could I …?"

"Get me a drink, please?"

"It's right in front of you."

"Could you pour me some?"

"Me?"

"Yes."

Annie looked at the table, an arm's length away from them both. "It's just there, Sophs, help yourself."

"No task too big or too small, did you say?"

"I meant for the actual wedding."

"Ah, caveats, of course."

Annie huffed as she leaned forward, picked a cup out of the plastic tower, and shook each box of fruit juice. They were all empty. She huffed again. Olivia and Faye stifled giggles, the others just watched, enthralled.

"They're empty," she said.

"There's some more in my fridge," said Beth.

Annie gave a little smile and said, "Could you go and get it?"

"It's just there." Beth pointed back at her motorhome.

Annie glanced over and frowned. "I don't really like going into other people's caravans, or whatever you call it."

"No, you're fine," Beth told her, struggling not to laugh, "It's not locked, help yourself."

Faye started saying, "I could–" before Brian gave her a quick shake of his head.

"Oh," said Annie, spying the coolbox in Brian and Faye's awning, "How about some Prosecco, Sophs? You've got a bottle of Prosecco in your cooler thingy, haven't you, Franny?"

"It's Faye."

"It's only midday!" Sophie cried. "I can't get sloshed, I'm getting m-married tomorrow."

"Deep breaths, Soph, deep breaths."

"O-kay!" Annie rolled her eyes, huffed, and stomped off to the Beth's motorhome like a stroppy teenager. "Where's the bladdy fridge?" she hollered from inside.

Beth was too busy clasping a hand to her mouth to answer. There came the sounds of cupboard doors furiously opening and closing, and then Annie huffed her way down the steps and back to the table. She slammed a carton of orange juice down, fiddled with the cap for a while before Jim leaned forward and pulled it open for her, and sloshed juice into a glass. She held it out towards Sophie, who, without moving, gently raised a hand, millimetres out of reach. Annie took a stomp sideways and placed it in her outstretched fingers.

Sophie sipped it slowly.

"You're welcome!" Annie snapped.

"So annoying, isn't it," Faye said, "When you do something for someone and they don't even say thank you."

"Bladdy rude."

"First time you've ever done anything for anyone else, is it?" Tel was dying to laugh.

"Of course not! I once made a sandwich for a boyfriend, *and* one time I cleaned out a stall when the stable-hand was projectile vomiting across the yard."

"Wow," said Tel, "Almost a philanthropist."

Annie stuck her tongue out at him.

Brian, looking over at the newly arrived campers, hauled himself to his feet. "Just going to lend a hand," he said, "I can't sit here and watch people with no common sense trying to reverse a car into a massive parking space."

"That'll be Sophie's relatives," Tel laughed, jumping up and joining him.

Mark looked over and saw people struggling to put up gazebos. He stood up. "Jim?"

"What?"

"Want to lend a hand?"

"Want to?"

"Come and help your fellow campers?"

"Go on, babes," Beth said, pushing him, "Us women want to talk."

Jim sighed and reluctantly dragged himself out of the chair.

As the men wandered off, the women quickly changed seats and gathered around Sophie.

"What's your dress look like?"

"What shoes are you wearing?"

"Veil? Tiara? Tell us *everything*."

"Well, I can't say too much, but the dress is–"

"Sophie!" cried her mother, hurrying over from the pack of relatives, "We need to sort out–"

Faye jumped up. "Cup of tea, Mrs Forbes?"

"No, thank you, so much to–"

"Coffee?" asked Olivia.

"No, thank you, dear, I don't really–"

"Fruit juice?" Beth asked, raising a carton.

"No, I–"

Tel came sprinting back. "Did you bring the suitcases from our flat, Camille?"

"And the dress?" Sophie added, "Did you pick the dress up from the shop?"

"Yes, we went to your apartment, as instructed, though why you had to dash away so quickly is beyond me, but we've brought everything. It was very last minute, Tel, it's quite an irresponsible thing to do so close to the wedding."

"It was necessary."

"But you picked up the dress, right?" Sophie asked again, "You definitely have the dress?"

"Oh yes, yes, don't worry, first thing we did."

Sophie exhaled with relief.

"Now, I've checked everything's ready at the hotel, it all seems to be running smoothly so far, just a slight problem with–"

"Stop!" Tel cried, holding up a hand. "No talk of problems or glitches or disasters with the flowers–"

"There's a disaster with the flowers?" Sophie gasped.

"No, Sophs, but if there is a problem with anything we'll cope. We're going to take it all as it comes. We're going to sail through the day, come what may, and enjoy every minute of it, warts and all."

"Hardly the right attitude to take for a wedding," Camille said.

"It's the attitude we're going to take."

"Oh." She eyed Tel. He eyed her back. "Well, it's your wedding–"

"Yes, mum, it's *our* wedding."

"It's time to enjoy the fruits of our labour and a good

chunk of our finances," Tel said, "And that's exactly what we're going to do, enjoy ourselves, and hope everyone else enjoys themselves too."

"I see." Camille pursed her lips together for a moment, then looked at Sophie. "Do you want to check we've brought everything?"

"We'll drive up to the hotel in a little while, mum."

"See you there then." She gave a tight smile at Tel, which suddenly turned soft and genuine. She reached out and touched his face, saying, "I think you two are going to be very happy together, I really do."

"Thanks, Camille."

"And give me lots of gorgeous-looking grandchildren."

"Mum!"

"I'll see you up at the hotel," Camille said, giving everyone a little wave as she turned and clambered back into her car.

Tel turned to Sophie. "I think she's mellowed."

Sophie shook her head. "It's the calm before the storm."

"You think?"

"I know."

"How are we getting to the wedding tomorrow?" Olivia thought to ask. "I don't want to drive if we're drinking. I suppose we could walk if it's not too far, but I'm wearing heels with my dress."

"I have *Louboutin's*," Annie smirked.

"Is that contagious?" Faye asked, and Beth splurted out the fruit juice she'd been drinking.

"They're designer *shoes*, Fran."

"It's *Faye*."

"No driving or walking required," Tel said, "I've got some fancy VW minibuses picking everyone up at twelve-thirty sharp, so be ready." He smirked and looked at Faye, unable to resist. "What's coming tomorrow, Faye?"

"VW minibuses."

"Buzzes!" they all laughed, making buzzing noises and swatting at invisible bees.

"Shut up, the lot of you!"

"So," said Beth, turning back to Sophie, "About the dress?"

"I can't tell you now, Tel's here!"

"Go away, Tel."

Tel laughed and wandered off towards the sound of Brian bellowing, "Left! Not that much! STOP! Did you actually pass your driving test?"

* * *

Eventually, the new arrivals were set up and were sitting outside their static caravans clinking glasses. The women were satisfied with the details of Sophie's wedding ensemble, and the men were knackered. Brian glanced at his watch. "Too early for a–?"

"It's four o'clock, Bri!"

He jumped up and strode defiantly to his coolbox, saying, "It's five o'clock somewhere." He dragged it back to the table and the men helped themselves.

"We'd better be off," said Sophie, standing up. Tel pointed at his just-opened can of beer, his mouth filled with the first gulp. "I need to check our luggage, and there's a rehearsal dinner at six. Sorry you can't all come."

"No, that's alright," Brian said, sniffing and wiping at his eyes, "We understand."

"Stop, you'll make me feel bad! I'd much rather stay here."

"We're good," he winked, "We're going to have a pre-wedding barbecue in your honour."

"Sounds more fun than a sit-down meal with a bunch of relatives that don't get on. Tel?"

Tel upended the can against his mouth and gulped furiously before standing up. "See you tomorrow, plebs," he burped.

"Later, posh git."

"Oh, are you staying at the hotel too?" Faye asked Tel.

"Yes, but my best man and I are staying in a room at the far end of a long corridor. I think Camille's arranged to have barbed wire fencing erected in the middle and a security guard posted outside our door all night."

"It's a lovely hotel," Sophie said, "More of a stately home really, insanely gothic, you'll love it."

They all stood up and hugged.

"It's going to be wonderful."

"You'll look so beautiful."

"I'm really looking forward to it."

"Free bar, is it?" Jim asked, and Beth pushed him. "What? I was just asking!"

Sophie went over to Fi, still asleep in the chair. "Fi?" she whispered, shaking her, "Fi, we need to go now."

Fi stirred, snorted, and opened one eye. "Is it an emergency?" she croaked.

"No, just a short trip to the hotel."

"Hotel?" Fi sat up and looked around. "Where am I? How did I get here?"

"Come on, I'll help you to your car, unless you want to come in our car and we can pick yours up tomorrow?"

"This is our last chance for an earnest snog for the next twenty-four hours," Tel shouted over, "Not sure Fi will appreciate our frantic fumbling in the front seats."

"Come on, Fi-Fi," Annie called, jumping into her little red sports car, "Let's get a wobble on."

"Get a wobble on?" Tel snorted. "Are you going native?"

"Nah, babes, I'm just fittin' in, ain't I."

"Hey!" Beth cried.

"Laters, people!" Annie waved, revving up her engine, as Fi got into her own car and started it up. "Race you, Tel?"

"I'll be taking the scenic route," he said, opening the car door for Sophie and kissing her as she got in. "The really *long* scenic route."

***

Tel pulled up outside the magnificent hotel almost an hour later. They both got out wearing big grins, looking flushed and dishevelled. Camille came running out to greet them, screeching, "Thank goodness you're here! I thought you'd run off again! Hurry up, you need to check out the wedding rooms and you'll have to change before dinner!"

They looked at the beautifully decorated reception room, Sophie vehemently avoiding the table decorations, and the ceremony room. Suitably impressed, they raced up one of the double staircases to Tel's room, snogged some more on a single bed, then hurriedly got ready to greet the family guests for dinner.

"Tequila shot to calm the nerves?" Tel asked, pouring drinks.

They clinked glasses. "To us," Sophie said.

"To our glorious, joyous future."

"Optimist."

"Realist," he winked. "The future looks bright from where I'm standing, Sophs, very bright indeed."

"We'd better wear shades then."

He took the glass from her and held her hands. "You okay now?"

"Yes, just a minor breakdown, hopefully no long-term effects, like becoming phobic about weddings or heaving at the sight of white dresses."

He kissed her. She kissed him back. And then Lucas, Tel's best man, burst into the room.

"Chap and chappess!" he cried, throwing his luggage down on the floor and wrapping his arms around them both. "The big day has arrived and I'm ready to partay!"

"Not just yet," Sophie said, kissing his cheek, "Pace yourself a little."

"You know me," he laughed.

"I do, which is why I'm asking you to pace yourself and show a modicum of restraint."

"I'll be as good as gold, Sophs, I promise. Which bed is mine, Tel?"

"The one we haven't just been snogging on."

"Right you are." He lifted his bags up onto the neat bed. "I'll unpack later, I'm famished. What time is dinner?"

"Six."

"Then let us depart our sordid bachelor pad and go eat. After you, lovely woman. You get more beautiful each time I see you, how is that possible?"

"It's a gift," she laughed, "From my mother."

As they left the room Lucas casually asked, "Is Annie here?"

"Yes, and she's still not talking to you after last time."

They were walking down the long corridor.

"Why, what happened last time?"

"Lucas!"

"What?"

"You called her 'posh totty' and told her that her magnificent breasts should be on display for all to admire."

"Her breasts *are* magnificent."

"Hardly the thing to be shouting about at Mrs Rudge's funeral though, is it."

"I can't help being a terrible flirt."

"You can, and you'd better."

"Scouts honour, Sophie, I'll be the perfect gentleman."

Tel laughed. "You weren't in the scouts."

"Wasn't I?"

"No, you insisted on going to Brownies and were kicked out for lifting the girls' dresses with a stick."

"Oh yes," he grinned. "But I still don't understand why Annie isn't speaking to me."

"I'm sorry, Lucas, she just doesn't like you."

"Bit cruel. Also, quite hard to fathom, everybody likes me, I'm practically irresistible."

"Not to Annie, you're not."

"She's just playing hard to get."

"Give it up," Tel said, "She's way out of your league anyway."

"I know, but I do like a good chase. I'll win her round

eventually, you'll see. I am nothing if not tenacious."

The rehearsal dinner in the dining room was an informal get-together. Charlotte, Camille's cousin, turned up drunk, still wearing her camping shorts and a stained t-shirt. Her husband, Ike, had made some kind of an effort and wore a dusty suit that was too small for him, topped by a permanently morose expression. Their son, Pete, the very epitome of a monosyllabic teenager, dropped his head to his phone and stayed like that for the rest of the night, occasionally picking at his food.

Sally, Camille's younger sister, shrieked and laughed and shrieked some more, forcing Sophie to discretely ask her mother if she was on any kind of medication.

"She's off her meds now," Camille said, as another high-pitched shriek echoed around the room, making several people touch their ears to make sure they weren't bleeding, "That's why she's like this."

Sally's husband, Harry, concentrated solely on his food and making sure his wine glass was filled each time a waiter walked by. After each course he sneaked outside for a cigarette. He spoke to no one. Sophie could never figure out if he was shy or just terribly rude.

On her dad's side, Aunt Mildred, a voluptuous liver consultant on Harley Street, regaled guests with her stories of the rich and famous. "He wanted a brand-new liver," she said, "Thought I could just magic one out of thin air for him and was genuinely shocked when I said he couldn't have one. 'Find me a donor,' he insisted, and I told him it wasn't a medical emergency and that if he stopped drinking so much his liver would restore itself, but he said he didn't have the time and it was just easier to have a new one."

"Who was this?" someone asked.

"I can't disclose my clients," Mildred said, "Confidentiality and all that. He's dead now, of course, refused to stop drinking." Several people put down their glasses of wine.

Mildred's husband, Carl, a rotund man with sparse hair,

spent the entire evening surreptitiously staring across the table at the contents of Annie's low-cut dress.

"See," Lucas whispered in Sophie's ear, "I'm not the only one enamoured by her assets."

"He's a plastic surgeon, he's used to looking at women's breasts."

"I bet he doesn't look at them the way he's looking at Annie's or he'd have been barred from medical practice by now."

The rest of the table were made up of various relatives and, Sophie noticed, a couple of high-profile business clients her dad had sneaked in. It was loud, chaotic, and jolly, apart from the spat about drinking too much which exploded between Sally and Harry, and the slurred bellowing from a very drunk Charlotte, mainly about how expensive weddings were and how some people had very little in the way of 'disposable income' in order to be able to afford a pretentious hotel room.

Pam, Sophie's old friend from university and mother of the two small bridesmaids, spent most of the time rounding up her two- and five-year-old daughters, who found it hilarious to dive under the table and tickle everyone's legs. Throughout the meal people suddenly jumped in their seats and cried out in alarm, followed by the giggling of toddlers.

Tel's brother, David, and his Texan boyfriend, Travis, had wildly animated conversations with everyone around them, frequently bursting into squeals of laughter. His dad didn't speak, his mother wouldn't stop.

"Bit of a motley crew, aren't they," Tel whispered to Sophie.

"Which ones, yours or mine?"

"Both."

"Have you seen my dad's cousin, Charlie? I don't know why he thinks dressing up in a cowboy outfit is suitable attire for a rehearsal dinner. I'll have to talk to him about what he's wearing tomorrow."

"I'm betting a Star Wars theme," Tel said, glancing down the table, "Darth Vadar, or Chewbacca."

"Oh, it doesn't bear thinking about!"

In a deep voice Tel breathed, "I am your cousin!"

"Stop it! I can't look at him now without laughing."

"It's good to see you happy again, Sophs."

"It feels good. We're here, the wedding's tomorrow, there'll be no more changes and–"

"Have you had second thoughts about the live band?" Jacquie butted in from the left. "It's not too late to bring in the chamber orchestra, you know."

"It is, mum, and no, we haven't changed our minds."

"Your cousin's on standby if you do, just let me know."

Tel shook his head. Sophie rolled her eyes, straight round to her mother, who leaned towards her and said, "I know it's a bit last-minute, darling, but–"

"No."

"I haven't said what it is yet."

"I don't need to know. Nothing is changing. Nothing."

"Well, okay, I just thought Tel arriving at the ceremony on a black stallion would be very dramatic, that's all."

Sophie turned to look at Tel, who stared at her, open-mouthed. They both burst out laughing.

* * *

Meanwhile, back at the camp, Brian and Mark had set up identical barbecues; tripods with a chained grill hanging over a fire pit.

"Towsure deal of the week?" Mark asked.

"Special offer from Aldi," Brian said, stoking up his briquettes.

"How much?"

Brian told him and Mark sucked in air – he'd paid twice as much! "M&S extra special beefburgers," he said, holding up a couple of frozen boxes.

"Almost out of date, take your chances section at Asda," Brian said, pointing at the boxes in his open coolbox.

"Best sausages money can buy from the local farm shop,"

Mark said, holding up a pack of eight.

"Meat man on the car park in Longbridge," Brian said, lifting up a heavy plastic bag. "Includes chicken legs, chicken wings, chicken kebabs, minty lamb chops, and twenty-four pork sausages."

"Ciabatta Rolls from Waitrose."

"Pack of twelve seeded buns for a quid at Iceland."

"What *are* you two doing?" Faye asked, coming over with bowl of salad.

"Bit of 'my meat is better than your meat' banter," Brian laughed.

"Horn locking, you mean?"

"He's a mate, he can take it."

"I can't take it!" Mark cried dramatically.

Faye tutted and wandered off to get cutlery. Mark picked a plastic box up off the table and said, "The best barbecue ribs on the planet, made by my very lovely girlfriend."

"Give it up, Bri," Faye shouted from their caravan, "I can't compete with Liv's cooking."

Olivia giggled as she came out of the motorhome with more plastic boxes. "Potato salad with bacon and buttermilk dressing," she said, putting them down, "And sweet potato salad with sage, speck, horseradish, and soft-boiled quails eggs."

"I love having barbecues with you," Brian sighed, licking his lips, "Best cook on the planet."

"Excuse me?" Faye huffed out of the caravan with a tray full of foil-wrapped objects and started slapping them on the edge of the grill. "Probably overcooked baked potatoes, cheap from the market." She pointed at her bowl on the table, adding, "Salad, by Faye. Hand-shredded iceberg lettuce, with vine-picked tomatoes and delicately-sliced cucumbers, finished with an Asda's own-brand Ceasar dressing."

"Outstanding," Brian grinned. Then, turning from turning beefburgers, he glanced back at Jim and Beth, casually sitting on chairs behind them. "Your contribution, Jim?"

"To what?"

"The barbecue."

"Contribution?"

"Am I speaking too Yorkshire for you?"

"Must be a speech impediment," Beth laughed. "I've brought six bottles of Dom Perignon champagne, should be enough for you lot. I'm detoxing."

"Detoxing?" Faye asked.

"Yeah, just thought I'd cut down for a bit, maybe lose some weight."

"You're perfect as you are," Jim said, kissing her cheek.

"Yeah, but I wanna see if I can be a bit perfecter."

"Not possible."

"Jim?" Brian said again, "What have you brought?"

"Just my skintitilating … skindeflating?"

"Scintillating, babes."

"My scintillating company."

Mark laughed. "What's that worth, half a beefburger?"

"Looks like you'll be going hungry then, lad."

"What?"

"No bring, no eat," Mark explained.

"I can't have anything?"

"They're joking," Olivia said, putting down yet more boxes. "There's more than enough for everybody. Grilled halloumi with a peach, ham and mint salad, and marinated lamb cutlets with herb dipping sauce."

"Invite us to every barbecue you ever have," Brian said, salivating.

"Oh, don't worry about me," Faye huffed, "I don't feel at all left out, under-appreciated or offended by your flattering comments about another woman's cooking."

"Oops, upset the wife," Brian said, quickly putting down his tongs. "Jim, take over while I appease the old ball and chain."

"What?" said Jim.

"The barbecue!" Mark hissed, "Take over the barbecue!"

Faye was already trying to hide a smile as Brian swooped down on her, wrapped her in his enormous arms and said, "You make the best …"

Faye pulled an arm free and glanced at her watch.

"The best …"

"What am I supposed to be doing?" Jim asked, prodding at a sausage.

"Turning," Mark told him, "Keep turning the bloody meat."

"It's not bloody, looks cooked to me."

"Cooked, except they've been on the grill for two whole minutes and they're still pink on top."

"I like mine well done," Beth said.

"Waiting," Faye sighed.

"The best … bread and butter pudding!" Brian cried with relief. "Yes, your bread-and-butter pudding is–"

"I've never made bread and butter pudding, Bri."

"Haven't you?"

"No. Never. I don't like bread and butter pudding."

"Well, what's that creamy, fruity thing you make then?"

Faye lifted her chin and said, "Spotted dick."

"Is it?"

"Yes."

"Are you sure?"

"Positive."

"But it's got that runny sauce in the middle, like a chicken Kiev."

Faye lifted her chin higher. "That's the suet that hasn't cooked properly."

"Oh."

Mark, Olivia and Beth were now crying with laughter. Jim continued to prod things on the grill, saying, "How do you know when they're done."

"They'll look cooked," Mark snorted. "Have you not done a barbecue before?"

"No."

"How is that even possible?"

Jim shrugged.

Faye had untangled herself from Brian's arms and was now furiously pouting around the table.

"Sweetheart," Brian whined, "You know I love you to bits."

"But not my cooking, apparently."

"You can't be good at everything, love."

Faye's pout tightened and Brian quickly added, "I'm not saying it's terrible."

"What are you saying, Bri?"

"I'm saying … nobody's ever … died afterwards."

Mark, unable to control himself any longer, exploded with laughter until he'd run out of breath and was bent double. Olivia put a hand over her cute overbite. Beth was dabbing at her eyes with the hem of her blouse and crying, "Stop, please, me makeup!"

"That's the best thing you can say about my cooking, Bri, that it doesn't poison people?"

Brian took a deep breath, held it, exhaled, threw his arms up and said, "Your toast is amazing, if a little on the dark side. Shall I put myself in the naughty corner or will you be using a cattle prod to guide me there?"

Faye considered this as she absently opened up a plastic box and put something in her mouth. Her face immediately changed. Her eyes bulged. She turned to Olivia and gasped, "What is this?"

"It's the grilled halloumi with a peach, ham and mint salad."

"Oh my God!" she cried, picking up the box and staring into it, "It's *amazing*!"

Brian hurried over. Faye clutched the box tight to her chest. "Mine!" she cried, "It's all mine!"

"We share *everything*."

"Not this. I'm not sharing this. Liv, just so you know, we're available for invites to dinner at your place at any time, day or night, just say the word and we'll be there."

"They live in the Cotswolds!" Brian said.

"Day or night," Faye repeated, lifting halloumi into her mouth as Brian tried to reach over and grab a piece.

Blushing, Olivia said, "My mum taught me to cook, she's much better at it than me."

"How is your mother these days?" Brian boomed.

"She's fine, happy, in love, still travelling and–"

"We should visit her sometime."

"Yes," said Faye, "Any time, day or night."

"Well, she's bought a villa in the South of France."

"Not a problem," Faye said, "We can stay in the caravan."

"It'd never make it that far," Mark laughed, "You'd arrive with just a chassis."

Brian, hungry, opened up another box, took out something on a stick, put it in his mouth and groaned with happiness. "Divine," he said.

"That's the marinated lamb cutlets with a herb dipping sauce," Olivia said, "You're supposed to cook them first."

Brian stopped chewing, took the bone from his mouth and placed the half-masticated cutlet on his grill.

"Pressure!" said Jim, jabbing it.

"Do you have a signature dish?" Olivia asked Faye, attempting to make things better.

"Salad!" Brian cried, and started running.

CHAPTER SEVEN

Saturday – The Day of the Wedding

Sophie opened her eyes and wondered where she was as her fingers stroked the unfamiliar white sheets. Then, reaching out a hand into the empty space beside her, she wondered where Tel was.

Rolling onto her back, she remembered where she was and why she was here, and a wave of abject panic washed over her, followed by a gentle buzz of exhilaration, and finally a sense of resignation and acceptance.

Today was the day. By the time she got back into bed again she would be a married woman, she would be a wife and Tel would be her husband.

Her heart rate increased. She felt exhilarated and terrified at the same time.

"Mrs Sophie Okenado," she breathed. Or maybe she'd keep her own name. "Mrs Sophie Forbes." Or perhaps a hyphenation to acknowledge her marital status and Tel's importance in her life. "Mrs Sophie Forbes-Okenado." Probably should have thought about it earlier, but then there was the chaos of organising and the chaos of the mothers, and then, of course, the nervous breakdown, there really hadn't been time. She'd think about it later.

She clambered out of bed and took a deep, calming breath. Today was the day. Everything had been planned and set in stone, nothing could change now. As Tel had said to her mother, all they had to do now was enjoy it. She felt immensely relieved.

Until her mother burst into her bedroom.

"Sophie!" she cried, "You're up! You're awake!"

"Not fully conscious yet, mum." She stood up and slipped the silk dressing gown over the long, sexy negligee she hoped Tel would like later. "Don't hit me with anything drastic or horrendous, no deaths in the night or the arrival of Tel's hitherto unknown first wife."

"No, no, everything's fine." Camille, already dressed in her mother-of-the-bride outfit, complete with a jaunty fascinator on her newly primped hair, hurried over to tie up her dressing gown and place a gentle hand on her shoulder. "Just have to get you ready." She dabbed at her eyes.

"Are you crying, mum?"

"My baby's getting married, of course I'm crying."

"With happiness or with inconsolable misery."

Her mother pushed the hand on her shoulder. "With happiness, of course!"

"No last-minute cries of 'Don't do it' or 'He's not the one'?"

"You're definitely doing it, and Tel is, without doubt, the one. You picked well, my child," she winked.

"Oh, cool."

With her mother obviously in her element, perhaps the day wasn't going to be so bad after all. In fact, Sophie felt quite hopeful and optimistic about it.

"So, where are my bridesmaids to pamper me and make me beautiful?" she grinned.

"Couldn't wake Fi, and Annie is still in the bathroom throwing up."

"Are you sure Fi's just sleeping?" She wished she hadn't said anything about people dying in the night.

"I checked, she's breathing."

"And Annie throwing up?"

"Too much to drink last night."

"Shocker. Just you and me then, mum."

Camille hugged her. "Love you, darling," she sniffed. "I just want you to be happy. I think Tel will make you very happy."

Sophie hugged her back. "Love you too, mum. I am, and he will."

"Your dad threatened to take his kneecaps off if he didn't."

"He never did!"

"He did. He was joking, of course. At least, I think he was joking."

"Mum!"

"Come on, no time to pither and dither, you've got a wedding to get ready for."

And the process began.

* * *

Meanwhile, back at the camp…

They were sitting on the grass, sipping coffee and munching butter-drenched toast, the women chattering about the wedding and what they were wearing and how exciting it was and how gorgeous Sophie was going to look, and Tel too.

Amidst the shrieks of excitement and the hand waving, Brian suddenly leaned forward in his chair and lifted up his bare foot, saying, in a high-pitched voice, "I've got these *divine* black lace-up shoes that really show off my legs."

Mark laughed and raised his own foot, running a hand up his hairy calf and saying, in an equally squeaky voice, "I've got some *adorable* La-Buttons that make me walk like a farmer with haemorrhoids but they do *wonders* for my pins."

"Pins?" said Jim.

"Legs," Beth said.

"What are you wearing, Jim?" Brian shrilled, waving a limp hand at him.

"Blue shoes."

"Suede, are they?"

Jim shrugged. "No, leather, I think." He turned to Beth. "Are they leather?"

"Yeah, babes."

"But do they make you look *gorgeous*?" Mark asked, laughing and quickly adding, "Although it would take more than a pair of shoes to make you look anywhere near gorgeous."

"Jim *is* gorgeous," Beth said, leaning over to kiss his cheek, which made him smile and flutter his eyebrows at Brian and Mark.

"As long as you think so, that's all that matters," Brian said.

"I do, and it is."

"Kiss me, woman!" Brian cried out to Faye, "I'm feeling left out!"

Faye leaned over, nearly falling off her chair, and planted a kiss on his beard. Mark turned an expectant cheek towards Olivia, who said, "Oh, you've got butter on your face."

They all watched in horror as Olivia pulled a square of kitchen towel off the roll on the table, licked it, and wiped his face before kissing it.

"Me mom used to do that," Beth said.

"Horrid."

"Very unhygienic."

"I like it," said Mark, "Makes me feel special, pampered." He planted a smacker on Olivia's mouth, making her giggle.

"I wonder what they're doing now," Faye breathed.

"I wonder what they're eating for breakfast," said Brian, smacking his lips.

"You've eaten *four* slices of toast, Bri, how can you still be hungry?"

"It was three, and I'm always hungry, don't you know that by now?"

"Is it because Faye's such a bad cook and you've got to eat when you can?" Jim laughed. Beth froze him with a look. He raised his palms up to her and mouthed, 'What?' Faye looked away and jutted her chin in the air, sniffing.

Mark said, "If Faye cooked as well as Olivia, Bri, you'd be the size of–"

"A barn," Beth cackled.

"A brick sh–" Jim started to say, silenced by a sharp elbow in his ribs which made him go sh-*oomph*.

"Zeppelin," Mark said.

"A whale," Brian laughed, rubbing his tummy.

Faye got up and walked into their caravan. Brian hesitated for a moment, then gave chase.

"My cooking isn't that bad," Faye hissed at him inside the caravan.

"No, love, it isn't. We were just having a laugh."

"At my expense?"

"Laughing *with* you, Faye, not *at* you."

"I wasn't laughing, Bri."

"Look, love, if it wasn't for you I wouldn't be the attractively thin and delicate man I am today."

"You know we can all hear you out here, don't you?" Mark shouted.

There followed some whispering, some hissing, a lot of murmuring, and then Faye came out of the caravan again, smiling.

"I have learned the error of my ways," Brian said, meekly following her. "And, as my beautiful wife so succinctly pointed out, a public apology and a meal at the restaurant of her choice is a small price to pay compared to the cost of a divorce solicitor."

"Sorry, Faye," said Mark, "We weren't being mean."

"It's because I can't smell," Faye said. "You can't be a good cook without a sense of smell."

"Can't smell the burning, can you," Jim said, matter of factly, and they all sucked in air and held it, peering at Faye from the corner of their eyes.

"I could show you how to do make grilled halloumi with a peach, ham and mint salad," Olivia offered. "It's really easy and I have some ingredients left."

Brian inhaled, ready to say, 'Not another grill fire,' but thought better of it.

"Oh, thanks, Liv," Faye said, and they all exhaled. "Don't look so worried," she added, "I know I'm not the best cook. I'll certainly never reach Liv's standard. I haven't taken offence …

much."

Mark looked up at Brian, standing with his hands on his hips, and said, "Looking good there, mate."

Brian threw back his broad shoulders and sucked in his tummy. "Thanks, it's the wife's cooking." He glanced at Faye's puckered face and quickly added, "Too soon?"

Faye leaned forward in her chair, pulled out the cushion from behind her, and lobbed it at him.

* * *

Back at the hotel, Fi had emerged from her coma and Annie was out of the bathroom, looking pale and horribly hungover. Camille slotted her iPhone into a mobile speaker, and suddenly the room was filled with the sound of Vivaldi's *Concerto in G*.

"Right!" she cried, "Let's get on with it then!"

Annie groaned. Fi rubbed her eyes. Sophie said, "Miserable bridesmaids I've picked for my wedding! Where's the joy? Where's the excitement? You're supposed to be happy for me, instead, you look like a couple of kids stuck in detention."

"Soz, Sophs," Fi yawned, "I was up half the night with emergency phonecalls."

"I thought you were supposed to be having the weekend off?"

"An A&E doctor is never 'off'. I'm always on call."

"Then turn off your phone."

Fi, who was clutching the phone in her hand, immediately looked mortified. "But ... but what if there's an emergency? What if I'm needed?"

"What if *I* need you, right here, right now?"

Fi glanced wide-eyed at her phone, which, as if she had willed it, started to ring. She had an emergency siren ringtone which bounced around the hotel suite.

Annie, perched on the edge of the bed, hung her head in her hands and croaked, "Make it stop!"

"Don't answer it," Sophie snapped.

Fi stared at Sophie. Sophie stared at Fi, who surreptitiously moved a thumb. The emergency siren stopped and Fi brought the phone up to her ear. "Hello, Doctor Braddock speaking."

Sophie crossed her arms and stood on one leg, impatiently tapping the foot of the other.

"Yes, Doctor Michael is the best person to call. Stop any bleeding and have them sent for a scan to check for any internal bleeding, especially around the–" Fi caught Sophie's piercing gaze and quickly said, "Doctor Michael can deal with anything else." She hung up.

Sophie held out a hand, grimacing. Fi looked at her phone again, and reluctantly handed it over. Sophie slipped it into the dressing table drawer and turned to face her Matron of Honour and Chief Bridesmaid. "Right," she said firmly, "This is my wedding day, my celebratory weekend, and nothing, *nothing*, is going to ruin it. Do I make myself clear?"

Fi nodded. Annie said, "Yah."

"Fi, stagger down to the dining room and drink black coffee until it comes out of your eyeballs. Annie, get yourself a full English breakfast to soak up that alcohol. Let's try this again in an hour, smiling and happy and excited for the day ahead this time, shall we?"

They shuffled off, Annie holding a hand to her head, Fi glancing down at her empty one.

"Shower, darling?" Camille said, "Before the hairstylist and makeup girl get here?"

Sophie took a deep, calming breath, and headed into the ensuite bathroom.

* * *

Faye came rushing out of the caravan wearing a floaty summer dress, her hands shaking on either side of her head as she screamed, "Liv! Beth! I forgot to bring hair grips!" Her pitch of hysteria increased as she cried out, "Has anybody got hair grips? *I need hair grips*!"

Brian sauntered out of the caravan behind her, tall and distinguished in a dark grey suit and tie. "Your hair looks fine," he said.

"No, it doesn't! I can't pin it up, I forgot the bloody hair grips!"

"Leave it down then."

"I can't!"

"Why not?"

"Because I have to have it *up* for the *fascinator*!"

"If you don't calm yourself, woman, you're going to implode and stain that lovely dress."

"You're not helping, Brian!"

"I am but a mere man."

Faye screamed again, wordless this time. Beth, wearing a dressing gown and curlers, her face like a blank canvas, came running over with a plastic box of hair grips, thrust them into Faye's hands, and rushed back again. Faye dashed into the caravan.

Mark sauntered out of the motorhome, resplendent in a pale blue suit and tie. He ambled over to a chair and sat down. "Women seem a bit stressed," he said. "Olivia's tried on three dresses and still can't decide which one to wear. She's treating it like a life-or-death situation."

"First wedding with a girlfriend?" Brian chuckled.

"Yeah, apart from my own, of course."

"It's all part of the 'getting ready' process; abject panic, hysteria, meltdowns. Just ignore them, they'll eventually calm down."

They didn't.

"Bri! Bri!"

"What? What?"

"Can you help me with my hair?"

Brian looked at his massive fingers and yelled, "No."

"Coming!" Beth cried, running over again, this time wearing a very tight, pale blue dress with an embroidered bolero jacket. One eye was outlined in makeup, the other naked, like a cyclops who'd had a stroke. She held onto her breasts as she ran.

"Blimey," Mark said, "Hope that dress has some sturdy straps on it."

"It has," Beth said, dropping one side of her jacket to show the thin straps digging into the flesh on her shoulders.

"Are those strips of cotton up for the task?"

"If they not," she puffed, rushing past, "I've got a whole roll of tit tape underneath, I might never get it off again."

"Mark!" Olivia cried, standing at the door of the motorhome and breathing as if she'd just finished running a marathon, "What do you think of this dress?"

"It's nice."

"You said that about the other two."

"They're all nice, you look lovely in all of them."

"Do you think the green one is better? I'm not sure if it's bad luck or not to wear green to a wedding."

"Then wear that one."

"But which looks better?"

"They're all lovely."

"Oh, you're no help at all!"

"Have you ever watched at TV programme called *Say Yes to the Dress*?" Brian asked, as Olivia started banging around in the motorhome.

"No, I can't say I have. Sounds right up my street though."

"Very good for picking up tips on what to say, apparently."

"BETH!" Jim yelled from inside their motorhome, "WHICH SOCKS SHOULD I WEAR?"

"ANY."

"I DON'T WANT THEM CLASHING WITH MY SUIT."

"THE BLACK ONES."

"ISN'T BLACK FOR FUNERALS?"

"THEY'RE SOCKS, JIM, JUST PICK A PAIR! LIV, DID YOU WANT ME TO DO YOUR NAILS?"

"OH, MY NAILS! I FORGOT ABOUT MY NAILS! WILL WE HAVE TIME?"

"I THINK SO."

Brian glanced at his watch. "Only three more hours to go."

Jim came out of the motorhome adjusting his suit jacket. Brian and Mark stared at him as he strutted over.

"What in heaven's name are you wearing?" Mark gasped.

"Nice, innit. Good fit, too."

"It's ..." Brian turned to Mark. "What would you say that was, chequered or tartan?"

"I'd say a mixture of both, in fifty shades of–"

"Blue?"

"I was going to say purple, but maybe it's some weird shade of mauve that only women know the name of."

"Mauve," Brian said, nodding his head.

"Do you like it?" Jim asked, posing like a catalogue man in front of them. "Beth picked it out for me."

"From a Scottish tailor selling off his back room rejects?"

"It was very expensive," Jim frowned.

"Saw you coming, mate."

"IT'S VERY *ON TREND*," Beth shouted through the caravan window.

"It's definitely on something," Mark laughed.

"Drugs perhaps?" Brian said.

"Made by someone who was clearly colour blind."

"Or just blind."

"HE LOOKS VERY SMART AND YOU'D BETTER STOP PICKING ON HIM OR I'LL COME OUT THERE AND SLAP YOU BOTH," Beth hollered.

"Smart?" Mark sniggered, "It's going to take more than a purple tartan suit to make Jim look smart."

"I CAN STILL HEAR YOU!" Beth yelled.

"PACK IT IN, YOU TWO," Faye added, "WE'VE ALREADY GOT ENOUGH TO COPE WITH."

"Okay, we'll stop." Brian looked up at Jim. "Sit down," he said, "Take the weight off your psychedelic apparel. Come and clash with this recliner here."

Smiling, as proud as punch in his new suit, Jim threw himself into it and it immediately tipped backwards, leaving him looking up at the sky.

Mark burst out laughing. "Chair thinks you're a blanket."

"Mark," Olivia said from the motorhome doorway.

"Liv?"

"This is my emergency backup dress, what do you think?" Olivia stood in the motorhome doorway wearing what looked like a Charleston fringe dress in royal blue, with sequins.

"Nice," Mark said, struggling and failing to stop an eye twitching from the glare.

Olivia looked like she was about to burst into tears, her curly black hair, normally held up in a clasp, cascading down around her shoulders.

"The pink one," Brian said, "I think I liked that one the best."

"Oh, did you?"

"Yes, definitely the pink one, brought out the colour of your cheeks, Liv."

Smiling now, Olivia disappeared back into the motorhome to change again.

"Be decisive," Brian said to Mark. "You can't like everything, you have to pick one, any one, or they'll never stop mithering."

Mark nodded. "I'll include that in my Little Book of Men's Answers."

"Oh, you've started your own?"

"You wouldn't lend me yours."

"I give excerpts when required. Maybe we can compare notes later?"

"Metaphorically speaking, I'm only three pages in. How many pages does yours have."

"Bloody millions," Brian sighed.

They sat and watched the women flitting from caravan to motorhome, squealing and panicking, oohing and aahing. Jim continued to lie horizontal on the chair, possibly in contemplation of life, the universe and stuff, but more likely he'd fallen asleep. Beth disappeared into her motorhome for a short time, returning with both her eyes fully made up and her blonde hair perfectly coiffed in a 1950s pin-up style. She placed a plastic case on the table and dashed into Brian and Faye's caravan.

Olivia still couldn't decide between her four outfits and kept changing, asking them what they thought, before giving up and rushing over to ask the opinion of the relatives in the other caravans, who were much too busy getting themselves ready to even look – except for Charlotte, who glanced at her briefly and said, "It'll do, I suppose."

"It'll do!" Olivia repeated, dashing back with wide, tear-filled eyes, "She said it's an 'it'll do' outfit!"

"Who, the woman wearing a white blouse with a stain on the front, blue knee-length shorts, and trainers?" Mark asked.

"Yes."

"Has a keen eye for fashion, does she?"

Olivia looked back, confused and uncertain. Beth yelled, "DEFINITELY THE PINK ONE, LIV," and Brian said, "See, the pink one, definitely the pink one." Olivia dashed off to get changed again.

Faye and Beth hurried over to the table and threw themselves into chairs. Beth opened up the plastic case, revealing a plethora of nail tools and varnishes. She started furiously filing Faye's nails, then buffing them like she was cleaning shoes in a hurry.

"What colour varnish?" she asked.

There followed a 15-minute discussion on which colour best suited the flowery, floaty dress Faye was wearing, during which Mark wandered into the motorhome for a cup of tea and was promptly kicked out again for 'taking up too much space'. Brian made tea, returning with three mugs in each hand, just as Faye picked a 'mango' varnish.

"Hope we're not having mango for starters at the wedding breakfast," Brian said, "You'll be chomping on your own fingernails."

"Don't be silly, Bri."

"Silly is all I have left after the sense of humour packed up and left earlier."

"You've still got it," Mark said.

"Ah, but it's not like it once was." He started off into the distance. "I miss it."

Jim struggled to sit upright in his chair in order to reach his tea. Mark had to reach out and push down on his feet, jettisoning him forward. He sipped at the mug. "No sugar in this, Bri," he said, holding it out, "I take three."

"Get it yourself!"

"I might stain the suit."

"Then spoon carefully!"

Jim wandered into the caravan. "Where's the sugar, Bri?"

"In the drop-down cupboard on the left where we keep the booze."

"You got a lot of booze in here, Bri."

"Emergency purposes only, like late afternoons or pre-wedding nervous breakdown, stuff like that."

Jim came back holding the mug of tea at arm's length with both hands, well away from his suit. He sat down in the chair and spilled a single drop onto his knee.

"Oh!" he howled, "It's ruined now!"

"Oh babes!"

Mark peered closely at the cloth-clad knee. "Can't see anything."

"I can, just there, see? It's ruined!"

Olivia came to the door of her motorhome and threw something at Jim, which made him jump, which made him spill another drop of tea onto his thigh, burning him and making him cry out as he pulled a damp cloth off his face.

"Dab, don't rub," she said, disappearing again.

Jim diligently dabbed. Beth delicately painted, telling Faye to "Stop shaking!"

"I can't help it, I'm so excited!"

"Can you do mine afterwards?" Olivia shouted.

"Yeah, babes, if Faye ever keeps her fingers still."

Faye closed her eyes and took deep breaths. Brian

hummed, "Omm, omm."

Mark glanced at his watch. "Two hours to go."

"Do you think we'll make it?" Brian asked.

"I doubt it."

"Doubt what?" Jim asked.

"Doubt you'll get through the day without at least one person asking what statement you're trying to make with that suit," Brian laughed.

"Oi!" Beth snapped, holding up a nail file, "I have a weapon and I know how to use it."

"Death by nail file," Mark pondered, "Never saw that on *Dexter*."

"It might start a trend."

"Bit of a slow death though, plenty of time to fight her off and escape."

"Did you see how fast she filed?" Brian said, "She'd have your head off in seconds."

"While I calmly sat here and let her?"

"Are you willing to take that risk?"

"Nah, Sophie would be furious if I turned up headless and covered in blood."

"What *are* you two wittering on about?" Faye said.

"Just chewing the cud, love."

"I'd rather be chewing on a Big Mac," Mark said.

"Oh, now you're talking." Brian hauled himself to his feet. "Anyone for a MacDonalds?"

"Bri! You'll ruin your appetite for the wedding breakfast!"

"Growing lad needs to keep his strength up for the big day ahead," said Mark, following Brian to his car.

"Wait for me!" Jim cried, giving chase.

"Slouch down in the back," Brian said, "A suit like that could ruin my street cred."

* * *

The bridal suite was full to capacity as various women swirled and fussed around Sophie, except for Fi, who lay on the bed like a dishevelled Sleeping Beauty. Sophie stood in front of a full-length mirror waiting for them to slip the gorgeous wedding dress over her head. It swished as it moved. Dozens of tiny diamantes flashed as they caught the light from the window. The material felt luxurious beneath her fingers. She felt like a princess about to marry her prince.

When the women started to gently ease it over her head and slip it down her body, it stopped. They couldn't get the embroidered bodice passed her chest. The full skirt slipped down to her knees in a desultory fashion.

"Damn!" she hissed.

"What size is it, darling?" Camille asked from the other side of the room.

"Ten, mum."

"But you're a size twelve."

"I know, I was aiming for ten!"

"Crap aim," a woman laughed, pulling on the material, which refused to unbunch from under her armpits.

Sophie looked at the woman, didn't recognise her, and said, "Who are you?"

"Sue's my cleaner," Camille said, "I said she could come."

"Not being rude," Sophie said, glancing at Sue, "But why?"

"She's a very good cleaner and good cleaners are hard to come by. You have to give them incentives to stay or else they'll be poached by other employers offering better enticements and you'll be left with an untidy house. You'd be amazed what good cleaners get given."

"Me mate was given a car," Sue said.

"We've discussed this," Camille said, "It's a rental, and you don't need one."

"But me mate's got one."

"Because she does the school run and all the household errands. Anyway, you've got the use of the Daimler when you need it."

"Can't park a Daimler in London."

"You can't park any car in London, you get a taxi."

"If we could just focus on the problem in hand?" Sophie said, looking back at the mirror and her scrunched-up dress. She braced herself and cried, "Pull!"

"We're pulling," Annie said, "Suck in a bit."

"Breathe out, not in!" Sam, Sophie's oldest friend, cried, "You'll expand like a balloon if you fill yourself with air."

Sophie exhaled and held it, half hunched, as the women around her gently tugged on the ivory satin. It stuttered over her chest, sailed passed her waist, and came to a dead stop around her hips. Sophie, almost fainting from lack of oxygen, gasped in air and looked at herself in the mirror; tall, elegant, hair and make-up perfect, dress bunched up like a giant tutu with the skirt hanging down at a jaunty angle. "Not quite the look I was going for," she grunted.

"It's very ... grungy," said Tam, the New Zealand friend Sophie had met whilst backpacking a decade earlier.

Camille left the room as the women tugged, gently at first and then more desperately. It wouldn't pass her hips, and the back pieces would not come together no matter what they did.

"Have you put on weight?" Sue, the cleaner, asked.

"No, I've lost a few pounds actually."

"Did it fit you when you first tried it on?" asked Sam.

"Well, yes, but that was a size twelve and I thought a size ten would look better."

Sam and Annie swapped a look and just the teensiest eyeball roll.

"Have you evacuated this morning?" Pam, her university friend and mother of the two small bridesmaids, asked.

"Evacuated what?"

"Your bowels."

"I know we've been mates for a long time, Pam, but I don't think we've reached the age yet where we can comfortably discuss our bowel movements."

"One good evacuation could lose you two or three pounds."

They all turned to glare, horrified, at Pam.

"That's a bag of sugar!" Annie gasped. "What the hell are

you eating?"

Pam shrugged. "It was just a wild guess, it's not like I've ever pulled one out of the bowl and weighed it or anything."

"Ugh!" Sophie cried.

Tam surveyed the gap in the back of the dress, running her fingers over her chin. "We could sew ribbon across the gape in the back?" she suggested, "Make it look like a loosely tied corset?"

"Or go punk and hold it together with giant safety pins," said Annie. "Very Elizabeth Hurley."

"Or kilt pins," Sam said. "Are any of the men wearing kilts?"

"No," Sophie sighed, "I asked them not to."

"Oh, pity."

As Sophie stared miserably into the mirror and the women stared at her stuck dress and gaping back, Camille slipped back into the room with a zipped-up dress bag identical to the one the wedding dress had come in, complete with the Chanel logo printed on the front.

"I've brought another one," Camille said, holding it up.

Sophie turned from the mirror. "Another dress?"

"Yes. The shop said whichever one you didn't wear you could return."

Sophie stared at her mother. "You've brought another wedding dress?"

"Yes." She lay the bag down on the bed, next to a sleeping Fi. "I'm not interfering, really I'm not, but when I picked it up I saw that you'd ordered a size ten and I thought you'd made a mistake, or the shop had. Luckily, they had the same dress in a size twelve in stock, so ... I brought it, just in case."

"Mum!"

"Yes, Sophie?"

"You're a bloody genius!"

"Thank you, darling."

"Okay, girls, let's get this dress off."

It took ten minutes of wriggling and manoeuvring,

pulling and tugging, until Sophie was finally free. They slipped the size twelve over her head and it fell perfectly into place, skimming effortlessly over her hips. Pam and Annie crawled on their hands and knees to put the short train into place around her stilettoed feet.

"Oh Sophie!" Camille cried, lifting her hands to her face, "You look beautiful."

"You have the perfect body for a slinky Chanel dress," Annie sniffed.

"Can I 'ave it after?" Sue, the cleaner, asked.

"I've just this second put it on!"

"I know, but when you've finished and the wedding's all over and everythin', can I 'ave it?"

"No!"

Sue shrugged.

The make-up woman and the hair stylist rushed over to repair anything the dress had misplaced. The stylist placed a sparkling tiara on top of her head, adjusted some locks of hair, and draped the exquisitely embroidered veil over it. Camille's cries got louder. Annie continued to sniff. Pam and Tam dabbed at their eyes.

"You look bloody bonzer, mate," Tam said.

Sophie looked at herself in the mirror and smiled.

It was perfect.

* * *

"I'm going to be sick."

"Don't be sick, Tel."

"Telling me not to be sick is not going to stop me feeling sick."

"Are you having doubts?"

"God, no."

"Because I'm quite happy to take your place if you want to do a runner."

"Very comforting."

"That's what friends are for."

"She wouldn't have you anyway."

"I'll charm my way into her affections."

"You're not helping, Lucas."

"No, you're right, she's way out of my league and definitely a zillion miles out of yours."

"Thank you for reminding me. I'm a very lucky man."

"You are. So why do you feel ill?"

Tel rested his elbows on his knees as he sat on the edge of the bed. "What if I trip up? What if I ... oh no, what if I faint before saying my vows?"

"You won't."

"I might."

"Here, drink this, stay hydrated."

Tel looked suspiciously at the glass Lucas had handed him. "Is this whisky?" he asked, sniffing it.

"Only the best on your wedding day. Hundred and fifty quid a bottle, that is."

"It won't help. Alcohol is a diuretic, and I don't want to be lurching down the aisle shouting 'Bring me my bride!' before passing out from dehydration."

Lucas, already in his Ralph Loren suit with an equally expensive blue tie, opened up the mini fridge at the bottom of his bed. "Tonic water? Ginger ale?"

"Ginger ale might settle my stomach."

Lucas brought the bottle over and handed it to him. Tel opened it and guzzled it down. "Any more?"

"No, only a bottle of champagne I'm cooling for us later."

"I won't be here later."

"Won't you?"

"No, Lucas, I'll be with Sophie in the bridal suite."

"How quickly I'm forgotten," Lucas sighed. "Guess I'll have to drink it all on my lonesome then, unless I can persuade Annie to join me for a nightcap."

"You're making me feel sick again."

"Pull yourself together, Tel, you're only getting married, not having open heart surgery or being launched into space, destination, Mars."

"I'm going to do something stupid, I just know it."

"It's not like you to suffer from nerves like this."

"It's the biggest day of my life. I'm marrying the woman I love, I can't let her down in any way, today or any other day. Oh, I can actually hear my heartbeat in my head, I'm not sure it should be pounding that fast. What if I have a heart attack during the ceremony?"

"You won't have a heart attack, Tel."

"How do you know?"

"What are the odds?"

"You're right, I'm sure you're right, unless," he said, clutching his chest, "I have an undiagnosed heart condition."

"I doubt it."

"You're a doctor, are you?"

"No, I'm your occasional jogging partner and you're perfectly healthy. Now calm down."

"Okay." Tel took some deep breaths, then said, "Can you get me some water from downstairs?"

"Sure." Lucas headed for the door, then turned. "I've got your back, chap. If you faint, I'll hold you up. If you have a heart attack I'll massage your organ and give you mouth-to-mouth; reluctantly, you're not my type, but I'd do it."

"Brain haemorrhage?" Tel asked, raising a hint of a smile.

"Oh, don't worry about that, you never use it anyway."

With a burst of laughter, he disappeared through the door in search of water.

CHAPTER EIGHT

The Ceremony

At midday, four pastel-coloured VW vans decorated with streams of paper flowers and heart-shaped bunting puttered onto the campsite and lined up on the driveway between the static caravans. When the drivers pulled back the side doors there were two padded benches inside, enough for six people.

"Herd 'em up, move 'em out!" Brian hollered at everyone.

Faye tottered over in flowery sandals to match her flowery dress, the heels a good two inches higher than what she was used to; she felt like she was walking on stilts.

"Does my hair look alright?" she asked.

"Looks perfect, lass."

"Are you sure? Feels funny having it up."

"Looks fine."

"Fine? You said perfect before. Is it coming down?"

"I have never seen such perfect hair, and the fascinator is outstanding. Now stop fussing."

"I can't help it, it's a big, posh wedding. I'm going to look scruffy if my hair starts falling down, and I'm going to sound so common when I open my mouth and Brummie falls out."

"Fink I'll get the award for that," Beth laughed, picking her way over the gravel driveway in her stiletto heels, a vision of loveliness in pale blue, holding onto the arm of a very 'trendy' suited Jim, both of them smiling and looking calm.

By comparison, Faye was constantly touching the back of her head to see if the hair grips were still holding everything in place, frantically using the VW bus mirrors to check the angle of her fascinator.

"If you keep doing that it's going to drop off," Brian told her.

"That's what Liv keeps saying," Mark laughed, holding Olivia's hand as she struggled to walk in high heels.

"Maybe I should put my flat shoes on and avoid death by falling," Faye said.

"Don't have time," Brian insisted. "Hobble into the van, woman."

"Can we all fit in?" Beth asked.

"We can," Mark said, "Brian will have to shrink himself to half his normal size and sit next to the driver at the front though."

"Oh!" Faye cried, running back towards the caravan.

"I've locked it!" Brian boomed.

She ran back to him as best she could with wobbly ankles, took the keys he held out like she was in a relay race, and wobbled off again.

"Hair!" Beth shouted, "Don't upset the hair!"

"How do you upset hair?" Jim asked.

"By running like that."

The rest of them piled into the VW bus and settled down as Faye jumped into the caravan, banged around inside for a bit, and jumped out again, seemingly empty-handed.

"What was that little burst of panic in aid of?" Brian asked, when she tottered back.

"Forgot my lipstick."

"Get in, lass, the other buses are leaving."

"Have you got everything?" she asked, as Brian closed the side door and opened up the passenger door.

"Phone," he said, tapping his breast pocket. "Funds." He tapped the inner pocket for his wallet. "Female," he said, nodding at Faye. "Yep, got everything."

"Go for it, Bri," Mark said.

Bri glanced at the driver before he began his ascent into the van. He was a middle-aged man who looked a bit alarmed at the enormity of his passenger. Brian slowly lifted himself up. The van tilted, the suspension creaked. Putting his head down as low as he could, he gently eased his torso onto the seat and sat down. His head pressed against the roof. The van groaned in protest. Brian awkwardly glanced at the driver again, who was now pressed against the driver's window by Brian's enormous shoulders. "All good?"

The driver said, "I think you'd be better off in the back."

"Tie him to the roof," Jim laughed.

"You want me to get out again?" Brian said.

"If you don't mind."

Brian huffed and extricated himself from the front passenger seat with some effort. Standing outside, he noticed all the other VW buses had left. He opened the side door and looked at the space on the end of one bench, instinctively knowing he wouldn't fit.

"You could lie on the floor?" the driver suggested, looking back. "Over the axle to evenly distribute the weight."

"I'm wearing a very expensive Matalan suit in pure polyester!"

The driver shrugged and tapped on the clock embedded into the dashboard.

"Sit on the end with your legs to the side," Mark suggested. "There's more space."

"Space is not a word I'd use in this context," Brian sighed.

Olivia sat on Mark's lap to give him more room. Almost bent double, Brian got inside to the sounds of the van screeching in protest, and perched himself on the end of the back bench with one bent leg in front and one angled to the side. It was very, very uncomfortable. Jim leaned sideways and pulled the door shut.

"OH!" Olivia suddenly screamed, "I've forgotten my earrings! I haven't put my earrings in!"

Mark said, "Get them for her, will you, Jim?"

"Why me?"

"You're nearest the door."

Jim huffed and opened the door again. "Where are they?"

"On top of the drawers next to the bed," Olivia said, handing him keys.

Jim got out, ambled over to the motorhome and disappeared from view.

"HURRY UP!" Brian shouted, "I'M IN A GREAT DEAL OF PAIN!"

Jim eventually yelled, "THEY'RE NOT ON TOP OF THE DRAWERS NEXT TO THE BED, LIV."

"LOOK INSIDE THE TOP DRAWER."

"NO, CAN'T SEE ANY EARRINGS. I CAN SEE A LOT OF OTHER THINGS THOUGH."

"SHUT THE DRAWER!" Mark suddenly shouted, making everyone jump.

"They're in the bottom drawer, darling."

"Oh. AS YOU WERE, JIM!"

"WHAT DO THEY LOOK LIKE?"

"THEY'RE DANGLY WITH PINK DIAMANTES."

"PINK WHAT?"

"SHINY BITS!" Mark bawled.

"THERE'S SOME GOLD STUDS IN THE KITCHEN AREA, IS THAT THEM?"

"NO, THEY'RE PINK. LOOK IN THE KITCHEN DRAWER."

"WHICH ONE?"

"ANY ONE!"

Brian tried to shift into a more comfortable position but couldn't. He felt wedged, his legs pressing against the wall of the bus, his back in a position it didn't much like. One small bump in the road and his spine and at least one kneecap would be done for.

"FOUND SOME LONG, PINK THINGS," Jim cried.

"THAT'S THEM!"

"OH NO, THEY'RE HARIBO HAPPY CHERRIES. NICE."

"Give me strength," Brian hissed.

"Stay calm, Bri."

"I'm so sorry," Olivia said.

"GOT THEM!"

"PRAISE THE LORD!" Brian cried, as loud as his crushed lungs would allow. "COME ON, JIM, GET IN, GET IN!"

Jim leisurely wandered back to the van, got in and passed the earrings to Olivia.

"Are we all ready now?" asked the driver.

They all muttered that they were.

The VW van started up and slowly pulled away, leaning to one side from the flattened suspension beneath Brian's bulk. It was only a five-minute drive, but Brian was acutely aware of every imperfection in the road juddering up his spine.

He whimpered the entire time.

* * *

"It's time," Lucas said.

Tel stood up. "I'm ready."

"This is it, chap."

"I know."

"Do you have everything?"

"I don't need anything except the ring."

"Right."

"You have the ring, don't you?"

"Me?" Lucas' eyes widened, as did Tel's.

"I gave it to you last night," Tel said. "I put the box in your hand and said, 'Don't lose this.'"

"Did you?"

"Yes!"

"I don't recall."

"Now is not the time to joke, Lucas."

Lucas patted the pockets of his suit. He pulled his suitcase from under the bed and put it on top, rifling through the contents, pushing his hands deep into the pockets.

"Lucas?"

"Just a sec."

Lucas opened the drawer of the bedside cabinet and shuffled through his loose change, his car keys and his phone, which he dropped into his jacket pocket.

"Lucas!"

"I put it somewhere safe. I'm sure I put it somewhere safe."

Tel pulled the duvet off the bed, then dropped to his knees to search underneath. Lucas scoured the room, then dashed into the ensuite bathroom. "Got it!" he cried.

"Show me!"

Lucas came back into the room holding a purple Asprey box. "It was on the shelf under the mirror. Don't remember putting it there."

"Open it," Tel gasped.

Lucas did, and the gold and diamond band inside glittered in the sunlight pouring through the window. Tel slumped onto Lucas' bed, breathing hard.

"Phew," Lucas said, "Bit of a panic on there for a minute. Look, watch me, I'm putting the ring in my right-hand jacket pocket, do you see? Right-hand jacket pocket."

"Push it down, you don't want it falling out."

Lucas laughed. "My last girlfriend said something remarkably similar. Oh, the ring is bulging my suit."

"I'll bulge you if you lose it again."

"It's there. Deep down inside. Safe. Are you ready?"

"As I'll ever be."

"Come on then, Tel, let us leave your sordid bachelor life behind and make that gorgeous girl your wife. Oh wait, I'll just check she's still ferreted away in her room and hasn't left yet, you don't want to bump into each other on the stairs or have her hysterical when she finds you're not waiting for her at the altar thingy. Stay here."

Tel slumped back on the bed as Lucas galloped off to the far end of the corridor.

* * *

He opened the door and quickly stepped inside. There followed a lot of screaming, some cushion throwing, and a hoard of women rushing up to him screeching, "What are you doing here?"

"You're not supposed to see the bride until she walks down the aisle."

"That's the bridegroom, I think, not the best man."

"He could give Tel *details*! He could be a *spy*!"

On the double bed Camille, who was fully dressed, pulled the duvet up around her neck, hissing, "Lucas! Why are you here?"

"We could have all been naked!" Annie cried.

"Damn, am I too late for that?" he grinned. "Just wanted to check everything was … oh my God!" Lucas saw Sophie, standing resplendent in front of the window, her outline glowing in the sunlight and her dress and veil sparkling like a million tiny bursts of magic. Always beautiful and elegant, she looked beyond stunning, her face highlighted by an enigmatic smile. "You look like an angel," he gasped. "I've never seen anything more beautiful."

"Thank you," Sophie said, her smile broadening.

"Tel is going to crumble at your feet when he sees you."

Sophie laughed. "He does that anyway. Do I look okay?"

"Okay?" Lucas gently pushed his way through the throng of women, who cried, "Lucas! You're not supposed to be here!"

"Get out!"

"No men allowed!"

"You look *spectacular*!" Unable to tear his eyes away from her face, Lucas blindly reached out to take her hand, lifted it and kissed it.

Then the women grabbed hold of him and physically bundled him out of the room, slamming the door. Lucas opened it again and poked his head in. "We're leaving in two minutes," he said, his eyes still transfixed by Sophie. "I'll bang on the door when we're heading down, don't leave the room until then."

The door was pushed shut by three women, who kept their backs to it to prevent him from breaching again.

"I'm not sure if that's bad luck, having a man in the bride's room," Jacquie fretted, searching Google on her phone.

"It's fine," Sophie said, quietly flattered. "It's all going to be fine."

* * *

"Tel!" Lucas gasped, bursting into the room.

Tel jumped up. "What? What's wrong? Has she left? Has she changed her–?"

"You are one very lucky man."

"She's still here?"

"Of course she's still here."

Tel flopped back onto the bed and said, "Don't scare me like that! I nearly had a heart attack! I thought something had happened."

"Something has happened," Lucas said, sitting down next to him. "Sophie looks absolutely *stunning*."

"She always looks stunning."

"Not like this, Tel."

"Don't tell me anymore, it might be bad luck or something."

"I can't wait to see your face when you see her. Are you ready?"

"No."

"Come on, let's go."

Tel stood up again, wavering. "I feel sick."

"It's just nerves."

"I really think I'm going to throw up?"

Lucas opened one side of his jacket like a man selling fake watches. "As your best man I'm prepared for any eventuality. I have sick bags, smelling salts, miniature bottle of brandy, one of those battery fan thingies, and emergency services on speed dial on my phone. Short of dragging a defibrillator down the aisle there's not much more I can do."

"I-I'm not sure I can do this," Tel gasped. "I can't move my legs."

Lucas gripped his shoulders and peered into his eyes.

"What's going to happen today is going to change your life, Tel. Prepare to have your world rocked. Marrying Sophie is the best thing you'll ever do. If you don't do it now, someone else is going to snap her up; me, possibly, I'm suitably attired and more than willing to step in at a moment's notice, just say the word and I'm there."

Tel grinned. "Are you secretly in love with her, like that bloke in *Four Weddings and a Funeral*?"

"Totally adore her. And it's *Love Actually* where the bloke is secretly in love with the bride, *Four Weddings* is where the groom abandons the bride at the altar, and again, if that happens, I'm more than happy to step in. I take my best man duties very seriously and I'll make sure that, at the end of today, Sophie marries someone, hopefully me, but more likely you."

Tel laughed. "Now I know why I wanted you as my best man."

"Because of my innate charm and wit?" Lucas winked, "Or because your brother didn't want to do it?"

"I didn't ask my brother."

"Oh, I'm honoured."

"Don't be, he told me ages ago he didn't want the responsibility. He's also crap in a crisis."

Lucas laughed as he put his arm across Tel's shoulder and said, "Come on, chap, let's do this."

* * *

"Wow!" Faye gasped.

"Is that the hotel?"

"Gothic mansion, more like," Olivia breathed.

"I'm sure I've seen that house in a horror film," Jim said.

They were crawling up the driveway of Sumsuch House, a resplendent red-brick building complete with turrets and spires and several high-pitched rooves above a multitude of tall windows. On either side of the driveway was an expanse of tended lawns, topiary trees and bushes, and elaborate concrete balustrading. The driveway opened out in front of the house, where there was a sweep of concrete steps leading up to the main door.

"We're late," Faye cried, glancing at her watch.

Brian, who'd been trying not to breathe in too much during the journey for fear of expansion, gasped, "Open the door."

Jim jumped out, as did the others. Outside, they looked back at Brian, who was trying to extricate himself from the van but couldn't.

"Little help?" he puffed.

"How?" Mark asked.

"Just pull."

"Pull what?"

"Pull anything, just get me out of here."

The driver came round to help and, between the six of them, they managed to pull Brian out by his arms and legs. It wasn't elegant. Brian took a moment to straighten his spine and allow blood to flow back into his buttocks, before they all hurried up the concrete steps to the open door.

They were first astounded by vast expanse of marble flooring, a split, wrought iron staircase rising up on each side of the foyer, and the height of the ceilings, from which hung sparkling chandeliers. As they rushed in with their mouths already open, they stopped dead in their tracks. Sophie, a vision of loveliness in a figure-hugging ivory gown covered in sparkles, was delicately making her way down the right staircase, one hand holding the arm of a tall, very handsome man, the other holding a teardrop bouquet of cream and mauve flowers. At the bottom of the staircase stood two women and two small children, all wearing matching mauve dresses.

The women immediately gasped and started dabbing at their eyes.

"She looks so beautiful," Olivia sniffed.

"*So* beautiful."

"Is it bad luck to see the bride before the groom?" Jim asked.

"Avert your eyes, just in case," said Brian.

As they turned to search for the wedding room, a suited man wearing a headset with a microphone in front of his mouth hurried over and hissed, "You're terribly late. Follow me." He raced off into the first room on the left, which was brightly-lit, impressively decorated, and full of people. Flowers and drapes were everywhere, and chandeliers twinkled in the sunlight from the patio doors. Two blocks of seats were separated by a pristine white carpet that led down to a table, behind which stood a woman. Tel and his best man were standing at the front, both looking nervous and shifting from foot to foot.

"Sit here," the man hissed, pointing at the empty seats at the back.

They sat, the women still sniffing.

The man closed the doors.

* * *

Tel glanced over his shoulder and spotted the campers entering the room. The women appeared to be crying and dabbing at their eyes. He sucked in air and spun round to Lucas. "There's a problem," he gasped.

"What?"

"Women are crying."

"Women always cry at weddings. I'm quite prone to the odd sob myself."

"They're crying *before* the ceremony," Tel insisted, "That can't be right, can it?"

"Women are complicated creatures, who knows why they do the things they do."

"Unless they know something we–"

Gentle music started playing. Everyone looked front right, where a woman in a long gown rocked backwards and forwards on her seat as she strummed on the strings of a harp.

"Ah," Lucas whispered, "Pachebel's *Canon in D*, one of my favourites."

Terrified to the core of his soul, Tel stiffly did a half turn and saw the double doors open at the back of the room. Seconds seemed like hours as he waited. He forgot to breathe. He thought his heart might have stopped. He willed himself not to faint.

And then he saw her. Sophie. His Sophie. Beyond beautiful in a figure-hugging dress, her hair piled high, a tiara glittering in the sunlight, a veil over her face. But the most attractive thing about her was her smile, her smile was sublime. He had never felt such love.

As he watched her slowly walk down the aisle with her father, followed by two small bridesmaids and Fi and Annie, a tear slipped from his eye and trickled down his cheek.

The room suddenly became filled with the murmur of deep voices, high-pitched sobbing and the sniffing of women. Sophie gently turned her head to smile at everyone. Tel had never seen so many fluttering handkerchiefs. He wiped another tear from his cheek.

Behind Sophie, two small bridesmaids carrying wicker baskets threw confetti into the air with wild abandonment, covering the seated guests in coloured paper. The smallest went up to people to personally present them with a handful. The guests laughed and threw it up in the air. The bigger one, whose basket had quickly emptied from enthusiasm, tried to take some from the smaller one's basket. A fight broke out, halted only when Brian bawled, "Pack it in!" from the back of the room. Annie picked them both up off the floor by their arms and hissed, "Behave, you little monsters." The children continued to push each other as they were dragged down the aisle.

And then she was there, beside him. Her eyes sparkled. She was, he thought, the epitome of perfection. His heart swelled with emotion as another tear slipped from his eye.

"You okay?" she mouthed.

He nodded and whispered, "You look amazing."

"I love you."

"I love you."

"Ladies and gentlemen," said the woman behind the table.

* * *

The ceremony was… eventful. It was accompanied by the soft wheezing of Fi, splayed out on one of the front seats, fast asleep. When Annie pinched her, she woke with a tiny scream and looked around, muttering, "Sorry. Sorry." Minutes later, the soft wheezing began again.

Just as Sophie was about to say 'I do', a long burst of flatulence echoed around the otherwise silent room, and everyone burst out laughing as the smallest bridesmaid cried, "Mummy, do poo-poo."

Pam, Sophie's university friend and mother to the toddlers, bent double in an effort not to be noticed as she rushed up to the child and whispered something in her ear. The child shrieked, "No, do poo-poo *now*!"

Another burst of flatulence, quite loud for such a small person. People in the front rows started wafting their hands in front of their noses, and a murmur of dismay rolled in like distant thunder. David, Tel's brother, who looked like he was wearing a coat of many extremely bright colours, with sequins, coughed and cried, "I can't breathe!" Travis, his boyfriend, similarly attired, dry heaved and cried, "Gosh darn it, that sure does stink!" Both Camille and Jacquie held tear-dampened handkerchiefs to their noses. The men remained stoic as the waft of rancid air stung at their eyes.

Pam picked the child up to soothe her, and the sound of a two-year-old exploding into a nappy reverberated off the walls. It was incredibly loud and sounded incredibly wet. A giant boom of laughter erupted from the back row, joined by others as everyone lost the fight to contain themselves. The laughter stopped abruptly when the smell hit them; except for Faye, who couldn't smell and continued to wipe away tears of laughter, wondering why everyone had suddenly gone quiet. Mark dry heaved.

Pam rushed off down the aisle holding the child, who was still fervently relieving herself.

"Mummy?" cried the other small bridesmaid, left all alone at the front.

"Daddy's here, darling," a man said, standing up. "It's okay."

The child promptly burst into tears, which quickly grew into hysterical crying and ended with the girl throwing herself down on the floor in a massive strop. The man hurried to pick her up. When she wouldn't stop crying he carried her, legs kicking, fists pounding, down the aisle. When he opened the door everyone could hear the toddler in the corridor still evacuating into her nappy.

"What have they been feeding it?" Jim asked out loud, and everyone was laughing again.

"If we could have silence to suit the solemnity of the occasion," the registrar said firmly, and they all quietened down, except for Sophie, who couldn't stop snorting, and Tel, who felt the solemnity of the occasion was long gone and thank goodness for that.

"Do you, Terence Albert Okenado–"

There was a brief explosion of noise from the back of the room as Brian clasped a hand against his laughter. He was instantly silenced by a withering look from the registrar.

When Sophie said 'I do', David stood up from his seat, threw his multi-coloured arms in the air and cried, "Yay! I have a sister! I finally have a sister!"

Everyone stood up and applauded as, now legally married, Tel kissed his beautiful bride. The registrar motioned them behind the table and they both sat down to sign the certificate. A photographer bounced around, taking photographs from every angle. Once done, the man with the microphone on his face immediately started leaping about, opening the patio doors behind the table and waiting patiently as Tel and Sophie walked out onto the balustrade balcony that overlooked the garden. He held up a firm hand to keep everyone else in their place. "Give the happy couple a moment to reflect," he snapped fiercely.

The photographer, who'd been furiously taking pictures throughout the entire ceremony, followed them into the sunshine. Microphone man dropped his hand and started swishing it at his side, urgently urging people outside. It took a while as everyone congratulated the newlyweds as they passed. A line of waiters held trays of champagne and canapes on the balcony.

"Group photographs!" yelled microphone man. "Make your way down onto the grass area and follow my instructions."

Brian looked at his watch. It had been hours since he'd last eaten and he was hungry. He hoped the photographs wouldn't take too long.

They did.

"Now all the guests," the photographer said behind his tripod, and the man with the microphone screeched, "All together! Don't crowd the bride and groom. Squeeze in a little. A bit more."

The photographer stood up straight. "I know what I'm doing, mate."

"Yes, yes, but I'm the wedding planner, everything needs to be perfect, *perfect*! You dawdlers over there, step away from the champagne trays and join the crowd! Hurry up! Are we ready? Stop fidgeting at the back! Okay," he said to the cameraman, "Go!"

The cameraman slowly bent down to his camera, sighing heavily.

"I said stop fidgeting! Do you want to be in this photograph or not?"

"How much longer, do you think?" Brian asked Faye.

"How should I know?"

"I feel faint from hunger."

"You'll survive on your reserves," she said, turning to pat his tummy.

"I said *stop fidgeting*!"

"Bossy little bugger, isn't he," said Mark. "Feels like I'm back at school."

The cameraman stood up and said, "Do you want some informal shots now?"

Everyone cheered.

"Okay, go for it!"

Sophie lifted her ivory skirt and wrapped a long leg around Tel, who leaned her back in his arms. Everyone else struck ridiculous poses or pulled faces, except for the mothers, who couldn't quite figure out what was going on. Brian pinched Faye's bottom, the cameraman perfectly capturing her O-shaped mouth. Beth lifted her breasts and puckered her lips, as Jim appreciatively stared down at them. Mark stuck two fingers up behind Olivia's head, while Olivia did a rendition of Munch's The Scream. Camille huffed at the childishness of it all, while her husband, John, CEO of a top London law firm, fell to a knee waving jazz hands.

"That's enough tomfoolery," shouted the man with the microphone. "Make your way back towards the house. We'll be using the right patio doors, the patio doors on the *right*, into the dining room."

"Did he say right?" Mark said.

"I think he did," said Jim.

"Food," Brian gasped, glancing at his watch again, "Thank flip-flop for that, I didn't think I was going to make it."

Tel and Sophie led the way across the smooth lawn. The guests followed, chatting and laughing. Brian bounced up and down at the back, willing them all to Hurry the Hell Up! The newlyweds climbed the stairs up to the house, and then stopped and turned. The guests, some still holding champagne glasses, others running off to grab a new glass from the line of waiters, smiled up at the happy couple.

Brian started whimpering as a man in a flat cap walked

across the balcony carrying a small cage containing two white doves. There was some delay as the man carefully took the birds out of the cage and placed them in Tel and Sophie's hands. Holding the birds, they turned to face their guests.

"To symbolise harmony," Sophie said, releasing hers first. It flew off into the clear blue sky and landed in a tree, waiting for its partner.

"And peace," Tel said, throwing his dove into the air.

It went up, didn't flap, and came down again with a small thud on the concrete. The crowd gasped. The man in the flat cap rushed to the motionless bird at Tel's feet and started pumping its heart with a finger. The bird didn't move. Sophie gripped Tel's arm. The crowd fell silent. The man opened the bird's beak and, still pumping, gently blew into its mouth. The bird stirred. The crowd cheered. The bird flapped its wings and flew off, narrowly missing several fascinators. The man stood, stared up at the sky and, with a look of horror growing on his face, quickly turned to Tel and Sophie and guided them towards the patio doors. The guests watched the bird fly up, almost reaching the tree where its mate sat, before another, bigger bird swooped down and snatched it up. Everyone gasped again. Sophie turned to see why, but the hawk and the dove were long gone. Nobody said anything for a moment, and then they all made their way through the patio doors, chatting and laughing merrily.

It took ages.

* * *

"Line-up," Camille said to her daughter as they entered the dining room.

"Oh mum," Sophie wailed, "I said I didn't want a line-up."

"Everyone has a line-up at their wedding."

"We don't want to stand there for ages with rictus smiles while everyone says the same thing, 'Oh, you look beautiful', 'Oh, it was a lovely wedding', 'I hope you're very happy together'. It's boring."

"It's de rigueur, darling."

"It's outdated, mum." Sophie and Tel wandered off to stand in front of the top table.

Camille gently shouted, "The guests will expect it!"

"They won't, but feel free to stand there by yourself and welcome everyone in if you're so determined."

Camille turned as the guests came into the room and held out her hand. The first guest shook it and said, "Lovely ceremony."

"Wasn't it," she beamed.

She held her hand out to the second guests and they just smiled and nodded and walked by, heading towards the top table to congratulate the newlyweds. By the time the fifth couple had passed her without comment she gave up and said, "Just find your names on the tables. There's a floorplan over on the right."

David came swishing up to Camille and kissed her powdered cheek. "That child farting," he laughed, "Funniest thing ever."

"Sure did stink though," Travis added, waving his hand in front of his face for emphasis. "I can still smell it."

"The staff have assured me they've had the room and the foyer liberally sprayed with air freshener."

"I'll never be able to get that stink outta ma nose, ma'am, and I've worked with cattle."

Camille took a step back to look them both up and down, at their outlandishly multicoloured, diamante covered wedding suits, complete with lace cuffs and ruffled shirts. "Did you just come from the starring role in *Joseph and the Amazing Technicolour Dreamcoat*?" she asked.

"Do you like it?" David beamed coquettishly. "There's this *fabulous* tailor down on Old Compton Street in Soho who makes the most *amazing* bespoke suits."

"Bespoke?" Camille asked. "You mean, you *wanted* them to make something like ... this."

"It's flamboyant! We're just injecting our fun personalities into the proceedings to keep people alert and awake."

"Awake? They'll all have migraines by the end of the night."

"These aren't just *any* wedding suits," David winked, and Camille muttered, "Kill me now." "They're special suits with a special surprise for everyone later."

"It's not a male striptease again, is it?" she asked, flashbacking to the engagement party, "Only my poor sister, Sally, still suffers nightmares about the policeman that showed up and started taking his clothes off."

"Nightmares, or *fantasies*," Travis winked.

"She said the stripper was … very large."

"No," David shrugged, "Normal."

"Aunt Sally didn't seem to think so." They all glanced over at Sally and her husband, Harry, chatting with other relatives around a table. Camille lowered her voice and said, "Harry's taken to wearing an 'enhancement' down there ever since."

"What kind of enhancement?" David whispered back, "Like a jockstrap?"

"Socks, apparently, a pair of rolled-up socks. You'll see when he stands up."

As if on cue, Harry stood up and made his way across the room. David raised a hand to his mouth and said, "That's *got* to be football socks. He looks positively deformed!"

"Just keep it to yourselves, okay?" Camille urged, suddenly regretting her indiscretion.

"Oh, you can trust us, ma'am."

"You will be good boys, won't you?"

"We promised Sophie we'd be on our best behaviour."

They both swaggered off to find their seats, flinging the front of their long jackets over the heads of seated guests and dislodging a couple of fascinators.

"Lovely wedding," Brian said, approaching Camille, with Faye and the others in tow.

"I've never seen a more beautiful bride," Olivia sighed.

"Brought a tear to my eye," said Beth.

"Everyone was crying," Mark said, "Either from seeing Sophie in that dress, or from the pungent aroma coming from the small child."

"Who knew something so small could create so much *gas*!" said Jim.

"I'm used to it," Beth said, "Didn't affect me at all."

"Me neither," Faye laughed, "Anosmia."

"Anosmia?" Camille repeated.

"No sense of smell."

"How unfortunate for you."

Faye shrugged. "I'm used to it."

They wandered over to Tel and Sophie, standing in front of the long table. "Terence, eh?" were Brian's first words. "I did sometimes wonder what Tel was short for."

"If you ever call me Terence we can no longer be friends."

"Noted." Brian held out a huge hand and Tel took it, gripping it with both of his. "Congratulations to both of you. You make a lovely couple and we wish you every happiness."

"Thank you, Brian."

Sophie reached up and wrapped her arms around his huge neck. "Thank you for everything, Bri. I'm so glad you're here."

"Wouldn't have missed it for the world, lass."

"I notice the mothers are roaming free and not locked in a cupboard."

"I have the cupboard key right here," he said, patting his empty pocket, "And I'm not afraid to use it, just say the word."

"I'll keep you posted."

Letting go of Brian, she hugged Faye, then Mark and Olivia, and finally Jim and Beth. They all commented on her beauty and the amazing dress that now twinkled in the sunlight coming from the patio, giving her an almost ethereal glow.

"I'm not crying with emotion," Brian breathed, brushing away a tear, "I've got flatulence in my eye."

"Me too," Mark sniffed.

Jim said, "How can you get–?"

"Be quiet, Jim," said Beth.

They wandered off en masse in search of their table among a multitude of round tables, each seating eight guests. Faye dashed off to check the large plan at the back of the room.

David suddenly jumped in front of Beth. "Oh my Lord above!" he squealed, hands raised to his face, "You're Adele!"

"Nah, I just look like–"

"You can't fool me, I'd recognise that beautiful face anywhere."

"Nah, mate, I'm really not."

"Can I touch you?"

"What?" said Jim.

"Can I kiss the hand of the greatest artiste of this decade, if not this century?"

Beth rolled her eyes and held out a hand. "If it makes him happy," she told a perplexed-looking Jim.

"Oh, it does, it really does." He kissed it and then yelled, "TRAVIS! TRAVIS, QUICK!"

Travis – tall, muscular and square jawed – sauntered over. "Hi, ma'am," he said politely.

"Look who it is?" David urged.

Travis smiled politely.

"It's Adele! It's only *Adele*! Can you believe it?"

"Pleased to meet you, ma'am."

David started fanning himself with a hand. "Oh my goodness! Can you believe this? Adele, at my brother's wedding."

"I'm really not."

David winked at her. "It's okay," he whispered, "It must be difficult, being so famous. You're incognito, but fear not, I can keep a secret, I won't tell a soul."

"Everyone will know by the time y'all reach your table," Travis laughed.

"Come on," Brian said, "Let's sit down, I'm starving."

CHAPTER NINE

The Wedding Breakfast

When everyone was seated and settled at their tables – bedecked with a plastic pot of flowers, a tealight holder of some sort, and a bevy of red and white wine bottles in the centre – a line of bowtie waiters came through from the kitchen, bringing out the first course. A dish was placed in front of everyone and the room fell silent except for the sound of rustling paper as guests picked up the menu and stared at it, reminding themselves of what it was supposed to be.

"Sophie," said Tel, looking down at his plate. "Is it me or is this a little on the small side?"

"It's small, Tel."

"It's barely a mouthful. What is it?"

Sophie glanced at the menu and said, "It's the chargrilled asparagus with shaved Parmesan."

"Is this just a sample to make sure everyone likes it before they bring out the proper portions?"

"I don't know, Tel."

Camille leaned in. "Is this the menu you ordered?"

"Yes, mum."

"The *original* menu?"

"Yes, not one of the three menus you picked afterwards."

"Why is it so small?"

"I don't know."

Tel waved at a waiter and whispered in his bent ear. The waiter whispered back. Tel looked shocked for a moment, then whispered some more, as did the waiter, who then walked off.

Tel turned to Sophie. "We've screwed up," he said.

"Screwed up, how?"

"With this menu."

"But we chose this menu."

An increasingly loud murmur went around the room.

Tel said, "Do you remember when we went to the restaurant to try the menus?"

"Yes."

"Do you remember we tried a lot of dishes."

"I do," Sophie grinned, "And very nice it was too."

"And do you remember the portions they gave us were small, like this?"

"Yes."

"And we thought they were just giving us a sample."

"Get to the point, Tel."

"Do you remember at the end, when they asked us how many courses we wanted?"

"And we said three."

"And they looked surprised."

"And you asked how many courses most people ordered, and they said between twelve and fifteen."

"And I said nobody could eat twelve to fifteen courses."

"I don't see a problem," Sophie said. "We went, we tasted, we picked a wedding menu."

"We picked the gourmet cuisine tasting menu."

"Yes, and…?"

"The gourmet cuisine tasting menu …" Tel shifted awkwardly in his seat. "… consists of several bite-sized dishes, twelve to fifteen courses, that are served to guests as a single meal."

Sophie looked down at the two baby asparagus with a light shaving of Parmesan sitting in the middle of her plate. "You mean, this is it?"

"That's exactly what I mean."

"And all three courses are going to be miniature versions of one dish?"

"Yes."

Sophie's mouth moved but no words came out.

Camille leaned in and said, "The guests are all complaining. I hope the main menu is going to be bigger."

"It's not, mum."

Camille's eyes widened. "I told you to get the–"

"Now is not the time to say 'I told you so,'" Tel said.

Sophie lifted up her fork, speared the two baby asparagus and the light shaving of Parmesan, and put them in her mouth. She chewed a couple of times, then swallowed. "Lovely," she said.

"It's a simple mistake anyone could make," Tel said to Camille. "I've never even heard of a gourmet tasting menu before."

"Is this a gourmet tasting menu?" asked Lucas, sitting next to him.

"It is," Tel sighed.

"Excellent, I love variety. How many courses have we got to look forward to?"

Tel looked up at the ceiling and said, "Three."

There was a pause. "Three?"

"Yes."

"Ran out of money, or you just thought we all could do with losing a bit of weight?"

By now, everyone had eaten their one bite of starter, mostly in silence, and were now looking at each other, perplexed. The waiters hurried in and took their plates away, immediately returning with what everyone assumed was the main course.

It wasn't.

* * *

On the far side of the room at table twelve, Brian stared down at the white canape spoon sitting on his plate holding what looked like crushed green ice, and picked up the menu again. "Palate cleansing Cucumber and Riesling Granita," he read. "Palate cleansing? The first course barely touched the sides."

"Don't cause a scene, Bri, just eat it."

Brian picked up the spoon and put the green ice in his mouth. It melted immediately. He didn't even have to swallow, it just slid effortlessly inside him. "A mouthful of sweet slushie. No, wait, I think the single taste bud it managed to hit can detect a hint, just a hint, of cucumber."

"Brian!"

Brian, who was hungry and annoyed, hissed, "Faye!"

"It's ... different," Mark said, putting his spoon down.

"I like it," said Olivia.

"I know," Mark winked, and Olivia turned puce.

"Is this like a children's menu?" Jim asked.

"Something like that," Beth replied.

"But I'm not a child."

"That's debatable," Mark laughed.

"Maybe each course gets bigger," Faye suggested.

"It certainly couldn't get any smaller," Brian huffed, "Not unless they provide us with a magnifying glass." He searched the table for a bowl of nuts or crisps to stave off starvation, but there were none. He considered chewing on a plastic flower as his stomach, teased with a modicum of sustenance, growled loudly for more. He held up his plate and caught Tel's eye.

'What's this?' he mouthed, pointing at it.

Tel shrugged and looked away. Brian scoured other tables for bowls of nuts or crisps, or even olives; he didn't like olives but he was starting to feel slightly desperate. He was a big man, he needed big portions. He briefly wondered how long he could physically survive without food and decided it wouldn't be more than a day. He hoped today wasn't that day.

The waiters came out to retrieve the plates. Brian asked one of them, "Any beer?"

"Beer, sir?"

"Yes, beer; brown, fizzy, a thousand times more palatable than wine."

The waiter haughtily nodded his head sideways and said, "Perhaps the lounge bar could accommodate you, sir."

"The lounge bar?"

"Yes, just through the door on the end, sir. They serve beer in the bar, I believe."

"Beer?" someone at another table cried, and there was the scraping of a multitude of chairs as a mob hastily made their way through a door in the partitioning wall into the lounge bar.

Brian stood up, huffing that he couldn't keep this special secret to himself and would, instead, have to wait in what would now be a very long queue.

"Get me a gin and tonic, would you, love?" Faye said.

"Ooh, me too," Olivia said.

Mark also stood up. "I'll help get the drinks in. Beth?"

"Oh, I'm dying of thirst, I'll just have a pint glass of water please, with ice."

"Are you sure?"

Beth patted her stomach. "Bit of an upset tummy."

"Fair enough. Etta?"

Etta, Sophie's secretary, who was sitting at their table and had already announced that she didn't drink, said, "Pineapple juice, please."

"Mute teenager with phone?" Brian said.

The teenager next to Etta looked up. "I'll just have a Coke, thanks."

"Jim?"

"I'll have–"

"No, come and lend a hand."

Jim reluctantly got to his feet and followed Brian and Mark into the lounge bar, which was heaving.

"Where are they all going?" Sophie cried from the top table.

"They're campers," Tel said, "Where do you think they're going?"

"Oh, right."

***

The bar staff looked surprised as a large group of people came charging towards them. When Brian finally got to the front, he slammed his hand down on the counter and boomed, "Stella, and lots of them."

One barman started pumping into pint glasses, the others took a flurry of orders.

"Two gin and tonics," Mark said, "A pint of water with ice, and …" He turned to Brian. "What did Sophie's secretary want?"

Brian shrugged. Mark ordered another gin and tonic.

At the end of the bar a tall, distinguished man flicked a credit card out of his wallet and put it on the counter in front of him. "Put them on … my tab," he said.

"Cheers," Jim shouted, walking away with his free drinks.

"Who do we thank?" Brian boomed over the heads of everyone else.

"Henry," said Henry, "Father of … the groom."

"Much appreciated, Henry."

"No … problem."

The barman handed him his card back and said, "All drinks are on the house, sir."

The man with the microphone came scurrying into the bar area. "Come on, come on!" he screeched at everyone, "You're keeping everyone waiting. They're about to serve the main course!

"I can barely contain my excitement," Brian said, deadpan, as he walked back.

A mob of people hurried into the dining room carrying trays of drinks. There was a buzz of excitement as they were passed out, and then everyone stared in anticipation at the swing doors that led to the kitchen. The silence was heavy, the expectation great. The doors finally burst open and a line of waiters brought the main meals to the tables.

Brian looked down at the small cube in the middle of his

plate, like a postage stamp in a sea of porcelain, and checked the menu again. "Sea bass in a pistachio crust with olive polenta." He looked at his plate again and started to laugh. "Have they just divided one sea bass into 150 pieces? This is death by torture. Tel and Sophie must really hate us, hate everybody, and we bought them a lovely gift as well. What did we get them, Faye?"

"A George Foreman grill."

"A George Foreman grill. Just a tiny one, is it? They don't seem to like normal portions."

"You okay, Bri?" Mark asked, "Your left eye is twitching."

"It can't believe the horror it's looking at, and I'm *hungry*."

"Here, have mine," Olivia offered, and Beth pushed her plate towards him as well, saying, "I don't like fish anyway."

"That's very kind of you both, but you eat what you can, while you can, before death takes us all."

"Little dramatic, Bri."

"Little desperate, Faye."

Brian lifted up the tiny, crusty fish with his fork and pushed it into his mouth, where it sat on his tongue like something he'd picked out of his teeth. He tried to chew it, to get the most out of it, but it dissolved and slipped down his throat before any flavour could be detected. Infuriated, he lifted the plate and licked it. The other people at their table – Etta and the floppy-haired, phone-immersed teenager who hadn't introduced himself – were rubbing their plates with their fingers and surreptitiously licking them. The atmosphere in the room was quiet and ominous.

The waiters returned for the plates. As they left, Brian shouted out, "I'll have a twelve-ounce steak, with mushrooms and chunky chips, a great pile of them." The room laughed nervously. The waiters immediately returned with tiny white dishes, complete with more canape spoons. The room fell silent again as they contemplated the offering, apparently served on dollhouse tableware.

"Palate cleansing blood orange sorbet with Aperol and

Thai basil," Mark read.

"What?" Brian grunted, glaring at an orange blob surrounded by a green goo with two tiny leaves floating in it.

"A palate-cleansing blood orange sorbet with Aperol and–"

"What's Aperol?"

The teenager, hunched over his iPhone, read from his screen, "Aperol is an Italian bitter aperitif."

"Bitter!" Brian hissed, "It doesn't know the meaning of the word!"

"Brian, can you stop complaining and just eat it!"

"Eat it? I can barely see it."

He started to lift the dish up.

Faye hissed, "Don't you slurp it straight into your mouth!"

Brian lifted the dish a little higher and Faye growled, "Don't you *dare*!"

He lowered the dish to the table with a grunt. Picking up the tiny spoon between finger and thumb, he lifted the orange blob and put it in his mouth. His mouth detected some horrible taste before it dissolved and was gone. The green goo with leaves followed it in two tiny spoonfuls, each of them equally horrible. He tossed the spoon into the tiny dish and growled, "If the desert course isn't the size of my head there's going to be trouble."

"Brian!" Faye snapped, staring at the two other guests sat at their table, "You're scaring the people who don't know you that well!"

"*And* the people who do know you," Olivia said. "I've seen you hungry before, Brian, but never like this."

"My apologies," he sighed, "My wife insisted I have a *small* breakfast so as not to spoil the breakfast dinner."

"Small?" Faye laughed. "Three pieces of toast *and* a MacDonald's!"

"It was just a Big Mac, and that was …" He glanced at his watch. "… almost five hours ago. Five hours! This," he spat, pointing down at the tiny dish, "This like feeding a peanut to an elephant."

Etta, who was as thin as a stick, said, "I know just what you mean, I'm quite peckish myself."

"Peckish doesn't even begin to–"

"*Brian!*"

"Pah!"

The waiters took away the dishes. Everyone stared at the swing doors to the kitchen, waiting for the final course, all thinking the same thing; maybe it was a joke and the bossy man with the microphone would come out and tell them the real meal was finally on its way.

He didn't, and it wasn't.

* * *

"People don't look happy," Sophie said to Tel.

"I know how they feel."

"What should we do?"

"What can we do?"

"I don't know. The evening buffet doesn't start until seven o'clock when the other guests arrive."

"Oh, it's not a miniature buffet, is it, where the guests are only allowed one vol-au-vent and a cheese stick each?"

Sophie's eyes widened. "I don't think so. I'm pretty sure the email said a normal buffet, chicken legs, quiche–"

"Pretty sure or positive?"

Sophie gave a little groan, just as Camille, sitting next to her, said, "You should do something before there's a riot."

"We know, mum."

"How could you have chosen a taster menu?"

Sophie's father leaned in. "It's like a scintilla of food artfully smudged across miniature dishes."

"Thanks, dad, really helpful."

"I'm giving my speech after this," Lucas said, "I was hoping for a full and happy audience, not a starving, drunken mob intent on revenge after being tormented by tiny bits of food."

"Some might take it as an insult," Annie hissed from the far end of the table. "'Come to our wedding, bring gifts, expect *nothing* in return.'"

Sophie looked down to the other end of the table at Fi, about to ask her what she thought and if she had any suggestions, but Fi had a hand to the side of her head and appeared to be muttering under her breath.

"Fi?"

Fi turned towards her, the edge of a mobile phone catching the light pouring through the patio windows.

"Fi!"

"I'm sorry," she said, "Could you just hold on for one second?"

"Me, or the person on the phone?"

"The person on the phone." Fi dropped her hands into her lap. "I went into the bridal suite for my bouquet and it was ringing in the drawer. I couldn't *not* answer it."

"Yes, you could. It's my *wedding day*!"

"I know, but there's been a bad RTA and it's Doctor Michael's weekend off."

"Lucky him! Isn't it your weekend off too, for my *wedding*?"

"Doctor Michael is in Scotland and I'm … not. Also, I'm the head injury specialist and this is … a head injury."

Sophie huffed and turned away. Fi raised the phone to her ear again.

John, her dad, started to rise from his chair, saying, "I'll have a word with the hotel chef, see if he can rustle up something quick."

"The kitchen staff went home when the outside caterers arrived," Camille told him.

"Oh, this is a nightmare," said Tel.

The murmuring in the room was getting louder. Someone shouted, "Is that it?" It was Uncle Charlie at table six, whom Sophie had tried not to notice during the ceremony but now couldn't avoid. He was wearing a voluminous Pierrot clown outfit, with black pom-pom buttons and red cheek circles on his otherwise white face.

Tel stood up. "Ladies and gentlemen, I'm afraid there's been a cock-up with the menu," he announced.

"Not sure you should say 'cock' at a wedding," said Jacquie, one seat down. "Bit crude, love."

"We apologise for the meal," Tel continued, "We didn't expect it to be quite so ... small."

"If you put it all together it wouldn't fill a side plate," Charlie huffed.

"I know, and we're very sorry. We're trying to work something out."

Tel called over the man with the microphone, standing nervously in the corner of the room, and he came tottering over.

"You're our wedding planner," Tel said, and the man instantly said, "I'm not responsible for this. I didn't pick the menu. This is not my fault."

"No, of course, but in your experience how would you handle this situation?"

The man tutted and said, "I've never come across a wedding where guests were deliberately starved."

"What should we do?"

"I've no idea," the man huffed, and walked off again.

* * *

When dessert was placed in front of Brian the whole table went silent. He looked down at the tiny pimple of white stuff topped with a molecule of red stuff and growled, "What new horror is this?"

"Vanilla panna cotta with raspberry coulis," Olivia read out.

Brian dropped his head to the plate and sucked it straight into his mouth. Faye, sensing the angst oozing from her husband, kept her mouth firmly closed. Brian felt nothing and tasted nothing as the thing gently slipped down his throat.

"Liv," he said.

"Yes, Brian?"

"Can't you rustle up something in the kitchen, like you did at the Woodsman?"

"Not for 150 people, Bri."

Brian made a noise at the back of his throat, a mixture of despair and hopelessness. "I'm going back to the caravan, where there's actual food."

"You can't *leave*," Faye gasped.

"I can and I am."

"Tel and Sophie will be upset if we just up and go."

"Not half as upset as my stomach is right now."

"It's just food, Bri."

"Look at me," he said, turning in his seat and holding his arms out. "Do I look like a man who can be satisfied with two baby asparagus, a tiny cube of fish and a blob of whatever the hell that was? I need food, woman, and I need it *now*."

"Deliveroo," said the teenager at the table.

"Deliveroo?" Brian said, slowly turning his head towards him.

"Yeah."

"Would you care to expand a little more?"

"Just order."

"Order what?"

"Food." The teenager lifted his eyes from the screen and laughed. "Have you never ordered from Deliveroo, or Uber Eats, or Just Eat?"

"You're just throwing random words at me now with no explanation."

The teenager laughed again and dropped his eyes from the face of the huge, hairy, highly agitated man, his attention span at an end. "It's like a takeaway," were his last words, before he started tapping on his screen again.

"Deliveroo!" Mark cried, pulling out his phone. "Brilliant!"

"Is it?"

"Have you got the Deliveroo app, Bri?"

"I don't know what Deliveroo is, and only a vague idea of what an app is."

"There's four Chinese, four Indian, two pizza places and a Mexican takeaway within three miles of here, and two fish and chip shops."

"And you know this how?"

"It's on the app." Mark looked up. Both Brian and Faye were looking at him and slowly shaking their heads. Olivia, Beth and Jim already had their phones out. "You order what you want and they bring it to you," he explained.

Brian sucked in air. "Bring it to you? Like ordering from a takeaway?"

"Exactly like that," Mark laughed. "Finger on the pulse of technology, you pair. Should I order just for us or for everybody? I reckon we could get maybe ten orders per takeaway for a quick delivery, so that's–"

"130 meals," Beth said, tapping on her phone. "I know you're all staring at me right now," she added, not looking up. "I ain't just a pretty face, y'know, I can do maffs an' stuff."

Mark stood up and quickly counted the tables around them. "18 tables of eight people each," he said, "Plus nine at the top table. That makes–"

"153," Beth said.

"130 takeaway meals aren't enough for everyone," Brian muttered.

"If we do a four-mile radius there's four Chinese, five Indian, two pizzas, one Mexican, and four chip shops," Olivia said.

"That's 16 takeaways," Beth said, "Ten orders each. 160 meals. More than enough, even for those with a big appetite." She winked at Brian.

He winked back and stood up. "TEL!" he bawled, and the whole room instantly fell silent. Would the big man be the first one to throw a fit about the food, they all wondered? Would there be chair tossing and tables overturned as the hairy giant turned into an enraged Incredible Hulk?

Tel looked over. Brian waved an arm, urging him to their table. Tel finished an animated conversation with the man with the microphone and hurried over, watched by the tense, almost silent room.

"We have a plan," Brian said, whispering in his ear. Everyone watched and waited. Tel turned to smile back at a nervous-looking Sophie, then said, "Everyone with a food delivery app on their phone, come with me."

* * *

Twenty-six of the guests had an app on their phone. They sat in a group at the bottom of one of the staircases in the foyer. Tel was saying, "Make an order for ten people, plus side dishes and rice, plenty of rice, or chips, or anything."

"What should we … order?" Tel's father asked.

"Anything. Their top ten dishes, ten random dishes, just a mix to cater for everyone's taste. No spicy stuff, like a vindaloo or madras, let's try to keep the death toll down to a minimum."

"I don't think people will be too fussed what we order," Mark said, "They're just hungry."

"Who's paying?" said Uncle Charlie, standing there in his Pierrot outfit.

Tel gave him his credit card. Tel's dad, Henry, gave his card to Lucas. Sophie's dad, John, pulled out his wallet, took out a card and put it on the step next to everyone. "Charge them all to me," he said. Then, counting out his notes, he added, "Tell them there's a ten-pound tip if they can get it here within the hour, twenty if it's within half an hour, and an extra tenner for the first one that arrives. That should spur them on a bit."

"Are you sure, John?"

"We want this wedding to be memorable for all the *right* reasons," he said.

"Thank you."

"I'll check the bar for any nuts and crisps to sustain them," Lucas said, striding off.

"And I'll get the caterers to set up the buffet table early," Annie said.

"We'll need plates," Fi cried, chasing after her, "Lots of

plates, and cutlery."

Tel, standing in front of the mob on the stairs, said, "Right, dad, starting at the top of the list, you order from ..."

As Tel allocated restaurants to most of them, John leaned into Ike, who had snatched up his credit card and was already busy on his phone. "My card is for food orders," he whispered, "Not Amazon."

* * *

There was a buzz in the room as people chatted animatedly.

"You should say something," Camille said to Sophie.

Sophie stood up. "If I could have your attention, please," she said, pretending she was in court. "As Tel has explained, our apologies for the mix-up with the meal. We're currently ordering takeaways to be delivered as soon as possible."

Some applause started at the back of the room, quickly dying away when no one else joined in. The chatter became more excited as waiters in bow ties started carrying in buffet tables and setting them out to Annie's clipped and precise specifications.

"Tablecloths!" she cried. "Plates! Come on, this might be impromptu but there's no excuse to let standards slide!"

Fi and two waiters brought out plates and cutlery and set them at the end of the table. Tabletop hotplates were brought out to keep the food warm when it arrived.

"Napkins!" Annie shrieked, "Where are the napkins? This is an emergency, step up or step out!"

Lucas burst into the kitchen next door with a box of crisps and various snacks on pub cards. "Put these in bowls and take them out to the tables," he said to the aproned caterers, "We can avert a catastrophe if we just keep them fed."

Nobody moved.

"That's not in our remit," said a woman, stepping forward. "We don't do *snacks*."

"Really? I'd poll the guests in the next room about that and see what they have to say about their bite-sized meals."

"They ordered the tasting menu and that's what we served."

"They want more, and we're going to give it to them."

The woman puckered her lips. The other white-clad caterers stood around the stainless-steel kitchen, watching silently.

"The choice is yours," Lucas said, opening up the box of crisps. "You'll either get 150 bad reviews on Google My Business, Facebook, Twitter and every other review platform on the internet, or you can get 150 good ones about how you stepped up in a crisis and saved a wedding. Which is it to be?"

Without taking her eyes off him, the woman reached up to a shelf and took down a stack of white bowls. The others followed and gathered around the table of snacks.

"Wise choice," Lucas said, ripping packets of Scampi Fries off a card. "Now load 'em up and get 'em out."

* * *

Thirty-five minutes after the first order was placed, a small moped, the rider wearing a boxy, pale blue backpack, skidded onto the driveway of Sumsuch House and roared up towards the building. It was followed by five more mopeds with blue, green or red top-boxes, four cars and three roaring motorbikes, all of them racing and slewing and overtaking in their haste to be the first to arrive at the house for the big tip. A car drove onto the manicured lawn, trying to overtake everyone else, and skidded to a halt in front of a wall encompassing a rose garden. Two mopeds jousted with their arms, trying to push each other off. The noise of screaming engines was deafening.

"THEY'RE HERE!" Lucas cried to the group of waiters and hotel staff waiting in the foyer. They hurried out to join him.

The first to arrive was a roaring motorbike. The rider leapt from the seat, opened the top-box, pulled out plastic bags of foil containers, and ran, slightly ahead of a moped rider, up the steps to the front door. The others followed hot on his heels, jostling for position.

"I was first!" said the motorbike rider, not letting go of his plastic bags until he received his tip.

"No, I was the first to *arrive!*" said the moped. "If you hadn't cut me off up the driveway I'd have been first at the door."

"First at the door is what counts," said the biker.

"First to *arrive* is what the order *said*," argued the moped, "And I came onto the driveway *first!*"

"But I was first at the *door!*"

"JOHN!" Lucas cried, and Sophie's dad pushed his way through the crowd. "Adjudication is more your area of expertise, and also, you have the cash."

Behind them, riders and drivers formed a disorderly group, each of them holding out plastic bags full of takeaway meals and shouting to be noticed and given their money.

"Get the meals on the table while they're still hot!" Lucas cried, and several waiters and hotel staff wearing white aprons took the plastic bags inside. When they walked into the dining room and started placing the foil containers and paper-wrapped chips onto the tabletop hotplates there was a burst of applause and some whooping and cheering. Everyone rushed to the buffet as curries and Chinese meals and starters and side dishes were laid out, their tops removed, along with a pile of fish and chips wrapped in paper, and a stack of pizza boxes.

"Women first!" Mark yelled, and a group of them hurried to the plate section. "Elderly next."

Brian pushed his way forward.

"Elderly?" Mark said.

"*Yes*," Brian snapped, "Old, grumpy, and very, very hungry."

"O-kay."

"What are they?" a woman asked Mark.

"Indian," he said, pointing at the curries, "Chinese, fish and chips, and there's pizza at the end."

"What type of curries are they?" she persisted.
"Do you want a menu?"
"Yes."
"There isn't one. Take pot luck and move on. There's tasting spoons in front, don't double-dip or the wedding planner will take you down."
The woman huffed and opted for the fish and chips.
"Are there any vegetarian meals?" a young woman asked.
"Or vegan?" asked another.
"Anything gluten-free?" asked Aunt Sally, a coeliac.
"Bugger," Lucas hissed at Mark, "I forgot about special diets."
"I ordered five vegan curries," shouted Uncle Carl, himself a vegan.
"Which ones?"
"Oh," said Uncle Carl, scanning the lidless tins on the hotplates. "They're here somewhere."
Guests started prodding the aluminium dishes searching for the veggie ones. "I think this is vegetarian," a woman cried.
Another woman prodded the same dish. "There's chicken in there."
"Vegetarians can eat chicken, can't they?"
"No!"
"Found one!" Cousin Mildred cried, and a woman hurried over to claim it. Another was located and they wandered off with their steaming plates of food.
"Gluten-free?" asked Aunt Sally.
Her husband, Harry, lifted up a fried rice dish and upended it onto a plate for her. "For you, my sweet. No soya sauce."
Aunt Sally wandered off, happy.

* * *

"Happy now?" Faye asked.
Brian didn't answer, he was too busy eating pizza slices dipped into curry sauce while choosing which accompaniment, onion bhaji or samosa, to eat next. He was

thinking he might try a bit of Chinese, there looked enough left. He just grunted and nodded.

* * *

"Happy?" Tel asked.

Sophie looked around the room, which was now pulsing with a party-like atmosphere as people dived into their takeaways and sipped at their drinks. "I'm happy that everyone is happy," she smiled.

"Thank goodness for that," Camille said, delicately nibbling on a sweet and sour ball skewered onto her fork. "I just can't believe you chose the–"

"Catastrophe averted," Tel cut in sharply. "All is well."

"Yes," she said. "Thanks to someone's quick thinking."

"Brian," he told her, "Our camping guru and man extraordinaire."

Tel looked over at Brian on the far side of the room. Brian, his mouth full, raised his beer glass in response. Tel stood up.

"Ladies and gentlemen," he announced, "I wonder if we could give Brian a round of applause for the wonderful meal now before us, it was all his idea."

There was rapturous clapping and cheering. Brian, looking surprised and quickly gulping down the food in his mouth, stood up and said, "No, no, I can't take credit." He coughed, then coughed again. With his eyes widening he started punching himself in the chest with one hand and pointing at his neck with the other.

"Brian?"

"Bri?"

"Choking!" he suddenly gasped, and Faye, Mark, and a man from the next table jumped up and started walloping him on his back. Fi raced down from the top table screaming, "I'm a doctor, let me through!" Standing behind Brian, she tried to wrap her arms around his body but couldn't, he was too big. Mark stepped in, his arms only just reaching. Faye was whimpering loudly.

"Make a fist," Fi instructed, and Mark did, just as Brian started wheezing and clutching at his neck. "Grab the fist with your other hand." Mark pressed himself against Brian's back, struggling. "Hard abdominal thrusts!"

Mark thrust once, twice, three times, each time accompanied by Faye crying, "Brian! Brian! Brian!" On the fourth attempt a piece of chicken flew out of Brian's mouth and landed in the lap of a woman at another table, who didn't look the least bit impressed and simply stared at the chicken lump before flicking it away with the tip of a finger.

Brian fell onto his chair, gasping for air. "Thank you," he croaked, feeling the impact of several thumps on his back. He gave a gentle cough and, standing again as the others dispersed back to their seats, he pointed at the teenager at their table, who had a Google result for 'How to stop a person choking' open on his phone.

"It was this young man here who suggested, what was it, dial-a-doo?"

The teenager went as red as a beetroot and tried to disappear inside himself. Another round of applause forced him to slowly slip underneath the table to avoid all the attention. When the applause had died away, Beth reached between her legs to pull him out and his face popped up in front of her chest. The teen didn't move. His eyes bulged. Beth, laughing, hugged his face into her flesh, and the teenager slowly disappeared beneath the table again, sighing softly.

"I fear the poor boy may need therapy to recover from such a close encounter," Mark laughed.

The boy crawled up onto his chair, a look of sheer bliss on his face. He abandoned his phone on the table and rested his head on a hand. He rolled his eyes towards Beth and kept them there, occasionally sighing. When Beth winked at him a delirious smile spread across his face.

"Ah, first love," Faye said. "Such a wonderful thing. Who was your first love, Liv?"

"Mark," she grinned, looking at him.

"No, I mean, your first love. You must have dated before you met Dick."

"I wasn't allowed to date, daddy wouldn't allow it."

"Oh." Faye stopped eating, intrigued. "What about Dick?"

Olivia shrugged. "Daddy decided on Dick and Dick agreed. Nobody mentioned anything about love." Mark reached over and squeezed her hand. "My first and only love is Mark."

"I'm honoured, Liv."

"That's so sweet," Beth cried. "I won't tell you my first love," she added, diving into her Chow Mein, "Jim gets all huffy about it."

"No I don't!"

"You do, babes."

"I don't!"

"Philip Raxter," she said.

"Hate him," Jim spat.

"How about you, Etta?"

"Still waiting for The One," she giggled, hiccoughing.

"One day your prince will come."

David suddenly came running over and crashed to his knees at Beth's side. "I know you want to stay below the radar and remain anonymous," he whispered, "But could you just ..." He put a pen and a serviette on the table in front of her. "... kiss this serviette and sign your name underneath?"

"What for?" Jim asked.

"So I can treasure it for all eternity."

"But I ain't her, babes."

"No, no, of course you're not." He gave her an exaggerated wink. "Do it for me, your biggest fan."

Shaking her head, Beth lifted the serviette to her lips and kissed it, leaving a lipstick imprint. David watched, waving his hands in excitement. She wrote her name and handed it back.

"Beth," he read adoringly, "Is that the name you use? I'll never divulge it. Thank you," he gushed, clutching it to his chest as he jumped up, "Thank you."

He hurried off.

"He really does think you're Adele," Olivia laughed.

"Wait till he tries sellin' my autograph on eBay, top bid, fifty pence."

"Ladies and gentlemen!" said the man with the microphone, into a hand-held microphone. "May I have your attention please? The best man would like to say a few words."

Lucas looked up suddenly, his eyes wide, his mouth slightly ajar as he gasped, "Would he?"

"You have prepared a best man speech, haven't you?" Tel asked.

"Yes, yes, of course I've prepared a best man speech."

He gave a little laugh, and stood up.

CHAPTER TEN

Lucas, tall, handsome, and looking very smart in his Ralph Loren suit, like some leading man in a romance saga, cleared his throat and awkwardly addressed the room.

"I'll keep this short," he began.

"Because he hasn't prepared a speech," Tel laughed.

"I have, it's all up here." He tapped his temple.

Tel groaned.

"I've known Tel for, what, twenty-two, twenty-three years?"

"Twenty-two," Tel said.

"We met at primary school–" A cheer went up from a table at the back. "–and went to university together." A cheer from a different table, with the added bonus of someone shouting, "Go Cantabrigians!"

"Remember the university years, Tel?"

"I do."

"Girls would throw themselves at our feet."

"They didn't."

"Okay, threw themselves at *my* feet."

"Still didn't."

"We took a gap year together in Asia. Oh, the tales I could tell you."

"Please don't."

"And then we entered the corporate world."

"And sold our souls," Tel howled, dramatically throwing his head into his hands. The room laughed. John didn't.

"Tel raced up the legal ladder, *not* aided and abetted by Sophie; in fact, I'd say she was more of a hindrance than a help in his legal career."

"Thanks," Sophie huffed.

"You know what I mean, darling Sophie."

"I do, lovely Lucas."

"No nepotism at Avery & Forbes," John shouted out, and half the room laughed, half the room smiled vaguely and threw frowns at each other.

"I exploded into the finance sector and, all modesty aside, made quite a name for myself." The private school and the university tables all cheered again. "Eventually ending up as a CFO for a prestigious financial services company, who shall remain nameless."

Tel reached up and tapped Lucas's arm. "This isn't the time to set your ego free, today is about us, remember?"

"And Sophie," Lucas said, turning to the bride. "What a catch! So beautiful, so elegant, so erudite and astute, and all-round amazing woman. I've known Sophie since Tel first met her, which was, what, three years ago, four?"

"Shall I give the speech?" Tel laughed, "I have all the relevant information."

"No, no." Laughing, Lucas turned back to the guests. "I've known Sophie long enough to think of her as my sister, and Tel, my brother. So this wedding today is almost like my brother marrying my sister, but without all the yucky stuff." More laughter from the audience, and a whoop of approval from David. "Two nicer people you will never meet, despite them being lawyers, and together they make, I'm sure you'll agree, a very splendid couple." There was an impromptu round of applause, made all the more rambunctious by the alcohol everyone was consuming. "And now that she has agreed to become Tel's wife–"

"I *am* his wife," Sophie laughed, holding up her hand and pointing at the wedding ring. "Did you not notice my sparkly white dress and the registrar saying 'I now pronounce you man and wife'? Try to keep up, Lucas."

"Now that the very gorgeous Sophie *has* married my very

best friend, I consider her to be my best friend also."

"Not before?" Sophie questioned.

"No, not before," he said, "You were just a girlfriend before."

"Oh, *just* a girlfriend."

Lucas shrugged. "They come, they go. No point investing time and energy until there's a ring on their finger."

Sophie threw up her hand again and pointed at the ring. "I am worthy!" she cried, and laughter echoed around the room. Someone at the back fell off their chair and crashed into the wall, and there was some commotion whilst people helped them up again.

"I just wanted to say," Lucas said, lifting his champagne glass and toasting the couple with it, "That I wish both of you a long life, long love, and–"

"Lots of grandchildren!" Camille cried.

"Mum!"

"– lots and lots of happiness. To the lovely couple!"

"To the lovely couple," everyone cheered, raising their various glasses in the air.

"Thanks," Tel said when Lucas sat down again, "I think. Short speech."

"Speeches are boring. Nobody likes long speeches."

"I'll just finish this up for you, shall I?" Tel stood up and said, "I'd like to thank everyone for being here today, we really appreciate you coming and helping to make our day really special."

There was a cheer and a round of applause, which was cut off abruptly by the man with the microphone, who spoke into a hand-held microphone. "And now a few words–"

"From our sponsors!" somebody cackled.

"– from the father of the bride."

"What?" John said, quickly looking around. "The father of the bride does a speech? I haven't prepared anything."

"Didn't stop Lucas."

John stood up and evaluated the room. "I guess, if I had

anything I wanted to say, it would be this. Sophie is our precious, beautiful child, our only daughter, and we love her very much. She is the light of our lives." Camille nodded her head, dabbing at her eyes with a napkin. "I'm very proud of her, and now, I am very proud of Terence–" There was a snort of laughter from the back. "–for taking on the huge and momentous task of *ensuring* her future happiness."

A chill ran up Tel's spine and his beaming smile dimmed a little. The room was dead silent, except for the sound of gently clinking glasses and somebody biting into a popadom. John broke into a huge, slightly sinister grin. "I'm joking of course," he said, quickly adding, "Or am I?" Tel's smile dimmed a bit more. John laughed and raised his glass. "Welcome to the family," he said, "May you both live happily ever after."

An enthusiastic applause followed, and then, when no one else stood up, the volume of their chatter peaked. Sophie glanced around at everyone having a good time and felt happy, relieved. Tel took her hand and kissed her cheek. "Love you, wife," he said.

"Love you, husband."

A luminous orange and yellow lycra-clad man wearing a cycling helmet wandered into the room with a large, square backpack and stood next to table twelve. He said something, but nobody heard. He said it again, and still nobody paid him any attention. Brian stood up next to him and said, "You lost, lad?"

The cyclist said something, and Brian had to put his ear closer to his face to hear above the noise. "AYE UP!" Brian yelled into the room, which immediately fell silent, "WHO ORDERED MEXICAN?"

"I did," shouted Uncle Ike, "About two hours ago."

The cyclist spoke again, Brian listened. "HE SAID HE'S HAD TO CYCLE DOWN FROM KENSINGTON."

"You ordered Mexican food from *Kensington*?" Mildred shrieked.

"They do the best quesadillas in London!"

"Yes, but we're not in London, are we! The poor man, cycling all that way." Mildred hurried over to the cyclist just as he was hauling off his giant backpack, and said, "Sit down, have a drink, have something to eat. Don't move until you're sufficiently rested. Yoo-hoo, man with the microphone on his face and in his hand, can you get this man something to drink?"

"Ask a waiter," he replied.

"I'm asking you."

The man with the microphone huffed and stomped off.

As the guests casually wandered over to the Mexican food now laid out on the buffet table, Ike digging in first, Mildred sat the cyclist down in Brian's chair. Brian lingered as she fussed over him, eventually leaning against the wall with his arms across his chest and his legs crossed. Mark stood up next to him, also crossing his arms and legs, both watching the room, at the people milling around in various stages of intoxication.

"Why is that man dressed in a clown's outfit?" Brian asked.

"No idea. There's always one eccentric relative at any family event, I guess he's it."

"I have a gurning uncle, takes his teeth out and looks like a gargoyle."

"My dad thinks he can sing like Tom Jones," Mark said. "He can't, completely tone deaf. I've seen people cry in pain when he spontaneously bursts into song."

There was a pause, and then Brian said, "Are you going to ask Liv to marry you?"

"I was thinking of it."

"Don't think too long."

"I won't."

Beth cackled uproariously at the table.

"I like her," said Brian.

"Yeah, she's a good egg. Known her a long time."

"Brilliant singer."

"Jim's a lucky man."

"He is."

They were silent for a moment, leaning, arms and legs crossed. A young woman in a skin-tight dress stood up from a table and sashayed across the room, leaving gawping men turning their heads in her wake and women swatting at them. Brian heard Faye hiss, "Stop staring!" and took no notice. They watched the waiters clearing up the buffet table, putting lids on containers and whisking them away.

"Late night snack later," Brian said.

"I couldn't eat another thing."

"All the more for me then. Faye won't approve, she says curries give me all-night flatulence, dangerous in a small caravan."

"No naked flames around your pitch then," Mark laughed, splaying his fingers and adding, "KABOOM!"

Faye looked up at them. "What are you two talking about?"

"Politics," said Brian, and Faye huffed and turned away, just as he knew she would.

Brian, tired of standing with no sign of the cyclist moving from his seat any time soon, waved a hand at microphone man, standing further along the wall and casting a severe eye over the proceedings. The man shrugged and held his hands out.

"Chair!" Brian hollered, "Need another chair over here!"

The man pointed through the double doors into the foyer. Brian looked, then shrugged. The man stomped over and said, "There's chairs in the foyer, go and get one of those."

"Get it myself?" Brian cried in mock horror, "But I'm a *guest!*"

The man tutted and stomped off through the doors, coming back dragging a chair behind him, which he abandoned in front of Brian and wandered off.

"Wonder how he got the job of wedding planner," Mark said.

"It was clearly his charm and sparkling personality."

Everyone scooted their chairs around to make room for Brian's extra chair. He sat down and sighed happily. Above the babble of multiple conversations and laughter he heard thuds from the room next door.

"That'll be the band setting up," Mark said, looking at his watch. "I think the evening reception starts at seven."

"Love a live band, me," said Jim.

The man with the microphone on his head stood in front of the top table and said, "Ladies and gentlemen, could you all make your way outside, please? Champagne and canapes will be served in the garden while the staff tidy up the room." He paused, looking at the takeaway-splattered tables, and added, "It might take them a while."

* * *

As the hotel staff cleared away and moved the tables, guests milled around the beautiful gardens, sitting on steps and picnic tables and the benches around a very pretty fountain. New guests joined them, smart and energetic compared to the stuffed and drunken afternoon ones. Microphone man approached Sophie and she nodded. He turned and loudly announced, "The bride will be throwing her bouquet. Ladies, gather over here. No, over here," he yelled at a woman heading towards the patio for a champagne refill. "Did I point over there? No, I pointed over here!"

The elderly woman stopped and turned and yelled back, "I'm eighty-four years old, you idiot, what do I want with a bouquet?"

The wedding planner pushed his nose into the air and walked off.

Sophie stood in the middle of the lawn with her back to a throng of excited women, including Faye, Beth and Olivia.

"I see Faye's looking to renew her wedding vows," Mark said to Brian.

"I'm looking to renew my caravan."

"Before it falls apart," Jim laughed.

"You'd know all about that, wouldn't you, Jim."

"Why is Beth up for catching the bouquet?" Mark asked.

"Dunno."

"You don't know much, do you."

"I know enough to marry someone like Beth."

"Fair comment."

Sophie cried, "One!" and swung her bouquet in front of her, "Two! *Three!*"

The bouquet sailed over her head. The women jostled towards it. Faye did quite an impressive leap into the air with a hand raised, and it sailed right passed her fingers. Beth, mindful of her low-cut dress and trying not to raise her arms too high, inadvertently bumped against a woman, who was catapulted sideways. The bouquet flew past her and continued its course.

Olivia was bouncing up and down on the spot, holding up her arms and squealing as the bouquet came straight towards her. A hand suddenly blotted her view and snatched it away. The woman who caught it screamed with joy as she waved it above her head and searched the crowds.

Across the lawn a man screamed out loud and started running like his life depended on it up the steps to the house, disappearing inside.

"BILL?" the woman yelled after him. "BILL, I CAUGHT THE BOUQUET!"

"He knows," a man laughed, "Oh, he knows."

"Is he coming back?" the woman asked.

The man shrugged.

"BILL!"

"Sorry," Olivia quietly said to her as the other women dispersed.

The woman thrust the bouquet at her with some force and said, "Take it, it's obviously no good to me."

Olivia turned to Mark with a huge smile on her face, holding up the flowers.

"You okay, Mark?" Jim asked. "You've gone a bit pale."

"I-I'm alright."

"Current emotional state?" Brian asked.

"Terror, panic, slight bit of excitement, but mostly panic."

"Are you going to ask her to marry you?" Jim asked.

"Not here," Brian said from the corner of his mouth as Olivia approached them. "You don't want to distract from Tel and Sophie's big day."

"No," Mark agreed. "I'll do it as soon as the terror and panic dissipate."

"Good man."

"I caught the bouquet!" Olivia squealed.

"Well done, love," Faye said, striding over.

"I think I fractured that woman's ribs," Beth said, looking back with concern as women fussed over the woman she'd catapulted across the lawn. "'Ope she's okay."

"She looks fine," Brian said, "Rib fractures are agony, had them a few times at the steelworks, and she's already sipping champagne and laughing, you can't laugh with a fractured rib."

"Thank God for that," Beth gasped, "I was worried she might sue me."

"That would look good in front of a judge," Mark laughed, "'I was chasing the bride's bouquet and was clobbered by a woman chasing the same bouquet. Sophie could be your witness and your defence lawyer.'"

Olivia snuggled up to Mark and again said, "I caught the bouquet!"

Mark felt an overwhelming urge to ask her. The time seemed right, the stars were aligned. He'd been meaning to ask her for months now but wasn't sure she was ready to commit yet, so soon after Richard – was a year long enough? The question danced around on his tongue, desperate to fall out of his mouth as she snuggled up to him with the bouquet. No ring, though. It would be an empty gesture without a ring, and Brian was right, today was Tel and Sophie's day, not theirs.

Jim took a couple of champagne flutes from a passing waiter's tray and handed one to Beth.

"I don't want it, babes."

"I'll take it," said Annie, walking passed and grabbing the

glass from Jim's hand, quickly glugging down the contents as she walked towards a waiter for another.

* * *

"I've been waiting for you."

"Have you?"

"I knew if I stood by the booze you'd come eventually."

"Charming."

"I am," Lucas said, stepping closer, "If you'd just give me a chance to show it."

"I'll pass, thanks." Annie picked a flute off a waiter's tray.

"Why do you treat me so cruelly?"

"It just comes naturally whenever you're around."

"Harsh."

"But true."

"Why do you hate me so much?"

"I don't hate you," she said, and Lucas smiled. "I'm completely indifferent. I feel no emotion towards you at all."

"Nothing?" he grinned.

"Not a thing."

Lucas gently trailed a finger down her bare arm. "How about now?"

"Irritating," she said, "Like you."

He leaned into her ear, his cheek brushing against hers, and whispered, "What about now?"

"Still irritating," she said, stepping away.

"How can you resist me?"

"It's easy. Watch." And she walked off.

"Can I just say," he called after her, "Your cleavage is looking particularly spectacular today."

Several women turned towards him with expectant smiles on their faces, turning away again when they realised he wasn't referring to them.

"I rest my case," Annie cried, raising her glass in the air.

Lucas stared after her, smiling.

"You're not still bothering Annie, are you?" Tel asked,

walking up to his best man.

"She challenges me."

"She'll punch you in the face if you don't pack it in."

"I'll take that chance."

"Why?"

"Because she's feisty and sexy and ..." Lucas sighed. "... totally irresistible."

"I'd give it up if I were you, mate. You're wasting your time, you're not her type, she seems to prefer older men."

"I'll win her over eventually, you'll see."

"I admire your confidence and your arrogance, but let me offer a word of advice."

"Word away, chap."

"Try playing it cool."

"I am naturally cool."

"Be a little less ... enthusiastic. Be vaguely disinterested and let her come to you, that'll tweak her interest."

"Come to me?" Lucas repeated. "I like the sound of that."

Tel patted him on the back. "Good luck, chap."

* * *

"Bloody creepy guy is chasing after me again," Annie growled, storming over to Sophie, who was talking to some of her relatives by a small pond with a fountain.

"Who? Lucas?"

"He's like a slobbering puppy desperate for attention. He wants to prove he can win me over and then he'll lose interest."

"He's just an incorrigible flirt, take no notice. Besides," Sophie added with a smile, moving away from the relatives and walking across the lawn, "You love it really."

"I don't! He's just said that my breasts were looking particularly spectacular today!"

Sophie looked down. "They are, very ... bouncy."

"I know, but he doesn't have to yell it across the lawn for all and sundry to hear. If breasts could blush mine would be purple."

"Wife," Tel cried, coming up behind Sophie and wrapping his arms around her waist.

"Husband," she laughed.

"A little bird tells me that Lucas has the hots for Annie."

"Oh don't," Annie sighed. "Was the little bird a great big bloke with predatory eyes and a ridiculously condescending smirk?"

"It was. You could do worse."

"I couldn't."

"He's not that bad," Sophie said. "He's quite charming, in an overblown, clichéd sort of way. I'm sure he thinks he's James Bond."

"And what, I'm his Bond girl? No thanks. Oh no, the bloody bugger's coming over."

"My ears are burning," Lucas said, swapping Annie's empty glass for a full one, "Are you talking about me?"

"No," Annie snapped, sipping her champagne. "We were talking about something far more interesting."

"There's that sharp riposte again. You know, there's a fine line between love and hate."

"It's not so much a line as a vast wasteland of nothingness, with tumbleweeds blowing across it and crickets cricketing, and in the background, sirens."

"Me thinks the lady doth protest too much."

"Me thinks the man doth wasteth his time."

"If this breaks out into fisticuffs," Tel said, "My money's on Annie."

"I would never lay a finger on a lady," said Lucas, running a slow finger down her arm again. "Not in anger, anyway."

Annie shivered and said, "Stop it, Lucas, you're making me feel nauseous."

"That's probably the curry you scoffed earlier," Sophie said.

"And the three magnums of champagne you've glugged since you've been here," Tel laughed.

"Not *three*!" Annie sighed, finishing her champagne, "Possibly two."

"Have you thought about having it intravenously pumped into your arm?" Lucas suggested. "It would save all the hassle of lifting that heavy glass to your mouth every three seconds."

"You're so rude!"

"Another?"

She handed her glass to him and he wandered off, laughing.

"Have you seen Fi?" Sophie asked.

Annie threw out her arm and said, "Last spotted sleeping on a picnic table over in that direction somewhere."

"Asleep? Again? I wonder if she's ill?"

"She is," Annie said, and Sophie gasped. "She's a necrophiliac."

"Narcoleptic!" Tel said. "Stop telling everyone she's a necrophiliac!"

"Whatever. Anyway, she's a doctor, she should know if there's anything wrong with her or not."

"Doctors are notoriously blasé about their own health," Sophie said.

"I've heard they're all hypochondriacs," said Tel.

"Either way, she does sleep an awful lot. I'll go and find her."

As Sophie was walking away, her dress glinting in the sun, Tel cried, "Miss you already, Mrs Okenado."

"Ah," she said, turning round and walking backwards across the grass, "We need to talk about that."

"About what?"

"My name."

Tel stared at Annie. "Her name?"

Annie shrugged and walked off in search of more champagne, thinking that Lucas couldn't be trusted to even fetch her a drink.

* * *

"Darlings!" David cried dramatically, mincing up to the camping group and extending a limp hand to each of them.

"We haven't been formally introduced. I'm David, Tel's baby brother. Are we all enjoying ourselves?"

"Very much," Mark said.

"It's a splendid wedding," said Olivia.

The others nodded.

"Sophie looks like a sparkly version of Audrey Hepburn, doesn't she, wandering around all sparkly and Hepburny. I'm beyond excited to have a sister at last. I wished for one every birthday, and even sent Santa letters, but I never got one until now. We've promised to take her shopping first chance she gets." David pursed his lips and gave them all the evil eye. "Don't think I didn't notice that heavy pause there. I know what you're thinking, Sophie doesn't need fashion advice from someone who looks like he's just run away from the circus." He swished the front of his multi-coloured jacket. "But colours are coming back, you mark my words."

"So many different colours, all at the same time?" Jim asked, shielding his eyes from the brightness.

"Says the man wearing purple tartan," Brian laughed.

Travis came striding over, nodding at each of them and displaying his white, very straight teeth.

"You ask Travis, my very hunky, very American boyfriend. Aren't colours coming back into fashion, Travis."

"Never left, as far as I'm concerned."

"I love your accent," Olivia giggled.

"Texan, ma'am."

"Ooh," she giggled again, "I love being called ma'am. Which part of Texas are you from?"

"All of it," he drawled.

"He's not the sharpest knife in the block," David said, raising an affectionate palm against his square jaw, "But he's very hunky and that almost makes up for it."

They swapped beaming smiles, then David turned back to them and said, "That horrid man with the microphone is going to descend on us at any moment, so be prepared to be whipped back into the house and punished if you don't do as he says fast enough. They've set out the buffet, if anyone's remotely hungry."

Faye looked up at Brian, who stared up at the house thinking he could probably eat *something*.

"And we have a surprise for you all later, haven't we, Travis?"

"We sure have."

David looked at Beth. "I think you'll like it," he breathed, "It might give you inspiration for your next album."

He hurried off before she could respond.

"My own real-life Adele," Jim laughed, kissing her cheek. "You're a lovely wife."

"And you're turning out to be quite a lovely husband."

"Oh stop," Mark cried when they started smooching. "Nobody needs to see that."

"Participation is better," Olivia said, turning his face towards her and kissing him.

"You're both ruining what was building up to be quite a decent appetite," Brian grumbled.

"Must you always think of food, Bri?"

"Yes, my love. I'd rather be snogged, but in the absence of any physical contact I'll take food instead."

Faye stood on tip-toes, wrapped her arms around his wide neck, and kissed him passionately on the lips.

"Ooh, am I on a promise for later?"

"Maybe, if you play your cards right," she winked.

"Feel the love," Tel laughed, walking over. "Nothing like a good wedding to put everyone in the mood, is there."

Mark grabbed hold of Olivia, who screamed out loud as he suddenly threw her backwards onto an arm. As he swished her up again her feathered fascinator fell out of her dark curls. Faye and Beth dashed forward to reattach it.

"Like a flock of birds," Brian laughed, as they squealed and fussed as if the worst-thing-ever had just happened.

"Pretty birds though," Jim grinned.

"That they are."

"Are you enjoying yourselves?" Tel asked.

"Your brother's just asked the same question."

"Ah, you've met David then?"

"And the very handsome Travis," Olivia, now resplendent in her fascinator again, giggled.

"Excellent wedding," Jim said. "It does feel a bit like we've been kicked out of the building for a playground break though."

"Enticed by champagne."

"My playground was never this lovely," Faye said, looking around the manicured gardens.

"Concrete playground in a concrete jungle?" Jim said.

"Hardly," Faye huffed. "There *are* trees and parks in Birmingham, you know. In fact, we have more green space in Birmingham than any other European city, and more trees than Paris."

"You've set her off now," Brian said.

"We've got more canals than Venice, *and* we invented Cadbury's chocolate, which is just down the road from us, isn't it, Bri."

"Yes, love."

"And the Bullring is one of the largest shopping centres in the UK. It's also where Ozzy Osbourne was born."

"What, in the Bullring?" Jim gasped. "I didn't know that."

"Not sure Ozzy Osbourne is something to boast about," Mark laughed, and Faye scrunched her eyes at him.

"I think Trevor Eve was born in Birmingham," Olivia said.

"Yes, yes, and the comedian, Frank Skinner."

"Again, not necessarily something you'd want to brag about."

"What's the public transport system like in Birmingham?" Tel asked with a grin.

"It's good," Faye nodded.

"What do you have?"

"The usual."

"Such as?"

"Oh, trains, planes, trams."

"And?" Tel persisted.

"I know what you're trying to get me to say," Faye sighed.

"Say it then."

"I won't."

"Apart from a train, a plane or a tram, what's the most popular, single form of transport up there in the Midlands?"

Faye lifted her chin up. "A bus," she said.

"A *buzz!*" they all laughed, except for Brian, who knew better. Mark and Tel started swatting at imaginary bees.

"Say it again," Jim urged.

Faye closed her eyes and turned her head away.

"Sorry, Faye," Tel said, "Couldn't resist. Anyway, you won't be out here for much longer, they're just setting up the room for the evening reception. The wedding planner, organiser, whatever he calls himself, will let us know when we can go back in again."

"Will he be ringing a bell?" Jim asked.

"No, he'll just be using the power of his enigmatic personality."

"And a big stick," Brian said, deadpan.

"So," Jim said, gently punching Tel's shoulder, "What's it like being a married man then?"

"Well, it's only been a short while, but yeah, I like it."

"You like it now, wait until the nagging starts." Jim's laugh cut off abruptly when he felt the force of Beth's withering glare upon him.

A magnified voice tore through the garden, making everybody jump and a few women scream out loud, including Olivia and Faye. "LADIES AND GENTLEMEN," the wedding planner hollered from the patio, "CAN I HAVE YOUR ATTENTION PLEASE!"

"Oh blimey!" Mark gasped, "He has a megaphone!"

"Very package-holiday tour-guide vibe," Brian said.

"IF YOU COULD MAKE YOUR WAY BACK INSIDE USING BOTH THE PATIO DOORS ON MY RIGHT." He indicated right

PITCHING UP IN STYLE!

with a flourish of his free arm. "AND THE PATIO DOORS ON MY LEFT." He flourished left. "DO IT IN AN ORDERLY FASHION, AND PLEASE, DON'T TRIP ON THE STAIRS, WE'VE ALREADY HAD THE AMBULANCE OUT ONCE THIS WEEK."

"We have been summoned," Brian declared.

"In an orderly fashion, no less," said Mark.

"We could charge across the grass, screaming and yelling, like a scene from a Zulu film," Jim suggested.

"Zulu film?" said Mark.

"Yeah, watched one the other day, had Michael Cain in it and he said 'Fire at will', and I always wonder who poor Will is and if he volunteered to be shot at or if he was forced to be the lead target. Had all these Zulus charging across ..." He noticed them all staring at him. "What?"

"I think we lack the necessary shields and spears for that particular scenario," Brian said.

"An' I ain't charging across no grass in these shoes," said Beth.

"Me neither."

Jim shrugged. "It was just a thought."

"Stop thinking," Mark said, "You'll wear your brain out."

"IF YOU'D LIKE TO HURRY YOURSELVES ALONG!" screeched microphone man, now upgraded to megaphone man. "LADY IN PINK BY THE FOUNTAIN, YOU'RE GOING THE WRONG WAY! COME TOWARDS ME! FOLLOW THE SOUND OF MY VOICE!"

The lady in pink said something, gesticulated a bit, then carried on walking the 'wrong way'. Megaphone man looked horrified, then resigned. The megaphone slumped to his side, then lifted to his mouth again. "YOU GUESTS WANDERING OFF INTO THE WOODED AREA, YOU'RE BEING *CALLED BACK INSIDE*. HELLO, IS THIS THING WORKING?"

"He's in the wrong job," Faye said.

"I doubt there's many vacancies for tyrannical dictators," said Brian.

"You've clearly never worked in the private sector," Tel

laughed briefly, before scouring the area for John, his boss and new father-in-law."

"On the subject of weddings," Olivia said, "Where *is* the wonderful wife?"

Tel burst out laughing again. "I thought you were going to say 'on the subject of tyrannical dictators, where's the wife?' She's circulating somewhere. I'll go and find her. You lot make your way inside before the megaphone comes chasing after you with a cattle prod."

CHAPTER ELEVEN

The Evening Reception

When they finally reached the top of the stairs and, after much discussion about it during their ascent, went through the double patio doors on the *right*, they saw that the tables had all been moved to the sides and the partition wall had been opened up to the large bar area. A live band fizzed excitedly on a low platform in the far corner, strumming the odd chord on a guitar and tapping lightly on drums. A disco ball strobed above a substantial dance floor. The space was enormous. New arrivals for the evening reception poured through the doors, distinguishable from the takeaway-stained, slightly dishevelled and squiffy afternoon guests.

"Beer!" cried Brian, striding off into the throng bustling around the bar. Mark and Jim followed.

"Where shall we sit?" Olivia asked, but Beth was already hobbling to the nearest table and flopped down into a seat. "Feet are killing me," she said, taking off her shoes. "All that standing around and pulling 'eels out of the ground, bloody nightmare."

The other women followed and sat down next to her, flicking off their shoes and flexing their naked toes. A passing Pierrot clown with ridiculously large feet stepped on Beth's big toe on his way past, and Beth yelled, "Oi, baggy man, mind where you're going, will ya!" The clown carried on walking. "Rude!"

Microphone man was fussing around the last few stragglers coming through from the garden, then racing across the room to herd the new arrivals into place.

"Can you get away from the patio doors and find somewhere to sit!" he screeched, rushing across the room again, "The bride and groom want to make their grand entrance! Is everybody here?"

"If they're not they wouldn't be able to say so, would they," Brian chuckled.

"Why *is* he wearing a microphone?" Beth wondered. "Who do you think he's talking to?"

Olivia giggled and said, "He's probably receiving spiritual guidance from Attila the Hun."

"Maybe he has a SWAT team on the roof ready to take down any stragglers," said Faye.

"E's just wearing it to make 'imself look important."

Microphone man stepped out onto the patio and disappeared, almost immediately coming back in again, hands wringing.

"He's very red in the face," Faye said, "He wants to be careful."

"High blood pressure," said Fi, slipping into a chair next to them and taking off her shoes. "If he carries on like this his head's going to explode."

"That's your medical diagnosis, is it?" said Annie, flopping into another chair, "Exploding head? Get a lot of those in A&E, do you?"

"'Is 'ead won't explode, will it?" Beth asked, horrified.

They all looked at Fi for confirmation. "No, of course not," she said, "It was my attempt at levity."

"Don't give up the day job is my advice," Annie cackled. "Anyway, did you have a nice sleep out there in the garden?"

"Yes, fine. Bit of sunburn on the back of my neck, arms and calves, but other than that, yes, very satisfactory, thank you for asking."

"Oh!" cried a woman behind them, twisting round in her seat, "Were you the young lady draped across the picnic table like a dead starfish? We were so worried." The woman immediately turned away before Fi could answer, feverishly waving at someone across the room.

"Not worried enough to poke me to see if I was still alive though," Fi said.

"It's that little noise you make when you're sleeping that gives it away," said Annie. "Like a little mouse having a terrible nightmare. You want to get that necrophilia sorted out, Fi."

"Necrophilia?" Olivia gasped.

"Narcolepsy," Fi sighed, "I keep telling you, Annie, it's *narcolepsy*, and I don't have it."

"There's definitely something wrong with you."

"Yes, my choice of friends for one!"

"Oooh," Annie sneered.

"What's up with you, anyway?"

"What do you mean, what's up with me?"

"I barely recognised you when I came in, there's no glass in your hand."

"Oh funny ha-ha," Annie sat up suddenly. "Here's my drink now," she said, watching Lucas striding across the room with four champagne flutes in his hands. She put on what she hoped was a slightly sardonic yet welcoming smile, and Lucas walked straight past without acknowledging her existence.

"Losing your touch there," Fi said. "Maybe he didn't recognise you without a glass in your hand either."

"Shut up."

Annie turned in her seat in time to see Lucas handing the champagne flutes to group of three women standing almost right behind her, who all giggled and fluttered their eyelashes at him. She heard Lucas say, "Sam, Tam and Pam?" and they giggled again, like a cackle of hyenas. One of them pointed at the other two and said, "Married, married, and," she pointed at herself and threw out her arms, "young, free and single!"

"Nice accent," he said, "Australian?"

"New Zealand."

Annie jumped up and stomped, bare-footed, to the bar, passing Brian, Mark and Jim on their way back to the table with drinks.

Microphone man popped in and out of the patio doors like a horizontal yoyo, finally waving at the band in the far corner and furiously nodding his head. The band started playing *The Wedding March* on electric guitars, Queen-style. Beth suddenly cried, "Oh blimey!" and pressed her feet into her shoes, quickly tottering off across the dance floor.

"Curry run," Brian said to Jim, "I'd recognise that urgency anywhere."

"Ladies and gentlemen," microphone man hollered above the music and the crescendo of conversations, "May I present to you, the bride and groom."

Tel and Sophie stepped through the patio doors and everyone burst into rapturous applause. Sophie looked positively radiant with the sun beaming behind her. Tel kept glancing at her on his arm and smiling proudly.

"Like an angel!" David screeched from across the room.

Both mothers instantly burst into tears as the couple walked out into the middle of the dancefloor. The applause thundered. Tel laughed and took a bow. Sophie just smiled, her face alight with happiness.

"Taking the dance floor for the very first time as husband and wife, Tel and Sophie," cried microphone man. "Please give them your heartfelt applause!"

During the ensuing ovation, *The Wedding March* stopped and a keyboard started playing a slow intro to a song.

"Oh, I know this one," Olivia squealed.

The room fell silent. A clear voice filled the room and Beth, holding a microphone, slowly walked up onto the small platform and stood in front of the band.

"Oh my God!" someone cried, "They got Adele to sing at their wedding!"

"Kudos!" someone else yelled.

"I spotted her first," David shrieked.

Staring at Tel and Sophie the whole time, Beth sang *Make You Feel My Love* to absolute perfection. Within minutes people were openly crying at the lyrics, the faultlessness of her singing, and Tel and Sophie's slow and loving dance around the room. The photographer flitted around and people stood recording it on their phones, switching from the couple to Beth and back again. Sophie lifted her arms from Tel at one point to wipe at her eyes. Camille ran over with a napkin.

Bar staff stopped serving, microphone man stood to the side unashamedly sobbing, and hotel staff crowded the doors, watching and listening.

"It's such a magical moment," Olivia sobbed, throwing herself against Mark, who wrapped an arm around her shoulders and hugged her tight, thinking, 'Now? Shall I ask her now?' A hitch caught in his throat. Not now, but soon.

"Are you crying, Bri?" Faye grinned.

"Isn't everyone? They look like film stars, and my God, that woman can sing."

"That's my girl," said Jim, letting the tears slip down his cheeks unhindered.

When the song ended the applause nearly brought the ceiling down. Everyone dabbed at their faces. People rushed over to hug the married couple and congratulate the singer. David fell to one knee in front of the platform, reached up to grab hold of Beth's hands, and screamed, "*Marry me!*"

Beth laughed. "Sorry, babes, but I already 'ave an 'usband."

"My heart is broken!" he wailed, "*Broken!*"

"Besides," Beth said, "Ain't you gay?"

"He is," Travis said, pulling David to his feet. "Get up now, Dave, you're embarrassing me."

"Says the man who thinks the Polly Darton outfit is perfectly acceptable to wear in Waitrose," David cried as he was led away.

The teenager from their table waited until everyone else had dispersed before walking up to Beth and saying, "Would you ever consider moving on with another man?"

"Man?" Beth said, trying hard not to laugh. "No, babes, I'm quite attached to me 'usband, as it 'appens."

"Oh," said the teenager, and wandered off, crestfallen.

"Hey," Beth said into her microphone, "I've got a funny story to tell you about that song." The room went quiet again. "Tel and Sophie both rang me, separately, and asked me to sing at their wedding. I was thrilled, obviously. They both asked me to sing the *same song*!"

Tel and Sophie stared at each other in surprise.

"I thought she was singing it for me," Sophie cried.

"I thought she was singing it for me!"

"Ain't that a match made in 'eaven?" Beth cried. "So, I asked Sophie to choose another song and she did, so you two get double the dancing, if the band's singer don't mind me pinching a bit more of her gig?" Beth turned to the young woman standing on the platform, who waved and nodded. "This is a favourite of mine, but I need a swig of something first to wet me whistle."

A man rushed forward and held up his pint of beer. "Nah, mate, ain't drinking alcohol, I'm detoxing."

A woman hurried over from the bar and held up her glass.

"What is it?" Beth asked through the microphone. "Ginger beer? Cheers, babes."

Beth took a gulp, handed the glass back, then nodded at the band. A guitar and a gentle drum beat started up. Tel and Sophie started smooching around the dancefloor. Glancing over at Jim and throwing him a kiss, Beth sang the Shania Twain song, *From This Moment On*.

The room fell to pieces. All that could be heard beneath Beth's beautiful singing voice were stifled wails and a lot of sniffing into handkerchiefs. When she finished both Tel and Sophie rushed over as she stepped down from the platform and hugged her tightly.

"Thank you," Tel said earnestly.

"I've never seen so many people crying at a wedding before," Sophie sobbed.

"I 'ad the room liberally sprayed with onion juice beforehand for effect," Beth laughed. "I know I ain't known you as long as the others, but I love you guys and I think you're going to be very 'appy together, I can feel it in me waters."

The band started playing *Love and Marriage*, just as a three-tier cake with lots of scrolled icing and pastel flowers was wheeled into the room by two waiters.

"Oh, the cake!" Sophie cried. "I'd almost forgotten about that."

"Relieved to see it's not a miniature one," Tel laughed.

They cut the cake, holding the knife together, to a round of applause and the feverish clicking of the photographer's camera. They each took a small piece and looked at each other.

"Oh, don't smoosh it in her lovely face," Faye cried. "Why do they have to do that? It's horrible."

"Such a waste of good cake," Brian said.

They held the piece out to each other and took a delicate bite.

"Classy," said Mark.

"When do we get some?" Brian asked.

"Brian!"

"I love wedding cake."

"You don't even know what type it is!"

"I'm not fussed," he shrugged, "As long as it's got icing on it."

"Like a Christmas cake?" Faye said.

"Yeah."

"Like the Christmas cake I make every year and you never touch?"

"Can't get a knife through it," Brian said, and Faye glared up at him.

"I'll never make it again," she cried.

"Oh, thank God for that. Another G&T, love?"

"Ladies and gentlemen," microphone man croaked through his emotions, "Can we have the father of the bride on the dancefloor please?"

John made his way through the crowds and gently led Sophie back onto the dancefloor. The band played *Isn't She*

Lovely, the female singer's voice echoing around the room. Guests cried again, and then, slowly, other people joined them on the dancefloor and the music changed to something more upbeat. The drummer, as if being released, went wild, sticks blurring in front of his tossed hair.

"He's never going to last the night at that pace," Brian said, watching him.

"He's like Animal from the Muppets," Mark laughed.

Faye was just resting at the table after a particularly exhausting boogie, kicking off her heels, when she spotted someone she thought she recognised on the other side of the room. She looked away, then looked back again.

A familiar face.

No, it couldn't be. Could it?

She sucked in air and held it. She sat up straight in her chair, her eyes wide. She stood up in bare feet and watched as the familiar face moved behind dancing couples and chatting groups, disappearing and then reappearing. There was no doubt about it.

"BRIAN!" she shouted, grabbing him as he jived by on his own. "BRIAN!"

He swivelled his head round, catching the urgency in her voice, then followed her gaze across the room. "What is it?"

"I think," Faye gasped, "I think Richard's here?"

"Liv's Richard?" Brian quickly searched the sea of faces, and then he saw him. Richard. Liv's ex-husband, making his way to the bar. Brian turned and caught Mark's eye on the other side of the table. 'Richard,' he mouthed, throwing his thumb over his shoulder.

'What?' Mark mouthed back.

'Richard's here.'

Mark shrugged and lifted his palms, unable to read the lips behind the beard. Brian hurried around the table and whispered into his ear, "We have a problem."

* * *

Annie was leaning against the counter in the bar area, sipping languidly on champagne, when she spotted Lucas striding towards her.

"Annie," he said, *not* smiling as he stood next to her, raising a hand to attract the barman's attention.

"Lucas."

He said nothing else. He didn't even look at her. Annie stopped leaning and watched, taken aback, as Lucas grabbed his drinks, nodded once at her, and walked off again.

That was twice he'd ignored her.

Intrigued, she slowly sauntered over to his group of chatting guests and wiggled her way in, laughing as Lucas finished a joke he'd been telling. She looked up at him and winked. He didn't wink back, he looked away.

What was going on?

She dashed to the Ladies loos to check that her makeup hadn't slid down her face, giving her panda eyes, or that her upstyled hair hadn't become a mess from all the dancing she'd been doing. As she gave herself the once over in the mirror, finding nothing wanting, she realised that, even though she'd glanced over at Lucas several times whilst she'd been 'strutting her stuff' on the dancefloor, he hadn't once been watching. He *always* watched her, his eyes like one of those weird portraits that seem to follow you around the room.

But not tonight.

Annie checked her eye makeup again. Perfect, as usual.

"What do I care?" she told her reflection, before strutting back to the party.

She marched over to Lucas' group again, snatching an empty glass off a table as she went. She stood so close to him that their bodies touched. To her surprise, he took a step sideways without even acknowledging her presence. She wriggled the glass in front of her.

"I'm empty," she shouted up at him.

"Vacuous?" he laughed, eyes averted.

"No," she whined, "I need another drink."

He still didn't look at her, staring instead at the throng around them, laughing, dancing, drinking. "Well," he said coldly, "If you take your empty glass over to the bar I'm sure someone will fill it for you."

"Will you fill it for me?" she pouted.

"Kind of busy," he said, suddenly smiling as he held a hand out towards the young woman with the fluttering eyelashes he'd been talking to earlier. "Dance?" he shouted above the noise.

"Bonza, mate," the woman giggled, and off they trotted onto the dancefloor, leaving Annie standing there, drinkless, with her mouth half open.

What the bloody hell was going on?

***

Brian and Mark hurried out of the room and into the foyer. "Richard's here," Brian said.

"What?"

"Richard's here."

"He can't be! Why?"

Brian shrugged.

"Where?"

"He's in the bar."

With a look of increasing horror, Mark hurried back to the door and peered inside. It took a couple of minutes before he was able to spot Richard's face at the far end.

"What the hell is he doing here?" he snarled, turning back to Brian.

"Dunno."

"Does Liv know?"

"I don't think so, not yet."

Mark took another look. "He *can't* be here. Why is he here?"

"Want me to find out?"

Mark nodded, standing in the doorway as Brian pushed his way through the crowds to the bar. Richard had his back to him when he approached. He tapped him on the shoulder and Richard turned with a blank expression, which turned into a look of surprise when he saw who was standing behind him. He stared up at Brian for a moment as if trying to place him.

"Big bloke," he eventually said, nodding, "From the campsite."

"Why are you here?"

"Quite frankly, it's none of your–" He stopped, his eyes widening. "Is Olivia here?" he asked, quickly scanning the room.

"Why are you here, Richard?"

"I'm a guest."

"A guest of Tel and Sophie's? They invited you?" Brian felt confused. Why would Tel and Sophie, knowing Liv's history with Richard, invite him to their wedding?

"I'm a plus one."

The woman standing next to Richard suddenly turned around. "Oh, hello," she beamed at Brian, the smile crinkling her eyes. "Fun wedding, isn't it? We've only just arrived, Richard got horribly lost on the way here, was convinced the sat-nav was taking us the wrong way, didn't you, Richard, but we made it in the end. I'm Lauren, friend of the bride's mother, we went to uni together, too many years ago to admit." She laughed and held out a delicate hand. Brian shook her fingertips, noticing that she seemed quite a bit older than Richard. "And this is Richard."

"Yes," Brian said, "We've met."

"Oh, have you? Small world, isn't it. Weddings can be terribly incestuous, can't they, everybody knowing everybody else, but I guess that's families for you."

"Is Olivia here?" Richard asked again.

"Did you know she was going to be here?"

"I did not."

"Didn't you recognise the names of the bride and groom on the invitation?"

"I didn't get an invitation," Richard snapped. "Lauren

asked me to accompany her to a wedding. Besides," he added, jutting his chin indignantly, "I don't know the names of the people on that horrible campsite, why would I? You were just *riff-raff*."

Mark suddenly came rushing over, pushing angrily through the crowds. Brian had to hold him back from actually barging into Richard with an outstretched arm. Mark thrust his face as close to Richard's as he could, and spat, "Why are *you* here?"

Lauren, looking more than a little confused, said, "I invited him. Why do you all seem so angry that he's here?"

"Get out before Liv sees you!" Mark hissed.

Richard sipped slowly from a champagne flute and said, "I was invited."

"Nobody wants you here!"

"We've only just got here," Richard sneered, "It was a long drive and we're certainly not leaving yet."

"Richard?" They all turned to Olivia, standing a short distance away looking dumbfounded. Faye and Beth stood either side of her, equally dumbfounded. "Why ... why are you here?"

They stared at each other for a moment, and then Richard drained his glass and turned to Lauren. "Would you like to dance?"

Lauren put her glass down and allowed Richard to lead her away, the confused look still on her face.

"What's he doing here?" Olivia squealed at Mark.

"Apparently a guest invited him as her plus one."

"What are the odds?" Faye gasped.

"He's a sneaky bugger," Mark growled. "He'll have instigated this just to get at Liv."

"Or it could be a genuine coincidence," Brian said.

"I wouldn't put anything past him!"

"I think the best thing to do," Brian said, "Is to ignore him and just enjoy the party."

"Ignore him? I want to punch him in the face for what he's

done to–"

"It's all in the past, darling," Olivia soothed, rubbing his arm, "I haven't heard from him in almost a year and we've both moved on. Brian's right, let's just ignore him and have a good time."

"I can't relax knowing *he's* here!"

"I think you'll have to," Brian said. "There's nothing you can do about it. We can't exactly kick him out, can we."

Tel and Sophie rushed over. "We've just seen Richard!" Sophie gasped.

"What's he doing here?"

"Your mother's university friend invited him," Brian said.

"Who, Lauren?"

"He's her plus one."

"You are joking! How does Lauren know Richard, althought that would explain why his name isn't on the guest list? Oh Liv, I'm so sorry!"

"Don't apologise, you weren't to know."

"Get rid of him!" Mark hissed. "I don't want him here!"

"I think it would cause a huge fuss," Brian said. "He seems quite content to stay and I don't think he'd go quietly."

They all turned to watch Richard and Lauren stiffly dancing, Richard's eyes flitting back to them every now and again, smirking.

"Maybe we should leave," Olivia suggested.

"We are *not* leaving!" Mark snapped, and a look passed over Olivia's face, a look he hadn't seen for a long time. Fear. He pulled her towards him and hugged her tightly. "Sorry, Liv. Brian's right, we should just ignore him, but if he bothers you," he added, his voice growing fierce again, "I'm going to punch his lights out."

"No, you're not," Sophie said, stone-faced and firm. "This is our wedding and there won't be any trouble, do I make myself clear?"

Mark dropped his head, nodding.

"Just stay away from him."

"I apologise," Mark said. "I'll go outside and calm down."
"Thank you."
Mark and Olivia walked away arm-in-arm.
"Blimey," said Jim, coming over. "Never expected to see that face again. What's he doing here?"
"I'll fill you in," Beth said, leading him away, passing the teenager who seemed to be following her wherever she went.
"Well, that was certainly a blast from the past," Faye said, as Sophie and Tel went off to mingle with their guests.
"We're all grown-ups, I'm sure it'll be fine," Brian said, but he crossed his fingers, just in case.
"Wanna dance with the old ball and chain?" she grinned, shimmying in front of him.
"Look at you, you drunken minx!" He grabbed her and spun her round on the spot, making her scream with delight.
Just as they reached the dancefloor, Tel's brother, David, having somehow gotten hold of microphone man's megaphone, brought the room to a shocked, silent standstill as he screeched, "We've got a surprise for the happy couple and all of you lovely people! Can someone bring a couple of chairs over? Hey, wedding planner, organiser, whatever, can you bring chairs over for the bride and groom?"
Microphone man rolled his eyes and dragged a couple of chairs over.
"What's he doing?" Sophie nervously asked Tel, "What's David up to?"
"You'll see."
"Do you know about this?"
"Kind of."
"It's not stripping, is it?"
"No, it's not a strip show."
"Can you promise me that there will be no naked men bandying their bits about and scaring the guests at my wedding?"
He took her hand. "I promise."
Sophie exhaled. "Okay then."

The chairs were placed on the edge of the dancefloor and Tel and Sophie sat down, holding hands. "I hope you know what he's doing," Sophie hissed from the side of her mouth

"I do. I think you'll like it. Now stop fretting and just enjoy."

Travis sauntered over to stand next to David in the middle of the now empty dancefloor, bringing multi-coloured Stetson hats with him. David boomed through the megaphone, "Can we have the lights down please? And can somebody draw the drapes at the window? Yes, wedding planner, I mean you, you're standing right next to them."

The place darkened. Everyone went quiet in expectation. David handed the megaphone to someone and hollered, "Okay, start the music! Three!"

In the semi-darkness, David and Travis struck a sideways pose and slammed the Stetsons onto their heads, holding the brim over their faces, Michael Jackson style. The hats lit up and everyone oohed.

"Two!"

They each raised a hand in the air, then brought them down in front of them and twitched their loins in unison. Their buttoned-up jackets immediately lit up with a multitude of coloured lights. Everyone oohed again, a few whistled, some held up their phones, recording.

"AH-ONE!"

Cotton Eye Joe burst from the speakers and the duo began dancing to the beat, totally in synch with each other. Sophie brought a hand up to her mouth and screamed, as did several other people.

"They've been practising for weeks," Tel yelled at her.

"Oh my God!"

The audience clapped along, hollering 'Yee-haa!' as David and Travis wowed them with their impressive moves, bouncing and flicking legs and arms, spinning, kneeling and jumping with a powerful, contagious energy. As the song neared the end it faded out and another song started, *Uptown*

Funk, and David and Travis spun their Stetsons off the dancefloor as the first bars played. The lights came on again and microphone man rushed to open the drapes. People began clapping and cheering.

And then Tel suddenly jumped up, pulled off his jacket, dramatically tossed it aside, and skipped across the floor to stand with them. Everyone screamed, Sophie loudest of all. Lucas appeared sans jacket and took his place at the end of the line, increasing the volume of audience participation. They all bopped and bounced in unison, marching and spinning, vigorously kicking out their arms and legs. It was very impressive and the room exploded. Sophie couldn't stop screaming as they thrust their loins, scrunched up their faces and bit down on their bottom lips, which Faye thought was the sexiest thing she'd ever seen in her life.

And then Annie and Fi jumped in, the skirts of their dresses pulled through their legs and tucked into their belts. The dancers' timing was near perfect, their movements smooth. Sophie jumped up, waving her arms in the air, whooping and yelling, until the dancers all fell to their knees in front of her, gasping and panting through huge smiles.

"You sneaky buggers!" she shrieked, as Tel got up and hugged her. "When did you plan that? *How* did you plan it without me knowing?"

Tel tapped his nose and winked. The others all hugged each other for a job well done.

When Annie went to hug Lucas he seemed stiff and eager to pull away again. He shot off to hug Sophie, leaving Annie bewildered. She wasn't used to being ignored, wasn't used to it at all.

Mark glanced across the room and saw Richard glaring back at him, smirking again. He pursed his lips and looked away, imagining all the things he'd like to do to him.

Richard caught Olivia's eye and his smirk disappeared, leaving him staring back at her darkly. She shuddered, then pulled on her smile and jumped back into the electric atmosphere on the dancefloor.

Faye grabbed Brian. "Scrunch your face and bite down on your lip," she demanded.

"Why?"

"Just do it. Are you doing it?"

Brian nodded. Faye ferreted through his beard until she found his mouth, and sighed. "It's not the same," she lamented.

He suddenly grabbed her posterior and pulled her in close to him. "I have other talents," he whispered in her ear, and Faye felt herself go a bit weak at the knees. "Congratulations, lass, you've pulled."

***

Microphone man suddenly yelled, "THE BUFFET IS NOW OPEN! FORM AN ORDERLY QUEUE, AND DON'T MAKE TOO MUCH OF A MESS, THE HOTEL'S ALREADY COMPLAINED ABOUT THE STATE OF THE AFTERNOON TABLECLOTHS. USE THE PLATES, FORKS AND NAPKINS PROVIDED."

"Is he calling us sloppy eaters?" Brian grunted at Mark.

"I think he is."

"I might discard the plates and forks altogether and eat directly from the table, just to annoy him."

"I'm going to eat with my hands."

They joined the surge of people making their way over to the now uncovered tables at the side of the room and, with two plates apiece, they picked their way along the vast array of dishes.

"What's this?" Brian asked, picking up a brown square and sniffing it.

"Label says Crispy Tofu."

Brian bit into it and pulled a face. "Tastes like a salty jelly cube."

Mark picked up a piece, smelled it and took a bite. "You're not wrong," he said, putting the remainder on his plate, planning to discard it somewhere at the earliest opportunity.

"Here, try an easily identifiable chicken leg."

Faye appeared behind them, bouncing up and down to see what was on offer. "Put some *quish* on my plate, Bri," she said, pointing, "I can't reach."

"Quish?" Mark laughed.

"She means quiche. These Brummies never learned how to speak properly."

Faye poked him in the back. "Says the man who announces time as 'nine while five' and has never uttered the word 'the' in his life. Oh, get me some spicy pasta, and a couple of slices of–"

Brian turned and handed her the plate. Faye wriggled in next to him, and someone further down the line, a woman who clearly hadn't eaten recently, displayed her 'hanger' by yelling, "Oi, you queue jumped!"

"Sorry," Faye threw over her shoulder, not sounding sorry at all as she scooped up sausage rolls and triangular sandwiches. "My husband was saving my place for me."

"You should have gone to the back of the queue!"

"We wanna be t'gether," Brian laughed.

"No, this isn't on!" the woman hollered, "You can't queue jump at a wedding!"

"Just did," Faye muttered.

"Hey, party organiser!" the woman called out, "That woman just queue jumped!"

The wedding planner/organiser/man with microphone still clamped to his head came running over. "What's all the kerfuffle?"

"That woman in the flowery dress, next to that big bloke who looks like Bigfoot's brother, just jumped the queue!"

"Madam," he said to Faye, and Faye slowly turned to look at him, feeling slightly guilty, but not guilty enough to leave her place at Brian's side. "I'm afraid you'll have to go to the back of the queue."

"I was saving her a place," Brian said.

Microphone man stared up at Brian – tall, wide and hairy – and bravely said, "We don't save places here and there'll be no queue jumping on my watch. I run an orderly queue. You'll have to go to the back, madam."

"But I've already got half a plate of food."

"Which you're welcome to eat as you wait in the queue for the other half."

"Get to the back!" shouted the woman. "And hurry up about it, we're hungry!"

Faye stared at the woman leaning out of the queue, stared at microphone man, and then said, "Oh, this is ridiculous! This is a wedding, not a prison canteen!"

With that, Faye quickly turned back to the table, grabbed two bread rolls, squeezed in next to Mark to snatch up some salad, then pushed her way down the buffet, eschewing the tongs provided and using finger and thumb to delicately pick up food and lob it onto her plate.

"*She's contaminating the food!*" the woman screeched.

"I've washed my hands *and* used sanitiser!"

"And we're supposed to believe a *queue jumper*?"

"I don't lie!" Faye snarled, "I've never practised it and I'm not good at it."

"She's not," Brian threw over his shoulder, trying to decide between an onion bargee and a vol au vent, eventually deciding to have both. "She's a terrible liar."

The woman huffed. "Clearly from the groom's side of the family, certainly not from ours. *We* know how to behave at a wedding!"

Brian was about to turn round in defence of his wife, when Jacquie, Tel's mother, turned in the queue in front of her and hissed, "Excuse me, Miss Fancy Pants, I'm the groom's mother!"

"My sincere commiserations."

Just as Jacquie took a step towards the whingey woman, Camille, Sophie's mother, came rushing over, putting up a hand up to Jacquie and stopping her in her tracks. "Elizabeth," she said firmly, grabbing the woman by her elbow, "A word please."

"I'll lose my place in the queue!"

"Come with me." The woman reluctantly followed her. The rest of the queue nodded and started chatting again. As Camille passed microphone man she hissed, "This is *literally* your job, to prevent any squabbles and keep everything running smoothly!"

Microphone man's bottom lip quivered for a moment, before he yelled, "ORDERLY QUEUE PLEASE! NO FIGHTING, YOU'RE NOT CHILDREN!"

"Then stop treating us like we are," Brian said, as he made his way back to the table.

"Impressively fast collection of buffet food, Faye" Mark said, as he handed Olivia a plate.

"They should make it an Olympic event," Brian chuckled. "They could call it The Buffet Run."

"First to fill their plate and not drop anything wins," Mark laughed

"Fill your plates!" Jim cried, "You son of a–"

"Jim!" hissed Beth.

"Is there a John Wayne season on the classic movie channel by any chance?" Mark asked.

"Yes, how did you know?"

"Oh, just a wild guess."

"What *is* this tofu?" Brian said, sniffing at the brown, half-eaten cube skewered to his fork. "It doesn't smell of anything, doesn't taste of anything except a slight hint of salt and ginger, and has the consistency of ..." He squeezed it between his fingers. "... soft cheese."

"It's for the vegans," Faye said, nibbling on a chicken leg. "Don't eat it if you don't want it."

"I was just curious as to why anyone would choose to eat such a thing." He inspected it as he turned it on the fork.

"Stop playing with your food, Bri."

"I wonder, if I threw it at a wall would bounce or stick?"

"It's just a cube of ... stuff. Well, half a cube with teeth marks down one side. Stop acting like a child."

"Says the queue jumper."

"Uh oh," Olivia said, "There's an angry looking woman heading in our direction."

"Which woman?" Faye turned and said, "Oh, *that* woman. Well, if she starts again I'm going to have to say–"

The woman, Elizabeth, flanked by Camille on one side and Jacquie on the other, came up to their table, wringing her hands. "I'm terribly sorry if I caused any offence," she squeaked. "I was just … hungry."

"That's okay," Faye said, giving her a huge, fake smile, "We understand how difficult it is for the middle classes to mix with the lower classes."

"Working," Brian said, chomping down on a slice of quiche, "We're working class and proud of it."

"Yes, yes, I'm so sorry," the woman said again, still wringing her hands. She turned to look at Camille, who nodded, and Jacquie, who remained poker-faced, and then she hurried away to the back of the buffet queue.

"Enjoy your meal," Camille winked, before she was snatched up by John and whisked away for a tango.

"Oh!" Faye suddenly cried, as the band launched into another song, "I love this one. Come on, Bri, dance with me."

"I'm eating!"

"Food can wait, the wife can't."

Brian reluctantly stood up, pushing a couple of sausage rolls into his mouth, before Faye dragged him onto the dancefloor. The others watched in increasing horror.

"I think we've just found the worst wedding dancer," Jim said, as Brian's giant arms were thrust into the air and his broad shoulders catapulted people in all directions.

"I fear lives will be lost," Mark laughed.

* * *

Annie sat alone at a table with her chin resting on a palm, watching everyone milling about, all of them with huge smiles. She wasn't smiling, she felt miserable. No one was flirting with her and she was bored. She was clearly losing her touch.

A couple walked past her table. It was the man she'd argued with about the noise the other night. She sat up, grinning, and cried, "I know what you look like naked." The woman he was with, presumably his wife, glowered at her and quickly bustled him from the room.

Bored again, she slumped, then spotted Lucas in the bar area and, with a rush of anticipation, hurried over to him.

"Lucas, darling," she cried.

"Annie, sweetheart."

Was that cynicism she detected in his voice or, worse, *exasperation*?

"Buy me a drink?"

"They're free, you just ask for what you want and they give it to you, it's really quite incredible."

"Ask them for me."

"Your cut-glass accent is perfectly capable of cutting a swathe through the screaming masses, Annie."

"You beast."

He turned to look at her then. "Beast?"

"Yah, you're beastly."

"Have I been transported back in time to the Bronte period?"

At least she had his attention now. "You've been ignoring me all night," she pouted.

"Well, you made it perfectly clear you don't want my irritating attention."

"I was just playing hard to get," she giggled, wondering if she'd had a little too much to drink, she wasn't prone to giggling, or confessing.

"I don't play games, Annie."

"Truce?" she asked.

"From?"

"Being beastly to each other."

"I've never been 'beastly' to you, Annie. I've always behaved like the perfect gentleman and you've always cut me down, so now I'm staying down and not bothering you anymore. You should be pleased."

She huffed, waving at a barman, who automatically brought her a flute of champagne.

"Fourth magnum, or fifth?" Lucas asked sarcastically.

"I don't like you like this," she said.

"You don't like me at all, or so you keep telling me."

"I ... I do like you."

Now Lucas huffed. He put down his glass and turned round to survey the party. "No suitable single men at this event, or are you just scraping the barrel purely for the fun of it?"

"You're being very mean, Lucas."

"I've lost interest, Annie."

"What?"

He turned his head to look at her. "I've been chasing you for years, and now, finally, I've lost interest."

Lost interest? How was that even possible? Men didn't lose interest in *her*, she lost interest in *them*. This was absurd. Ridiculous.

Not knowing what to say, she left her champagne glass at the bar and stomped off to sulk.

Lucas dropped his head to his chest, slowly shaking it. It was absolutely killing him, playing it cool and indifferent. Annie was beautiful, there was no doubt about that, and she was intelligent, loud, demanding and funny, and he really, *really* liked her. She was the type of woman you couldn't help but admire, strong and formidable, but with a certain softness about her deep down inside. For a moment he was tempted to go chasing after her, but didn't.

He swigged back his beer and joined a group of university friends on the dancefloor, trying to put the problem of Annie to the back of his mind.

Annie sat alone at a table, watching him.

CHAPTER TWELVE

Hot and sweaty from dancing, Olivia broke away from Mark and staggered, slightly unsteady on her heels, into the foyer, where it was marginally cooler. Just as she was walking down one side of the sweeping staircase towards the Ladies, Richard came out of a door next to it. She stopped dead in her tracks, as did Richard. They stood staring at each other; Olivia nervous, Richard with that dark, brooding look in his eyes that she was so familiar with. She wondered whether she should just turn and go back to the party, there was no one else out in the foyer apart from a receptionist at the other end. It was just the two of them, facing each other.

Her old fear seemed to peak and then dissipate. Suddenly she wasn't afraid of him anymore. Also, she was desperate for a wee.

"Richard," she said, taking a step towards the Ladies room.

He stepped sideways to block her path. There was a short distance between them and Olivia felt uncomfortable. She tried stepping around him, but again he stepped sideways and stopped her.

"Let me by, please, Richard."

"You took everything from me," he hissed, "*Everything*, and left me with *nothing*."

"Let's not do this again, Richard, we're way past that now." She was surprised at the calmness of her voice when her heart was pounding furiously in her chest.

"You might be *past it*, prancing around with your little *farmer* boy, but you *ruined my life*."

"I don't want to have this conversation with you, Richard,

not now, not ever."

"Easy for you to say, but I'm–"

"How's it going with the girlfriend?" she asked, to distract him. "She seems nice."

"Who, Lauren?"

"Well, how many girlfriends do you have?"

"She's just a friend from work who needed someone to go to a wedding with her."

"So you didn't know I'd be here?"

"I was as surprised as you were." He paused and looked at her intently. "Fate brought us together, Olivia, brought us together like this for a purpose."

"Coincidence, not fate, Richard."

"Destiny has given me a chance to tell you how I feel, to tell you how ... how *sorry* I am for the way I treated you. I'm a different man now, Olivia, I really am."

"I'm pleased for you, Richard, but I really don't care. If you'll just ex–"

"I think we should try again," he blurted.

"What?"

"I've had time to think, to re-evaluate, and ... I think we could make a go of it this time."

"Richard, it's too late! We're divorced!"

"It's never too late to start again," he insisted. "Let's start again. We can remarry! Yes, we'll remarry and everything will go back to the way it was before."

Olivia was struck dumb with the audacity of the man. Remarry? He must be out of his mind. If he was the last man on earth she'd still avoid him.

"I don't want to argue with you, Richard." She stepped sideways again. He stood in her path again. This time he reached out and took hold of her hands. She snatched them away. Her heart was beating so hard she thought he might hear it. She glanced around, searching for company, but even the receptionist had disappeared from behind the counter. It was if they'd been caught in a bubble of time, circumstances forcing them to meet up and have the same argument over and over again, like an unending episode of *The Twilight Zone*. Maybe this was her punishment for finally finding her voice and arguing back instead of relinquishing to Richard's every demand, or perhaps it was payment for her new and better life. Whatever it was, they were alone, she didn't like it, and she *really* needed the loo.

"Do you ever ... think about me?" he asked softly. "Do you ever regret what you did?"

"What *I* did? No, I don't dwell on the past, Richard."

"You should. You learn from the past. I've certainly learned my lesson."

"Good for you."

"I have regrets, of course I have regrets, and I'm sure you do too, Olivia."

"If I have one regret," she told him, and a smile twitched at the corners of his mouth, "It's that I didn't do it sooner."

His face contorted and there was a flash of anger in his eyes that she knew all too well. Then it softened when he said, "We were so good together, Olivia, you have to admit that."

"Time has put a rose-tinted hue to your memories, Richard. We were never good together."

"How can you say that?"

"Easily. You were a terrible husband."

"I can do better," he pleaded. "Let me prove to you I can be better. Give me another chance."

"Richard, my life began the moment you left, of your own volition, I might add. I'm not going back to that again. We're over. We're divorced. There are no second chances. This is it."

"How can you be so cruel?" he snarled.

"I learned from the best."

"You're still my wife," he growled, suddenly gripping her wrist.

Instinct kicked in. She didn't want him to touch her, to be this close to her. Putting her free hand firmly over his, she swung her head under their conjoined arms and grabbed hold of his wrist, pushing down on it until Richard was forced to a knee. She kept pressure on his arm, now half way up his back, holding him in place.

"I am *not* your wife!" she hissed, "And you can't bully me anymore."

Faye and Beth burst into the foyer at that moment, shrieking with laughter. They came striding over, barefoot, chatting, until they saw Olivia standing over Richard, who was still on a knee on the floor. Olivia let him go and he slowly stood up, rubbing his wrist, looking stunned.

Beth weighed up the situation immediately. "Babes!" she cried, rushing up and linking Olivia's arm, pulling her away from Richard's orbit as he scrambled to his feet, "Come and do a girly stint in the loo with us."

Slightly stunned by what had just happened, Olivia gratefully allowed herself to be led away. Faye glared at Richard as she passed.

Inside the toilets Olivia leaned back against the sink, breathing heavily.

"You okay, babes?"

"Oh Liv, are you alright?"

Olivia nodded. "Man's an idiot," she said. "He asked me for a second chance. He said we could remarry!"

"He never!" Faye cried.

"Looks like you put him in his place though, babes."

"I think I did." A smile crept onto her face. "I didn't think I'd ever be able to, but I did, thanks to those self-defence classes."

"Good for you."

Faye was heading towards the door, hissing, "Let me get my hands on him! Is that big knife still in the wedding cake?"

"No, Faye, it's okay. Honestly, it's fine."

Faye turned back again, her lips still tight.

"I'll just stay away from him. I don't want any trouble. And please, don't tell Mark."

"We'll form a shuffling barricade around you at all times,"

Beth cackled, dabbing mascara on her eyes, "He won't get nowhere near you again, babes."

"Man's a moron," Faye hissed. "The cheek of him, asking for a second chance after what he–"

"It's all water under the bridge now," Olivia said.

"Talking of water," Faye said, dashing into a cubicle.

* * *

"Happy?" Sophie asked Tel, when they finally managed to meet up on the patio after much mingling with guests.

"Never been happier in my life." He pulled her to him. "I'm so proud of my beautiful wife."

He kissed her, slowly, softly. They snuggled into each other, her head on his shoulder, his hands rubbing the back of her neck. They heard clicking nearby and pulled apart. The photographer, still on duty, was bouncing around them, taking pictures.

"I thought you were booked until eight o'clock?" Tel said, glancing at his watch. "It's almost nine."

"I know," the photographer said, still taking pictures of them both, "But I want to capture every moment, and there's so many good-looking people here I can't seem to stop."

"Stop," said Tel, and the photographer lowered his camera, looked disheartened for a moment, then spotted a couple walking across the lawn below. He shot off towards them and they watched as he bounced around, taking photos of them. Mildred and a less enthusiastic Carl started posing.

"Hope he's taken the lens cap off," Sophie laughed, "Or all this will be for nothing."

"We have 150 guests," Tel said, watching Mildred drape herself and her voluminous dress over a stone bench, while Carl awkwardly stood to one side looking like the man from American Gothic. "If each one takes at least twenty-five pictures on their phones that'll be ..."

"A lot of photos," Sophie finished for him. "Now, where were we?"

He was just leaning in for another kiss, when Mark stepped out onto the patio holding a pint. "Phew," he said, pulling at the tie already loose around his neck, "It's getting pretty hot in there, and out here too from the looks of it."

"What does a man have to do to get five minutes alone with his wife?" Tel sighed.

"You'll have plenty of time for that on your honeymoon." Mark leaned on the concrete balustrade around the patio area. Lots of people were milling around in the garden. A woman was sprawled on the grass having her picture taken. "Until then," Mark said, turning back and laughing, "It's all about us guests."

"Are you enjoying yourself?" Sophie asked.

"Best wedding I've ever been to."

"How many have you been to?"

"Well, just my own, so far."

They both laughed.

Jim burst through the patio doors, sloshing beer in his haste to reach them. "I've just seen something really interesting," he declared.

"It's not David and Travis stripping, is it?"

"No. Ugh, no. Just been wandering through the rooms across the foyer in search of my missing wife, when I caught a couple snogging. I mean, they were really going at it," he laughed. "They jumped away from each other when I opened the door, very suspicious like."

"Who was it?" Sophie grinned, peering through the patio doors at the dancing throng inside.

Jim turned and looked, then pointed. "It was her in the blue dress, and that man over there."

Sophie raised a hand to her face. "Are you sure?"

"Positive. You can't mistake a moustache like that, can you." Jim casually took a sip of his drink. "Are they married?"

"One of them is," Sophie snapped, stomping inside and shouting, "ETTA!"

Brian wandered out onto the patio area. "I wondered

where everyone had gone," he said. "Where's the womenfolk?"

"Here!" Faye cried, coming out with Beth and Olivia, all of them barefoot and squiffy. "Did you miss me?"

"Only just noticed you'd gone," Brian said. Then, noticing Faye's pouting lip, he added, "*Desperately* missed you. I was *bereft* without you by my side. I am but a mere man who needs to be guided and–"

"That's enough," Faye laughed, snuggling up to his huge body. "I think I'm a little drunk."

"I think you're a lot drunk."

"She's plastered," Beth said, sliding under Jim's arm, "Wanted to use the wedding knife in the cake to–" She stopped suddenly, glancing at Faye and Olivia's widening eyes. Olivia very slightly shook her head. "To cut herself a big slice," Beth finished.

"Help yourself," Tel said, "There's plenty of it."

"Maybe on the way out."

"I'm bloody boiling," Beth said, untangling herself from Jim's arm and taking off her bolero jacket.

Tel surveyed them all. "Have you noticed," he said, "That you're all cuddling up the ones you love and I, the bridegroom, at my own wedding, am standing alone?"

"Got to keep a firm grip on these women," Brian said, stifling a laugh as Faye poked him in the ribs, "They run amok otherwise."

"Amok, amok, amok," Faye cried.

"Where is the beautiful bride?" Mark asked.

"Gone to give her secretary a good thrashing I think."

"Is that 'ow they treat secretaries at your company?" Beth cackled, "One typo and they're hauled off to the thrashing room?"

"Pretty much."

"She's been a very, very naughty girl," said Jim.

"Who, Sophie?"

"No, the secretary."

Pierrot the clown wandered out onto the patio with his

white face and baggy outfit, and sadly peered at them all.

"Charlie," Tel said, and the clown turned his miserable face towards him. "Indulge my curiosity for a moment. Why do you always come to family events dressed up?"

Pierrot gave a mime shrug and said, "It makes me feel happy."

Jim sniggered, the others swapped looks.

"Makes you happy?" Tel repeated.

"Yeah." There was a long pause. "Family events are boring. I try to liven them up with my costumes. The kids seem to like them."

"There are no kids here, Charlie. This is a child-free wedding."

"I didn't know that when I picked my outfit, but if there were–"

"They'd be running away yelling their little heads off," Mark snorted.

Pierrot pierced him with a look from his doleful eyes.

"As I recall," Tel continued, "Your zombie outfit was not a hit amongst the screaming children at the last wedding we attended."

"You were a zombie at a wedding?" Faye gasped.

"He was," said Tel.

"I was the best man," Pierrot said. "The groom and I used to play Resident Evil together. It was kind of a joke thing."

"A joke that fell flat on its face when the bride saw you and sobbed her way down the aisle."

"Why are you trying to bring me down?" the clown asked. "I'm just trying my best to inject a bit of fun into otherwise dull proceedings."

"Dull?" Tel said, raising his eyebrows.

"Not your wedding, of course, your wedding isn't dull."

"And yet here you are, dressed as a clown to inject a bit of fun into otherwise dull proceedings."

"I didn't mean it like that."

He looked so sad beneath his makeup that Tel felt sorry

for him. "You dress however you want at any of our events, Charlie."

Charlie grunted and wandered off.

"Drinks!" Brian bellowed, dragging Faye back into the function room, closely followed by the others.

* * *

"What's up?" Fi asked Annie, throwing herself onto a neighbouring chair and supping at her sixth energy drink of the night. She'd only just discovered it and she was buzzing, more awake than she'd felt in a long time. "You look like you've just lost the winning lottery ticket."

Annie, chin resting on her palm, said, "Nobody loves me."

"I bet a third of the male population in this room have the hots for you."

"Not lust, *love*."

"Haven't you just broken up with your most recent husband, Lord what's-his-face, who wants you back because he loves you?"

"He doesn't count."

"They *all* count, Annie."

"I thought he was fun and spontaneous."

"He's in his fifties! You can't blame him for not wanting to bungee jump off bridges or do a spot of skydiving at weekends."

Annie sighed loudly, still watching the throngs on the dancefloor. Lucas was dancing with Miss Flutter-Eyes again. They looked like they were having fun. "Lucas doesn't fancy me anymore."

"Ah," Fi said, nodding her head, "Is that what's bothering you."

"I thought he'd cheer me up a bit since there's no one really eligible or attractive enough to get me through the night, but he … he rejected me, Fi."

"Oh goodness, how did that feel?"

"Horrible, just horrible."

"Karma gets us all in the end."

"What?"

"How many men have you rejected, or treated badly, or kept hanging on in the hope of–"

"Er, you're supposed to be on *my* side."

"Am I?" Fi looked briefly confused. "I don't think I got that memo."

"It's an unwritten law that bridesmaids must stick together at weddings."

"Again, didn't get the memo."

"You were probably sleeping."

"Touche, I'll give you that one. Quite clever for you, actually."

"Now you're being awful to me. Is it Be Mean to Annie Day or something?"

"No. Sorry. Poor you." She woodenly patted Annie on the back.

"Your bedside manner is appalling," Annie said, shrugging her off. "How do your patients put up with it?"

"They're usually on death's door and not all that bothered about bedside etiquette, to be honest, but I take on board your constructive criticism and will strive–"

"I just want someone to love me!" Annie whined. "Anyone!"

An elderly man bent his head down in front of her, displaying his grey, crooked teeth. "Can I be of assistance?" he leered.

"Ugh, no!"

"Annie, don't be so rude!"

Annie sat up. "I thank you for your very kind offer," she said brightly, "But on this occasion I'll have to pass on account of a very irate woman thundering towards us who is, I assume, your wife."

The man quickly straightened up and raced off in the opposite direction.

"I hate men," Annie snapped.

"No you don't."

"I do! I might go lesbian."

Fi burst out laughing, stopping only when Annie turned to give her the evil eye. "I don't think that would work for you," she said.

"Why not?"

"Well, possibly because you're not gay."

"I could transition."

"Not sure it works that way."

Annie sighed again. "Look at him," she hissed, staring balefully at Lucas, "Dancing there, all happy and ... *happy*."

"What about him over there?" Fi suggested, trying to be helpful.

"The bald bloke with the beer bulge?"

"No, not him, the one behind him."

Annie sat up, briefly interested, then slumped down with her chin in her palm again. "He's not nearly as attractive as Lucas."

"Or him?" Fi said, staring at a luminous, lycra-clad man wearing a cycle helmet, who was throwing wild shapes on the dancefloor. Annie just glared at her.

"Then charm your way back into Lucas's affections again, should be a doddle for you."

"You'd think, wouldn't you, but he's made it clear he's not interested."

"Or," said Fi, leaning in, "He could just be playing hard to get?"

Annie sat up again. "You mean, reverse psychology? Pretending not to want the thing you want?"

"Maybe he's acting cool and aloof to get your attention."

"Yah," Annie breathed. "It's the only reasonable explanation. I mean, I've never been rejected before, and who in their right mind could resist everything I have to offer."

"Who indeed?" Fi said, deadpan.

Annie jumped to her feet. "The night can yet be saved," she said. "Watch and learn, Fi, watch and learn."

***

Beth broke away from Jim mid-dance and wandered over to the teenager standing forlornly on the edge of the dancefloor, watching her.

"What's your name?" she asked the boy.

"Pete," he said, grinning from ear to ear at having her so close to him.

"Listen, Pete, babes, I can't have you ogling me all the time and lookin' miserable."

"I'm sorry, you're just so … *beautiful*," he sighed.

"I am," she winked, "But I'm a bit old for you."

"You're not. I could be your toyboy."

"I ain't in the market for a toyboy on account of me 'aving an 'usband."

"I'd be very discreet," he gushed.

Beth laughed. "Give it a couple of years and girls your age will start to look attractive."

"They won't look like you," the boy whined. "Nobody looks like you, and I can't wait a couple of years!"

"You're gonna 'ave to, babes."

Pete leaned forward and said, "I want you."

"You can't 'ave me. Now, be a good boy and go find someone your own age to ogle."

"There's no one here like you."

"There's no one *anywhere* like me," she laughed. "But look." She reached out and the boy briefly smiled, before she held his shoulders and turned him round. "There's two lovely young ladies over there and I think one of them fancies you."

"Which one?"

"The blonde one."

"Really?"

"Yes, really. Now, off you pop, go and practice them chat-up lines you've been reading on your phone all night."

The boy walked off with a smile on his face. Beth said, "Job well done, girl."

"Where've you been?" Jim asked, as she made her way back to him.

"Just putting someone out of their misery."

Jim huffed, then said, "Wanna dance?"

"You askin'?"

"I'm asking."

"I'm dancing. Can't raise me 'ands in the air though or me boobs'll fall out."

They wriggled and smooched to a couple of songs, and then Beth staggered to a chair and flung herself into it. "Knackered!" she cried, "And me bloody feet are killing me in these shoes."

"Beth," Olivia said, rushing over, "I need the loo again!"

Beth pushed her feet back into her shoes and said, "Coming, babes."

"You women do actually know how to go to the toilet on your own, don't you?" Jim laughed.

"Nah, babes, it's never 'appened. FAYE!"

Faye waited until Brian had finished dipping her backwards and up again before yelling, "WHAT?"

"LIV NEEDS THE LOO!"

Olivia cringed. Jim shook his head, thinking he might never understand women and their weird ways, and Mark, flopping onto a chair, said, "Miss you already. Oh, are you okay with *him* around? Want me to come with you?"

"Don't be silly," she giggled. "Besides, I have backup."

Faye hurried off the dancefloor, leaving Brian to boogie on his own. They tottered across the room, Olivia in front trying to set a quick pace. As Beth passed the bridesmaids, Annie and Fi, she said, "Ex-husband on the prowl," and they joined the group.

Out in the foyer they flanked Olivia on all sides as she scurried towards the Ladies. Next to it, the Men's door was slightly ajar and, as she approached, rather desperately, Richard came bursting out.

"Olivia!" he cried in mock surprise, stepping sideways to

cut her off again.

"BACK AWAY FROM THE WOMAN!" Beth hollered, and Richard almost jumped out of his suit. He stared at the entourage, his mouth falling open.

Olivia, beyond desperate now, pushed passed him and crashed through the doors to the Ladies. As it slammed shut behind her Richard faced the four fierce-looking women. He indicated the door Olivia had just gone through and said, "Do you all want …?" He snapped his mouth shut when he sensed the rising tension.

"Are you finished here?" Beth asked menacingly.

Richard frowned. "Well no, actually, not that it's any of your–"

"You need to step away from the door."

"Excuse me?"

"I said, you need to step away from–"

"I'm waiting for my wife!"

"*Ex*-wife," Faye snapped, "And she doesn't want to talk to you."

"I'd rather she told me that herself."

"She won't, because she doesn't want to talk to you, trust me."

"Trust *you*?" Richard suddenly hissed, "I don't trust any of you, especially you reprobates from that dreadful campsite, you're the ones who started all this in the first place."

"Reprobates?" Beth asked casually.

"I think he means commoners?" Faye shrugged.

"Unprincipled persons," Annie said.

"Oh," said Fi, "So you *were* paying attention at school then!"

"Yah, I wasn't behind the bike sheds *all* the time."

"Certainly seemed like it."

"Plebeians," Richard snapped, trying to fight them off with his superior intellect. He couldn't believe that four women were actually trying to intimidate him.

"Cad," Annie said, not taking her eyes off him.

"Boor," said Fi.

"Dick," Beth hissed.

"That's actually his name," Faye said, conversationally. "Suits him."

Richard, annoyed now, snarled, "How dare you try and tell me what I can and can't do, who do you think you–?"

"Right!" Annie barked, "He's gone into overdrive, it has to be a stiletto stand-off!"

The others looked at her, confused. Annie bent her left leg backwards like Betty Boop. They all did the same. She slipped off her shoe and brought it up in front of her with the slender heel facing Richard. The others did the same, except for Faye, who bent and fiddled with the straps on her sandal for a bit. Standing on her bare foot, one shoulder inches lower than the other one, Annie slammed the heel of her right foot down in front of her and yelled, "*Atten-shun!*" The others did the same, and the sound of four sets of heels hitting the marble floor at the same time ricocheted around the foyer.

"Louboutin's?" Annie asked, glancing at the red sole in Beth's hand.

Beth nodded. "New season. Yours?"

"Jimmy Choo"

"Nice."

"Gee-or-gee," Faye said, waggling her chunky heeled sandal.

Annie turned to Faye and repeated, "Gee-or-gee? Is that a new luxury brand?"

Faye, instantly ashamed of herself, said, "George at Asda."

"Asda? The *supermarket*?"

"Yes."

Annie took the sandal from her and gave it the once over. "You know, these are actually quite nice, I can see myself wearing these on some exotic beach, maybe Mauritius or–"

"Are you all completely mad?" Richard suddenly barked.

"Bloody fuming, mate."

"She definitely is," Fi said, hitching her head towards Annie.

Richard felt uncomfortable with the four lopsided women holding their shoes like weapons in front of them. They were clearly insane. With a huff and a tight pursing of his lips, he moved away, his steps gathering momentum as he hurried down the foyer and back into the reception room.

"At ease!" Annie cried.

"Oh, thank God for that!" Faye gasped, hobbling quickly into the loo.

The others stayed outside with their backs to the door, their eyes peeled, tapping the shoes against their palms. When Olivia and Faye came out again, they crookedly flanked her on four sides, hobbling up and down until they got to the door of the reception room where, leaning against the wall, they put their shoes back on again – Faye struggling with her straps – and sauntered back to the party.

Richard immediately headed across the room towards Olivia, pushing his way through the dancers in his haste to reach her before she reached Mark on the table near the patio doors. He stopped when four women briskly came towards him and surrounded him, piercing him with their eyes.

"Don't do it, Dick," Faye shouted above the music, "Leave Liv alone."

"I have military training," yelled Annie.

"You've never been in the armed forces!" Fi laughed

"I dated a high-ranking officer in the Royal Navy and he taught me how to look after myself," Annie said, bending her knees and doing karate moves in time to the music, "I know how to take down an enemy swiftly and efficiently."

Richard's eyes bulged as he searched for a gap in their defences.

"Stay away from Liv," Beth yelled at him.

Annie pointed at her eyes with two fingers and pointed at Richard with one, her face stern and determined. Richard angrily turned and left.

Olivia, watching them from the table, turned to Mark and said, "Darling, I think we need to talk."

"Sure."

They stood up together, Olivia nervous about telling him, Mark nervous about what she was about to say. Had he done something wrong? Had he shown himself up with his dancing and she'd decided she couldn't live with a man who bopped so badly? Had seeing Richard sparked something inside her? Did she still love him?

All this was in his head as they walked through the patio doors, down the sweeping concrete steps, to a wooden bench below, both in contemplative silence.

"Mark," she said, and he forced himself to look at her, bracing himself. "There's something I have to tell you."

* * *

While keeping one eye on Richard, Annie used the other eye to seek out Lucas. He was leaning against the bar, sipping on a pint and watching the dancers. She scurried into the space next to him. The barman automatically placed champagne in front of her.

"Are you and the eyelash flutterer an item?" she asked, spurred on by her victory with Richard and by her level of intoxication, which was just short of taking off her Coco de Mer thong and waving it in the air.

"Who?" Lucas asked, without looking at her.

"The woman you keep supplying with drinks and dancing with, while I stand here parched and danceless and apparently lacking in the eyelash department."

"I don't think we're an item," he laughed. "Why, has she said anything?"

"No, but she looks smitten."

"And you'd know that look, wouldn't you."

"What's that supposed to mean?"

"You're always surrounded by smitten people."

"Am I?"

"You know you are. You garner attention wherever you go."

"Being beautiful and intelligent is such a burden," Annie sighed.

"Poor you, my heart bleeds for your suffering."

There was a moment's silence. To fill it, Annie said, "You're not smitten?"

"By?"

"Me, of course."

"I am not."

"Why not?"

Lucas shrugged.

"But you were smitten?"

"I was, and then I came to my senses."

"Why?"

He looked at her then. "You're not interested. I thought I'd waste my time elsewhere in the hope of achieving better results."

"With eyelash woman?"

He turned his head to watch the dancers again. "Not especially."

Annie swigged back her drink and eyeballed the barman for another. "It just feels weird," she said.

"What does?"

"You being *unsmittened*."

"I doubt it's something you'll have to get used to."

Annie felt something inside her she'd never really felt before. Was that … nerves? Was she nervous, like when she thought she'd failed her exams at school and of course she hadn't, or that time the ski lift broke when she was half way up a mountain and her heart had pounded in her chest a few times before being rescued by some rather hunky men? It felt like a bowling ball was hanging heavy in her stomach – or was that all the booze? She emptied her glass and indicated for the barman to bring her another drink.

"I'm having to get my own drinks," she huffed.

"Couldn't keep up with your demand if I tried. Order a bottle and a straw, that should keep you topped up for a while."

"You could at least *try* and be nice to me."

"I am."

"You're not even looking at me."

He turned a deadpan expression towards her. "Looking," he said, immediately turning away again.

She huffed. Finished her drink. Raised her hand for another. The barman came over with more champagne and said, "I do have other people to serve, you know."

"Give the poor man a rest," Lucas laughed.

Annie turned and leaned against the bar next to him, thinking. It was hard to think when her brain felt like cotton wool was stuffed inside her head and everything around her felt slightly unsteady. She looked up at Lucas, who was determinedly looking everywhere but at her. She turned to face him. Putting her glass on the bar, she stood on the toes of her Jimmy Choo's, clasped the sides of his head in her hands and turned his face towards her. Look at me now, she thought.

And then, out of nowhere, she was pressing her lips against his and it felt nice, it felt soft and warm. She felt his hands slowly circling her waist and thought, 'This is it, he's mine.' The hands pulled her and the kiss away. Lucas stared down at her, aghast, amazed … delighted? No, that wasn't delight on his face, it was something she couldn't identify.

"What the hell are you doing?" he gasped.

Horrified, that's what the expression was, he was horrified that she'd kissed him. Now there was something she'd never encountered before.

"I'm kissing you," she said.

"I gathered that, but why?"

"I felt like it."

"You can't always have what you feel like," he snapped. "I know it's what you're used to, Annie, but not this time. Stop playing games with me!"

"I'm not!"

Lucas huffed, tearing his eyes away. She stood looking up at him, and he glanced at her from the corner of his eye.

Lifting her chin, she spun round and staggered off, feeling like Scarlett O'Hara to Lucas's Rhett Butler; a cruel, heartless scoundrel.

At the bar, Lucas watched her sashay unsteadily across the room and subconsciously pressed a fist to his aching chest. He tore his eyes away and lowered his head, hiding his pain. What the hell was he was doing? Rejecting women was definitely not his thing, playing cold and hard to get even less so. This hurt, it hurt a lot.

And she'd kissed him. He still felt that kiss on his lips.

He put down his glass and marched determinedly across the room.

* * *

"Okay," Mark said nervously, "I'm listening."

Olivia clutched his hand in both of hers and he thought, 'Oh, this is going to be bad.'

"Richard seems determined to cause trouble," she said.

"Cause trouble?" Rage exploded inside him. "Has he been bothering you?"

He started to stand up, but Olivia pulled him down onto the bench again. "I'm going to find him and smash his face in!" he snarled.

"No, you're not!" Olivia said calmly. "I'm perfectly capable of taking care of myself! I have lawyers, I've learned self-defence and know how to take a man down, quite well actually, and I have a personal alarm in my bag. I wanted a taser and some pepper spray but they're apparently illegal in this country." She rolled her eyes. "I'm only telling you this so he doesn't goad you into a fight, he *wants* you to react and cause a scene, but trust me, I have it all under control. What you *can* do, my little sex monster, is you can stop treating me like a feeble female in distress, beating your chest like a testosterone-fuelled gorilla, and just share my life with me, good and bad."

"That's you told!" Brian laughed from the balcony above

them, "You little sex monster."

"Er, excuse me!" Mark shouted up, "This is a private conversation, if you don't mind?"

"There's no privacy at weddings, lad."

"Apparently not!"

From up above they heard Brian holler, "Okay, you nosey people, step away from the balcony, there's nothing to see here."

There was a beat of silence, and then Mark yelled, "You're still there, aren't you."

"Aye."

"And Faye?"

"All of us," Brian said, and a gaggle of giggles floated down on them.

Mark looked at Olivia and frowned. "Beating my chest like a testosterone-fuelled gorilla?"

"It's the first thing I could think of," she laughed, "And you do look a bit like one when you're angry."

"A gorilla?"

"A silverback."

Mark pounded his fists into his chest and did a Tarzan cry across the garden. Several people turned to look at him, and he waved.

"Is that it now?" Jim called down. "Any more juicy gossip coming up?"

Mark craned his neck back and looked up at the concrete balustrade. Several faces peered over it. Beth's breasts looked enormous from this angle, gravity threatening to tip them out of her dress. As if realising, she straightened up, out of sight.

Mark looked back at Olivia. "Do you have any more juicy gossip coming up? Is your dad arriving later, or my ex-wife, anything like that?"

She laughed and shook her head. "No, I don't think so."

"We're all out of gossip," Mark shouted up. "But if you want to contribute to this apparently open forum, feel free."

Faye said, "Beth, is your dress shrinking or are your breasts actually getting bigger?"

"Thanks, Faye, now everyone's looking at 'em."

"I think the dress is forcing blood *up*, babes."

Footsteps clattered across the patio, along with the sound of a metal chair being dragged across flagstones. "Here, sit down, my gorgeous songbird," David shrieked, "Take the weight off your–"

"*Hey*!" Jim cried.

"Feet! I was going to say feet!"

"Whilst looking straight down at her–"

"I wasn't!"

"You were, and if you do it again I'm going to–"

"TRAVIS!" David shrieked.

Travis ambled over, nodding his head at the women and coming to a hunky stop in front of everyone.

"You'll what?" David asked, clinging onto Travis's bulging arm and adding, "Show him your biceps, Travis."

Travis bent his arms at a ninety-degree angle and flexed. The seams in both arms of his jacket immediately tore apart. David screamed, hands fluttering at his face as he stared at the tears in the material. "Do you know how much these jackets *cost*?"

"I do. I bought them."

"I gave you something towards them."

"The cash you gave me paid for …" Travis peered down at one ripped arm. "… this sleeve and a couple of buttons."

"Come on," David said, bustling Travis through the patio doors, "Let's see if reception has a needle and thread. You really should be more careful, Travis, you simply don't know your own strength!"

"Shall we go back?" Mark asked Olivia.

"Yes, it sounds far more interesting up there. You're okay with Richard though, aren't you? I really do have it under control, I just don't want him to goad you into doing something drastic."

"It's fine." He took her hand. "No response, no threats, and

definitely no fisticuffs. I am patience personified."
"Thank you."
Neither of them knew what was to come.

CHAPTER THIRTEEN

"Catch any interesting gossip whilst mingling amongst our guests?" Sophie asked Tel.

They were on the dancefloor, snuggled close and gently swaying to their own rhythm, whilst all around them guests bounced and jived like they were on pogo sticks as the band thrashed out some classic rock.

"You mean, apart from your secretary snogging Rupert?"

"He of the magnificent moustache."

"Whose wife, the very prim and proper Penelope, is currently cutting a very serious salsa across the dancefloor with Travis."

He spun her round just in time to catch Travis spinning Penelope down one arm, across his chest and down the other arm, expertly catching her at the end and almost giving her whiplash.

"Where is Etta?" Sophie asked, looking around.

"Current location unknown, last seen snogging the face off that bloke who brought the Mexican food. She seems so quiet in the office."

"She doesn't drink, so she says, completely teetotal. I can see why now, the girl is *rampant* under the influence of alcohol."

Tel gently twirled her round and pulled her back into his arms.

"How's your mother?" she asked.

"Squiffy and entertaining a group of our uni friends with customer horror stories. They're loving it, half of them have never been to a supermarket."

"Bit like us."

"Dad's had a whole pint of shandy and fallen asleep in the corner of the room. Look." He turned so she could see a pair of crooked legs on the floor next to the patio doors, the head and torso hidden behind a chair.

"Is he okay?"

"He's fine, he'll just sleep it off and be grumpy in the morning. How's your mother?"

"She's had *three* glasses of champagne and is what Beth calls 'as pissed as a fart'. Though, after the flatulence released during our wedding ceremony this afternoon, I'd say a fart is more inclined to make you cry and gag than piss yourself."

"Sophie!" Tel gasped, "Such crudeness! I expect my wife to behave with a bit more decorum."

"Yes, Mr Rochester." She listened to the music, looking around, enjoying the moment, then said, "Have you noticed something strange about the girls?"

"What girls?"

"Faye, Beth, Annie and Fi?"

"Strange, or stran*ger*?"

"They keep merging together."

"Like a coven of witches?"

"No," she laughed. "They'll be dancing, then they'll suddenly dash off, gather together in a group, then disperse again. It's really odd. Look, they're doing it now."

They both watched as the four women abruptly left their dancing partners and marched quite aggressively towards the bar area.

"Ah," said Sophie, suddenly realising. "They're keeping Richard at bay. He must be giving Liv a hard time."

"Maybe we should have asked him to leave when he got here. His presence is bound to cause some friction."

"Mark seems to be handling it okay though."

"You think?" Tel said. "Look at his hands."

Sophie saw Mark leaning against the far wall, watching

the women form a wall in front of Richard as Olivia hurried away from the bar with a couple of drinks. His fists opened and closed at his sides, and the muscle in his jaw twitched incessantly.

"It'll be fine," Sophie said, hoping it would be, "There's only a few hours left anyway, so let's just enjoy ourselves."

"I am. I can't believe you're my wife."

"I can't believe you're my husband."

"Feels weird, doesn't it."

"It does. Nice though."

They kissed.

"Your dad's on good form I see," Tel laughed, "He's doing his Cossack party piece again."

Sophie watched her father star-jump by them, squatting down with his arms folded and kicking out his legs to the sound of LMFAO's *Party Rock Anthem*. "He's convinced he has Russian blood in him."

"Russian vodka, more like."

"He'll do himself an injury."

"Excuse me, sir," said a man, coming up to them. Tel felt he'd seen him somewhere before but couldn't quite place him. "The nine-thirty minibus is outside if anyone wants to be driven back to the ..." The man paused and wrinkled up his nose. "... campsite."

"Oh, you're the wedding organiser!" Sophie said, "I didn't recognise you without your microphone. You look different, less tyrannical."

"Isn't it your job to tell everyone about the bus?" Tel asked.

"Yes, sir, the band are just about to announce it now." All three looked down towards the band, the drummer going wild on the cymbals. "After this song," the microphoneless man said, and walked away.

Tel rubbed his nose against hers. "And how is the very lovely Mrs Okenado?"

"Ah," she said, pulling away, "I wanted to talk to you about that. Would you be very upset if I didn't change my name and stuck with Sophie Forbes, or would you prefer a modern, power-couple hyphenation with Mrs Forbes-Okenado?"

"Or Okenado-Forbes."

"Either. Do you mind?"

"Call yourself whatever you want," Tel said, bending to kiss her, "As long as you're happy."

She kissed him back. "I am."

"Get a room, you two!" Brian laughed, dancing passed with a very red-faced Faye.

Sophie laughed, then looked beyond them. "Annie looks a bit stompy and unsteady." She watched her Maid of Honour flounce across the room with her arms outstretched for balance. "I hope Lucas hasn't upset her."

"He's playing it cool and composed to try and win her over."

"From her expression I'd say he's failing quite spectacularly. Oh, and there goes Lucas, chasing after her all flustered and panic-stricken. It's like watching one of those sickly-sweet TV dramas, will they, won't they?"

"I'm betting they will," Tel said.

"Really? I'm on the fence, it could go either way."

"I think you're underestimating Lucas' powers of persuasion."

"We shall see," she grinned.

* * *

Brian was dancing with Faye when he saw Richard's head making its way through the crowds towards Olivia, who was dancing with Jim. He kept his eyes on him as Richard went up to Olivia and started to put an arm around her shoulders, as if to lead her away.

He couldn't see what happened next, there were too many people between them, he just saw Olivia duck down and Richard's head suddenly drop from sight.

Brian danced casually but quickly through the crowd. Jim had stopped dancing, as had a few other couples nearby, and was staring, somewhat in awe, at Olivia, who had somehow flipped Richard to the floor.

"Oh dear," Olivia cried dramatically, "Are you okay? This floor is terribly slippy, isn't it. Here, let me help you up."

Richard furiously pulled away from her, his eyes shocked, pained and angry. He clambered to his feet and stormed out of the room, furiously rubbing at his arm.

Brian looked at Olivia, who immediately looked over at Mark, sitting and laughing with Beth at the table on the other side of the dancefloor, completely oblivious. Brian winked at her and she winked back.

Faye, happily being led around by Brian, didn't notice a thing.

"I'm flagging," she said, fanning her face with her hand. "I need to rest for a minute."

"Want to go outside for some fresh air?"

"No, I need to sit on something soft and comfortable. Those dining chairs are too hard."

"I could lay down on the floor and you could flop on top of me?"

She pushed his shoulder, still fanning her face. "It would look a bit weird in the middle of the dancefloor. Anyway, you're not soft and comfortable."

"Oh? I thought our whole marriage was based on the fact that I'm soft and comfortable."

Faye laughed. "I'm a bit tired actually."

"Tired?" Jim said, catching their conversation as he gently glided passed with Beth, "It's not even half-nine yet, you lightweights!"

"Come with me," Brian said, taking hold of Faye's hand and leading her off the dancefloor.

They left the room and crossed the foyer.

"Where are we going?" Faye asked.

"You'll see."

He opened a door on the opposite side, glanced into the darkened room, and pulled Faye in after him.

"Ooh, this is nice," she whispered.

It was a large lounge filled with soft, comfortable chairs and sofas around a large, unlit fireplace. A coffee table was piled with magazines. The drapes at the window had been drawn and it was so dark they could only see each other in grainy black and white. Faye threw herself onto the nearest sofa and sighed in relief. Another sigh echoed around the room and Faye jolted upright, whispering, "Is there an echo in here?"

Another, deeper sigh wafted across the soft furnishings, followed by a tiny gasp. Faye perched on the edge of the cushions, holding her breath.

"Could be old water pipes," Brian breathed.

"Sighing water pipes?"

There was a long exhalation from somewhere behind them, deep in the darkness, and Faye leapt up off the sofa, turning to face the black abyss and gripping Brian's arm.

"Hello?" Brian said, "Is there anybody there?"

There was a sudden shuffling sound, a cough, and some scraping of furniture on the wooden floor. The vague shape of a man wearing strangely baggy clothes hurried across the room, making Faye cry out in alarm and grip even tighter onto Brian's arm. As the man opened the door, blinding them with the light from the foyer, they could just make out the smudged makeup on his face and the clown costume he was wearing. Then he was gone, leaving the door open.

"Who was that?" Faye asked in a tiny, high-pitched voice.

Into the shaft of light shuffled a young woman with messy hair. She pulled up the straps of her blue dress and looked at them, smiled, hiccoughed, dropped her smile and picked it up again. "You won't tell my boss*h*, will you?" she slurred.

"Who's your boss?" Faye asked.

"S*h*ophie."

"Oh."

With a wiggle of her fingers, she bounced against the door into the foyer, pulling the door closed behind her and leaving them in darkness once more.

"Have they gone?" whispered a voice, and Faye's heart swelled to three times its normal size.

"I think so."

Rigid with terror and thinking the house was likely haunted, Faye forced out a hand to a lamp on a table next to the sofa and, after a bit of fiddling, turned it on.

The room was bathed in a dull light that didn't fully extend to the walls, but bright enough to see a couple snogging on a chaise lounge further back.

"Terribly sorry," said a man's plummy voice, "But would you mind turning off the lamp for just a moment whilst we rearrange ourselves?"

Brian blindly fumbled with the lamp until darkness descended once more. Faye's fingers dug into his arm.

"Thank you so much," said the man's voice, "We'll just be a moment."

There came the sound of movement, the rustling of clothes, and then a woman hissed, "I told you it wasn't a good idea, Michael!"

"Shhh, don't use my name."

"Why, are you married? Am I just your bit on the side, *Michael*?"

"Just hurry up."

"I *am* hurrying up."

Bare feet padded across the wooden floor, and then the door opened, light burst in, and two shadows flitted from the room, closing the door behind them.

"Rampant lot, these guests," Brian chuckled, sitting down again. "Come on, lass, put your feet up on the table."

"I don't think I can relax in here now," she said, slowly lowering herself onto the edge of a cushion, "There could be more."

Brian was about to assure her there wasn't when a head popped up behind the sofa on the other side of the coffee table. Faye screamed and pulled her legs up onto the sofa, clutching them with her arms and screaming again. Brian quickly leaned over and turned the lamp on.

"Mark?" he said, "Is that you?"

Mark's head rose like it was decapitated, his white shirt taking on an ethereal glow from the lamp. "Sorry, Bri," he said, "We were hoping you'd leave again."

"We?" Faye said, unscrunching herself. "That'd better be Liv you've got there with you!"

"Of course it's Liv!"

"Hi, Faye, Brian," Olivia said, standing up next to Mark and turning her back to him. "Could you just do me up, darling?"

Mark pulled up the zip on her dress and, turning to Brian and Faye, said, "So, what are you two doing in here then, eh?"

"We're old," Brian said, "We came in for a rest."

"A likely story," Mark jeered. "Ready, Liv?"

"Yes, darling."

"Catch you two in a bit, after your *rest*." Brian couldn't see the air quotes but he could hear them in Mark's voice.

They left.

"Scared the living daylights out of me!" Faye said, flopping back onto the sofa. "There's no more in here, is there?"

"IF THERE'S ANYONE THERE, PLEASE GIVE US A SIGN," Brian bellowed.

"Don't say that!" Faye cried, "We'll have ghosts coming out of the woodwork!"

"HELLO?"

"At least warn me before you shout!"

"I'm going to shout. HELLO? LAST CHANCE BEFORE THE OLDIES TAKE THEIR CLOTHES OFF!"

Faye punched him in the arm.

"Assault!" he cried. "I think we're finally alone."

"Thank goodness for that." She rested her head back against the soft cushions. "Oh, this is nice. Just five minutes and then we'll go ..."

Her unfinished sentence hung in the air as she drifted into unconsciousness, with Brian spread out next to her like a broken marionette, snoring loudly.

They didn't hear the band announce the arrival of the first minibus back to the campsite.

* * *

"Annie! *Annie!*"

She was halfway up the sweeping staircase, relying heavily on the banister to keep her upright and moving forward, and didn't stop. He ran up the stairs two at a time to catch her up.

"I don't want to speak to you!" she snapped, when they reached the top together.

"I'm sorry, Annie," Lucas beseeched, "I'm really, really sorry."

"For being so horrid to me?"

"Yes."

"For being rude and–"

He impulsively grabbed her shoulders and pressed his lips against hers. He couldn't help himself. She tasted of champagne and wine. He buried his fingers in her glorious red hair. She staggered backwards against the wall, inflamed with passion, both of them breathing heavily.

"Oh Annie," Lucas gasped, "I've waited so long for this."

"Shut up and kiss me."

They rolled along the wall, Lucas kissing Annie and Annie kissing Lucas, their hands clutching at each other's bodies.

"Come to my room," he panted, pulling away and grabbing her hand.

She let him pull her down the long corridor, kicking off her shoes as she went and almost falling over. After a brief, frustrating fight with the key card, they burst into his room, kissing and falling onto one of the single beds.

He was just caressing her neck with his mouth when he realised she'd stopped participating and was lying motionless beneath him. He leaned up to look at her face, her beautiful, delicate, porcelain face. He thought maybe she'd changed her mind and he'd find her glaring up at him coldly, but her eyes were closed, her breathing soft and regular.

She was out cold.

He gently pulled the duvet around her and sat on the edge of the bed, staring at her, before bending to kiss her forehead.

"My sleeping beauty," he said.

* * *

Tel and Sophie were sitting at a table, Sophie with her feet up on a chair, her beautiful gown bunched up to her knees and draped on the floor around her. They both looked shattered.

"It's been good, hasn't it," Tel said, popping a sausage roll into his mouth.

"It has. I think people enjoyed themselves."

"I'm glad. Oh, talking of glad, Charlie Pierrot certainly looks happy about something."

Pierrot, the sad clown, marched across the room to the bar with a certain spring in his step. His normally downturned mouth was stretched across his face in a big grin, and there was something glinting in his eyes.

"Wow," Sophie said, "I've never seen Charlie look that happy before, ever. I wonder what ... oh no."

"Oh no, what?" Tel turned in his seat to look where Sophie was looking. Etta, her temporary secretary, was just staggering into the room and bouncing against chairs, tables and guests. "You don't think–?"

"I do think," Sophie snapped, "Her track record hasn't been exemplary so far."

"But ... with Charlie?"

"She doesn't seem all that fussy, I think her only criteria is 'male, with heartbeat'. Also," she said, squinting her eyes, "There does appear to be white blotches around her mouth."

They both looked at Charlie, standing at the bar. When he turned around his face displayed some pink patches where his white makeup had come off.

"No!" Tel cried, grinning. "Etta the temp and Charlie the clown?"

"I wonder if you can still get chastity belts on Amazon?" Sophie mused, "Or is that kind of thing frowned upon nowadays?"

Etta glanced over as she picked at somebody's buffet plate, completely oblivious to their objections, and came unsteadily towards them.

"Oh no," Sophie sighed. "What should I say to her?"

"Stop snogging the guests?"

"S*h*ophie," Etta cried, falling into a chair next to them with her head nodding like a bobble doll and her eyes struggling to keep still – she seemed to be looking at both of them at the same time. "Brilliant wedding."

"You seem to be having a lot of fun."

"Oh, I am. At least, I think I am, I can't remember most of it."

"Maybe lay off the drink a bit?" Tel suggested.

"Ooh, drink!" she cried, standing up, then closing her eyes and clutching at the back of the chair to steady herself. "I'll jus*h*t wait for the room to s*h*top s*h*pinning first. It's very wobbly in here, is*h*n't it."

"It's not the room, Etta, it's you."

"Me?" She looked down at herself and oscillated on her feet. "I'm not wobbling, it's*h* definitely the room. You s*h*ould make it s*h*top, it might make people feel …" She obviously couldn't think of the right word and splayed fingers out in front of her mouth whilst making a retching sound. She looked down at the floor, at a dropped vol-au-vent and a half-eaten bread roll, and said, "I don't remember eating that."

"Etta," Sophie said, "*Stop drinking!*"

"Why?"

"Because you're drunk."

"That's*h* the point, is*h*n't it? Get drunk, get off with a bloke."

"*A* bloke! Just pick *one!*"

"I will when I find the bes*h*t kiss*h*er. I have to …" She wavered a little and her eyes widened. "… pick s*h*omeone who can …" She gripped the back of the chair again and did a long blink. "… kiss*h* properly, *s*ho I have to … tes*h*t them out."

"Test less, talk more," Tel laughed.

"You're very …" Sophie looked at Tel. "What's the word I'm looking for?"

"Promiscuous?"

"Yes, promiscuous when intoxicated, Etta."

"I jus*h*t love men," she wailed, burping loudly.

"Try not to love *all* of them. Show a little restraint."

Etta smiled deliriously at them both and staggered off towards the bar, bouncing off people on the dancefloor and draping herself around the neck of the lycra-clad man, before undraping and continuing her journey.

"GET A COFFEE!" Sophie called after her, "A STRONG ONE … OR TWO! Oh God, she's heading straight for Uncle Harry."

"I can't look," Tel laughed, burying his face in his hands.

"Aunt Sally is not going to like … No, Sally's spotted her, she's moving in to deflect. Harry looks deflated. Oh, bit of finger pointing, bit of head shaking, and yes, Sally's turned her away, and now she's … going after Uncle Ike. Charlotte's going to eat her alive."

"We should probably send her to bed," Tel said.

"She hasn't got a bed. She drove down, I assume she's going to drive … oh."

"Bit of a flaw in the plan there, Sophs."

"Yes."

"She'll probably fall asleep under a table or something, she'll be fine."

"Will she?"

"Yes, of course."

Lucas came rushing into the room and headed straight towards them. "Tel," he said anxiously, "Could I have a quick word?"

"It's not Etta, is it?" Sophie whined. "Tel me you haven't–"

"No, no, it's not Etta, whoever she is. I'll just steal him for a moment, Sophs."

"Steal away."

Lucas quickly guided Tel out onto the balcony.

"What is it, chap?"

"Something's happened."

"What have you done? Broken something in the hotel? Snogged someone's wife?"

"No, listen." Lucas sighed heavily and leaned on the concrete balustrade, staring out over the darkening garden as he tried to control his breathing.

"Lucas," Tel said, suddenly concerned. "What's happened?"

"I'm in trouble."

"With the police, the inland revenue, Interpol?"

"I think ... I think I'm in love."

"Well, that's not a bad thing, is it? Who's the lucky lady?"

"Annie. I'm in love with Annie."

"Well," Tel said, slapping him on the back before leaning on the balustrade next to him, "You've always had the hots for–"

"Not the hots, Tel. I mean, I know I'm always flirting with her and joking around, but it's just hit me, tonight. I kissed her–"

"And about time too!"

"Tel!"

"I'll be quiet."

"I kissed her and we went up to my room."

"You didn't! Sorry."

"We were kissing on the bed, and then she fell asleep."

"You're that good, huh?"

"No, she was drunk."

"Shocker."

"I ... I pulled the duvet around her and kissed her on the forehead, and then ... then I just sat there, staring at her face as she slept, and it hit me like a blow to the chest. I love her, Tel. She's the one, she's always been the one. I actually really love her."

Tel put an arm round his shoulders.

"It hurts, it physically hurts."

"I know, chap. Welcome to the wonderful, exquisitely painful world of lurve."

"I love her," Lucas said again, standing straight and smiling, "I bloody love her!"

"I'm really pleased to–"

There was a commotion from inside the reception room, the sound of glass breaking and raised voices. Tel and Lucas hurried back inside. The music had stopped and everyone was staring down at the bar area.

"IF YOU LOOK AT ME LIKE THAT *ONE MORE TIME* I'M GOING TO–"

"WHAT? WHAT ARE YOU GOING TO DO, EH? SHE'S MY *WIFE*!"

"YOUR *EX*-WIFE. WHEN ARE YOU GOING TO ACCEPT THAT SHE'S NOT–"

The sound of a skirmish and more glasses breaking. Tel and Lucas ran down and pushed their way through the crowd, who were watching Mark and Richard struggling to get near each other as bar staff and guests tried to hold them back.

"I'M GONNA WIPE THAT BLOODY SMIRK OFF YOUR FACE ONCE AND FOR–"

"MARK!" Olivia pushed her way through the bodies. "MARK, STOP IT! HE'S NOT WORTH IT!"

"OH, IT'LL BE WORTH IT, TRUST ME!"

Tel grabbed hold of Mark, who was lunging through fallen chairs. Lucas stood in front of Richard, who was literally frothing at the mouth.

"STOP IT, THE PAIR OF YOU!" Tel yelled.

"He started it, staring at Liv with his beady little eyes and–"

"You *stole* my *wife*!" Richard spat back, and there was some gasping from the watching crowd.

"*Saved* her, from *you*!"

"Mark!"

"It's okay, Liv," Tel said, "We've got this."

Sophie found herself standing next to the wedding planner at the back of the crowd. She glared at him as several guests brought the skirmish under control.

"I'm not security," he snapped. "If you wanted security you should have hired security. I'm just the planner, my job is to plan, not break up fights."

"You could have at least intervened."

"It's not in my remit to keep the peace at weddings."

Sophie tutted.

With brute force, Tel and Travis hauled Mark away from Richard. Lucas and Sophie's dad, John, indicated for Richard to follow as a furious Mark was bundled from the room. The two men were frogmarched down the foyer to the front door. A small crowd shuffled along in their wake.

"Take it outside!" Tel demanded, opening the door and pushing Mark through it. "Take it down the bottom of the garden! Take it anywhere but here at my wedding!"

Olivia clutched at Mark on the front patio, trying to calm him. Richard straightened out his jacket and smoothed down his hair. Lauren appeared at his side.

"Well, that was a frightful display of testosterone," she said curtly. "I never saw you as the fighting type, Richard."

"I wasn't the instigator."

"Yes, you bloody were!" Mark snarled. "Glaring at Liv all the time and following her around like a slavering wolf!"

"That's *enough*!" Tel yelled.

Richard grinned, and Mark lunged towards him again, held back by Tel and Travis and Olivia. "You smirking weasel of a human being!"

"Wolf, weasel, your metaphors are all over the place," Richard drawled.

"ENOUGH!" Tel demanded.

The crowd stood in the doorway, watching silently.

"I get the impression," Lauren said, "That you're not well-liked here, Richard."

"I don't tend to mix with *these* types."

"And what's that supposed to mean?" Mark barked. "Does your girlfriend know what you're really like, Richard? Have you told her what you did to–?"

"Oh, I'm not his girlfriend," Lauren said, glancing at Richard with a sardonic smile. "He's not my type. Not anybody's type by the sound of things. I'm his boss."

There was a stunned silence, and then Lauren said, "Richard, go get the car, I think you've outstayed your welcome."

With a final glare at Mark, who scowled at him, Richard marched off down the steps and across the gravel driveway.

Lauren looked at Tel and said, "Wonderful wedding." She turned and saw Sophie at the front of the crowd in the doorway. "Beautiful bride," she smiled. "Say goodbye to Camille for me, tell her I'll call her next week."

Sophie nodded.

A burgundy Bentley pulled up at the bottom of the steps. Richard jumped out to open the back door as Lauren descended, and closed it after she got in. With a final glare up at Mark, who flipped him a stiff finger, he got behind the steering wheel. Just before he put the idling car into gear he looked up at Olivia and mimed, 'Call me,' with a finger and thumb. Mark flipped the other finger and held them both up in front of him. Richard grinned and pulled away.

There was a beat of peaceful silence, and then Lucas said, "What's a wedding without a good fight or two?" He put his arm around Tel's shoulders and guided him inside. The crowd at the doorway parted and he said, "All over now, folks, let's continue with the boozing and the boogying."

Mark, calm now that Richard was gone, leaned against the concrete balustrade, breathing heavily.

"My knight in shining armour," Olivia said, crossing her arms and raising a cynical eyebrow at him. "Did you have to cause a scene like that?"

"He wouldn't stop looking at you and smirking at me?"

"So?"

"So I ... I got mad."

"Whilst I appreciate your gallantry," she sighed, "I did have a posse of women watching out for me, and a fully functioning knee I was more than ready to raise if he got too close. I don't need looking after, Mark."

"No. I'm sorry."

"It's not me you should apologise to."

"No, I know."

She leaned against the balustrade next to him. "You okay?"

"Yeah. Just wish I could have got a punch in."

"That's not the answer, Mark."

"No, but it would have felt good." He paused, looking down at his shoes. "Still love me?"

"No," she giggled. "Completely gone off you now."

"Don't tease, Liv."

She wrapped her arms around him and kissed his cheek. "Of course I still love you, silly."

"Would you still love me if I'd have hit him?"

"Of course."

"Wish I'd have hit him now."

"Well, I managed to get a couple of moves in, had him pinned to the floor with his arm up his back at one point."

Mark stared at her. "You never!"

"I did. My self-defence instructor would have been very proud of me."

"Good for you. I feel better for hearing that."

"And," she giggled, "I toppled him on the dancefloor too, he went down like a bag of potatoes."

"Go, Olivia!" he laughed.

"Come on," she said, grabbing his hand, "Let's forget about him and go enjoy ourselves. You can get me drunk and have your wicked way with me later."

"I like the sound of that!"

They kissed and wandered back into the hotel, passing the closed door of the lounge on their right, behind which Brian and Faye were peacefully sleeping.

They missed all the drama, and the ten-thirty bus ride back to the campsite.

* * *

"Beth," said Sophie, as she hurried back into the reception room, "Could you sing something to calm everyone down?"

"No problem."

Walking onto the raised platform, she asked the lead singer if she'd mind.

"Not at all, I could do with a break, and you have the most wonderful voice, I'm so jealous."

Checking that the band knew the song she planned to sing, she turned to face the chattering crowd filling up the room and raised an arm to beckon them over.

It all happened at once and as if in slow motion. There was the sensation of something snapping, something sticky being whipped off, and something flopping out. She felt a gentle breeze wafting over something that shouldn't be exposed to the air, and then Jim was suddenly thudding across the stage and lunging towards her, pressing his back against her with his arms outstretched. Beth didn't move, she stared straight ahead, her hand still in the air, holding the microphone. The whole room went deathly silent.

"Jim," she breathed.

"Yes, babes?"

"Has my boob just popped out?"

"Yes, babes."

"Oh my God!"

"Don't panic. If you could just pop it back in again, maybe?"

Beth slowly lowered her left arm and, using both hands, claimed back her modesty. The sound of flesh being pushed back into material echoed around the room. She still hadn't blinked.

"You okay, Beth?"

"Yeah, babes. Just tell me when the ground starts opening

up under me feet."

"Will do."

Beth brought the mic up to her mouth and cleared her throat. "I was going to sing a song to calm everyone down," she croaked, looking at them all as Jim turned to check she was decent, "But I'm too embarrassed now."

"Don't be," someone shouted, "It was very lovely."

"Thanks, but I'm not in the habit of popping my boobs out in public. I know some of you may find that hard to believe, me being all brash and everythin', but there's a reason why it fell out like that." Everyone was quiet. "This dress fitted when I bought it a couple of weeks ago. It's a bit tight now though, especially around this area," she indicated her cleavage, "and down here," she rubbed her abdomen.

Olivia suddenly threw her hands up to her mouth and made a tiny squeaking noise.

"What?" Mark whispered.

"Shhh."

"Are you okay?"

"Shush, this is important."

"What's important?"

"What she's going to say next."

"What's she–?"

"Listen."

"I wasn't going to say anything yet," Beth continued, "But I guess now is as good a time as any, since my 'usband is in merry mode from all the beer he's 'ad, and it's good there's people around to help him up off the floor when I tell 'im what I've got to tell 'im."

"No!" Jim suddenly cried, crumbling to his knees in front of her, "You're not leaving me, are you?"

"No, babes, I ain't leaving you. Now get up. I'd help you, but if I move it could fall out again and I might not be able to get it back in next time. Can someone give him a hand?"

A couple of men helped Jim to his feet.

"I'm sorry, Sophie and Tel, I didn't plan to intrude on your special day like this."

Sophie, who had tears running down her cheeks, shook her head and waved her hands for Beth to continue. She knew too.

"I've given up alcohol," Beth said into the microphone, "I didn't want to, I had to, but I quite like it. Good job really 'cause I can't have a drink for another six months."

Beth stared at Jim, who stared back at her with his mouth hanging loose.

"And I know I'm curvy," she said to everyone, "But I ain't put on weight 'cause I'm stuffing my face with pizzas and pies. Actually, I can't keep anything down on account of the morning sickness." She glanced at Jim. Nothing registered on his face.

Some women in the crowd started smiling and looking at each other. The men wondered what was going on.

"Who are these people?" a woman next to Mark asked the woman standing next to her.

"I heard they're gypsies."

Mark leaned into them and breathed, "Campers! We're *campers!*"

Standing in front of the band, Beth said, "I'm 'with child', babes." She patted her abdomen for emphasis, and a murmur started up all around them.

Jim shook his head and laughed like she'd just made a joke.

"You're going to be a dad."

There was a sudden surge of excited whispering in the crowd. Jim still looked blank. "A dad?" he repeated in a tiny, uncomprehending voice.

"Yeah, a dad."

"I'm going to be a dad?"

"Did you not do biology at school, babes?"

People had their hands raised in front of them, ready to clap as soon as Jim cottoned on to what Beth was trying to tell him.

"I'm having a baby, Jim."

"A baby?"

"Ah, come on, mate!" someone shouted, "Try and keep up. Everyone in the room knows except you."

"Babes, look at me," Beth said. "Listen to what I'm saying. I'm pregnant."

"You're ..."

"Pregnant."

"You're having ..."

"A baby."

"You're carrying..."

"A baby, yes."

"My baby?"

Beth pursed her lips, stared at Mark, standing behind Jim, and said, "Slap him for me, will ya? I'd do it myself but I've got body bits to keep under control."

Mark reached out a hand and whacked Jim up the side of his head.

"See if that knocks any sense into him," someone shouted, and everyone laughed.

"Have you tried turning him off and turning him back on again?" someone else shouted, and the laughter got louder. Jim still looked stunned, and now he had a pain in his head. The laughter died away.

"What do you think, babes?"

Several sets of hands were poised, ready to applaud the pregnant woman who looked and sang just like Adele. Everyone stared at Jim, standing there, immobile and apparently having an out-of-body experience.

"Whack him again," someone shouted.

Slowly, Jim's eyes started to move. He looked down, as if thinking, then back up to Beth. He gave a little gasp.

"I ... we ... you ... a baby?"

"Running out of patience here, babes. 'Appy, sad, indifferent? Shocked, 'orrified, checking exits for a quick escape?"

Everyone waited expectantly. Jim's gaping mouth slowly

turned into a grin. He threw his hands on top of his head and crouched down, emitting a strange, strangled cry. When he jumped up again his eyes were wide and moist. "You're *pregnant?*"

"That's what I'm trying to tell you, babes. We're going to have a baby."

"A baby! Oh my God! I'm going to be a dad!" He turned and started telling everyone, "I'M GONNA–"

"BE A DAD!" the crowd yelled, "WE KNOW!"

"You know?" Jim said, confused.

"Congratulations," Mark said, patting him on the back, "Didn't think you had it in you."

The applause and cheering started. People came over and heartily shook Jim's hand, just smiling at Beth, too frightened to touch her in case something fell out. Olivia rushed up and gingerly placed a kiss on her cheek. "I'm so happy for you I could burst," she giggled.

Sophie came over in her beautiful dress and gently took Beth in her arms. "I'm so pleased for you both," she said. "It's wonderful news."

"Thanks, Sophie. Sorry if I ruined anything."

"No, you made it better."

"Well done," Tel said, punching Jim's shoulder and winking at Beth.

"Oh," Beth said, carefully throwing her hands out in front of her, "It was nothing. Well, not nothing, it's always something, isn't it, but thanks."

"A dad!" Jim kept shouting, jumping up and down and furiously shaking people's hands, "I'm going to be a dad!"

"Could someone bring me my jacket?" Beth said into the microphone. "Gotta try and keep these puppies under control somehow before I get done for indecent exposure."

David came running over with her pink bolero. "Congratulations," he said, gently handing it to her, "It couldn't have happened to anyone nicer. Oh, do you need a hand with that?"

"She's fine," Jim snapped, standing between David and his wife.

When Beth had fastened up her jacket she said, "Can I have the stiletto brigade?"

Olivia and Fi went up onto the raised platform and she whispered something to them. While Olivia steadied her, Fi bent down to take off her shoes and lower her, very slowly and very gently, onto her bare feet. "No trips and *whoops*!" Beth cackled. "Now, who wants a song?"

Everyone cheered. Beth started singing, *Happy Days*, Barbra Streisand style. By the end, everyone was singing and waving their arms in the air, except Beth, who firmly clamped an arm across her chest and held it there.

CHAPTER FOURTEEN

It was almost midnight when the last minibus arrived to take the stragglers back to the campsite. Guests exited the hotel en masse, having been purged from the wedding room by staff wanting to clear up, and milled about the front patio as they waited for taxis and rides. They were still in party mode and very noisy. One of the long windows overlooking the patio opened up and a woman in hair rollers poked her head out, yelling, "Can you keep the noise down, some of us are trying to sleep!" The noise level remained at screaming laughter pitch. The woman huffed and slammed the window shut.

Beth was gently guided onto the bus by a super-attentive, still partially in shock, ecstatically happy Jim. He brushed the seat off before carefully lowering her down onto it. "You okay?" he asked, "Is there anything you want? Anything you need? Is the seat comfortable–?"

"Enough with the fussing, babes, you're driving me mad already and there's another six months left yet."

He sat down next to her, staring at her and smiling, reaching for a hand and holding it with both of his.

Mark and Olivia, both giggling hysterically as they tried to walk and kiss at the same time, clambered on board and resumed their snogging on the back seats.

"Could you do that somewhere else?" Jim said, turning round. "I've got a pregnant woman here."

"And?" said Mark.

"And I don't want her to see anything she's not supposed to see."

"She can't see anything unless she's got eyes in the back of her head, and I think she's already seen everything she's not supposed to see."

"I ain't bovvered," Beth said, "Snog away."

Mark cried, "Chocks away, chaps!" before resuming his face interaction with Olivia.

There were just three other people they recognised from the static caravans at the campsite, each of them at varying stages of intoxication; one man looked green and limp, a woman looked drunkenly furious at the green man, and a younger man had his head lolled back on the bar across the back of his seat, fast asleep.

"Where's Brian and Faye?" Beth asked, her arms clamped across her chest in preparation for any bumps on the journey back.

"Saw them earlier," Mark said, coming up for air. "They were tired. They probably caught the earlier bus."

The driver shut the door and started the engine. As the bus boinged and wobbled its way down a long country lane, Beth couldn't stop laughing as she fought to keep control of her bouncing breasts. Jim covered her up with his tartan jacket in case of further accidents.

The sleeping man's head pounded up and down on the back of the seat. He didn't wake up.

The green man vomited into a carrier bag.

* * *

"Brian."

"Uh?"

"Brian?"

"S'up?"

"I don't know where we are."

"We're in the caravan, love."

There was a long pause as Faye dragged herself into a sitting position and tried to get her bearings. "I don't remember putting an antique sofa in the caravan," she croaked, "And I certainly didn't buy these cushions."

Brian peeled open his eyes. It was pitch black.

"Where are we?" he grunted, hauling himself up.

"I remember dancing," Faye said, rubbing at her eyes. "I remember drinking and laughing, but ... I don't remember how we got back to the caravan."

"I don't remember leaving the hotel."

"I'm not sure we did."

Brian reached out and turned on a lamp. The room was bathed in a gentle glow. This was definitely not their caravan.

He lifted his watch and tried to focus on the face and the teeny-tiny hands. "Twelve-fifteen."

"Oh Bri!"

"We overslept a bit."

"A bit? The last bus back was at eleven-thirty. We've missed it. What do we do now, Bri?"

"I don't know."

"We could walk back?"

"Too far, too dark, and I don't know the way."

"What should we do?"

"I guess we just stay here."

Faye threw herself back down on the sofa and pulled the blanket off the back up under her chin. The door to the lounge suddenly opened and a shaft of light filled the room, blinding them.

The silhouette of a suited woman stood in the doorway. Behind her came the clattering sounds of a clear-up in the reception room on the other side of the foyer. The woman raised a hand and turned on the big light. Brian and Faye squinted at the sudden brightness.

"What are you doing in here?" the woman asked.

"We were resting," Faye said.

"Which turned into sleeping," said Brian.

"You can't stay here, it's against hotel policy."

"Could you ...?" Brian rubbed his face awake. "Could you make an exception? We were at the wedding and we're a bit hungover."

"Certainly not! Gather your things together and leave immediately."

The woman spun round and clattered off.

"She was friendly," Faye huffed. "What should we do?"

"I don't know."

"Where should we go?"

"I don't know."

"But you always know, Bri."

"I'm not conscious enough to know anything right at the minute, Faye. My head's banging, my mouth," he said, smacking his lips together, "is as dry as dust, and I think I lost my brain somewhere."

Faye threw back the blanket and stood up, wavering on the spot. "I'm still drunk," she said.

"I'm stuck between being drunk and suffering a hangover. It's grim." He staggered to his feet. "Come on, before shadow woman comes back."

"Come on where?"

"We'll figure something out."

Faye leaned against him, clinging to his arm, closing her eyes and wondering if it was possible to sleep and walk at the same time. Brian glanced at his phone to double-check the time, but it was flat and unresponsive. He knew Faye hadn't brought hers, there hadn't been room in her bag.

He began the long journey into the bright, dazzling foyer. Clattering, banging, scraping and chattering came from the reception room opposite. They both winced at the noise.

They made it to the reception desk. The woman who'd ejected them from the lounge using only the power of her charm looked up at them and turned on a faux smile. "Can I help you, sir?"

"We were just in the lounge."

"Yes."

"We were wondering you could order a taxi for us."

"Taxis won't come out here this late," she said, rather cheerfully. "They have to come from Epsom and it's too far, and even if they have a driver willing to come all the way out and back again it would be very expensive."

"Okay." Brian thought for a moment. The woman watched his face intently, her faux smile steady. "Can you give us directions to the campsite then?"

"I don't have that information to hand, sir."

"You could look it up." He glanced at the computer screen.

"It's not official hotel business," she said, "And I certainly don't deal with campsites."

Faye tugged on his arm and said, "I'm not walking in these shoes, in the dark, in the middle of nowhere. Could we get a room?"

"Do you have a room?" he asked the woman.

"Of course, sir." She clattered on a keyboard, glancing at the screen. "Single beds or double?"

"Double," Faye said.

"Ensuite?"

"Ooh, yes please."

"No," said Brian, "We don't need an ensuite."

Faye started whimpering. Out of the corner of his mouth he whispered, "Ensuite will be more expensive."

"We have a double room available for ..." She gave the keyboard a final tap, glanced at her screen, looked Brian dead in the eye and told him the price. Brian visibly blanched. He stared at the woman with wide eyes. She stared back, still with a fake smile pinned to her face; Brian briefly wondered if it was a smirk, before deciding he didn't care.

"*How* much?" he gasped.

She repeated the figure, seeming to take great pleasure from it.

"There must be some mistake," Brian gasped, half-laughing before the dryness caught in his throat. "I just want a room for the night, not shares in the hotel."

"There's no mistake, sir. That's our standard price for a double room."

"For one night?"

"Yes, sir. Shall I book it for you?"

The figure was still running around in Brian's head like a hamster in a wheel. He glanced at his watch again, vowing to get one with a bigger face at the earliest opportunity. "There's only half the night left, could we have it for half price?"

The woman raised one plucked eyebrow. "No, sir."

"Just book it, Bri."

"I'm not paying that much for a room for …" He glanced at his watch again but couldn't focus. "… a few hours." He looked at the woman. "Could you not charge by the hour? We could leave early."

"We're not that kind of establishment, sir."

There was a cough behind them and Brian glanced over his shoulder. A young woman, half asleep and stumbling like a zombie, staggered out of the reception room rubbing at her eyes with the heels of her palms. Behind her, a luminous lycra-clad man with a cycle helmet dangling from a hand wandered out into the foyer, looking around as if trying to figure out where he was.

"We're willing to share," Brian told the receptionist.

"Are we?" Faye asked, horrified despite the fog of alcohol.

"Two guests per room only," said the receptionist.

"What about a family room?"

"Occupied."

"Could we sleep in a cupboard? You must have a spare cupboard somewhere."

The receptionist stared at him blankly, the smile/smirk now gone. "If you're not a paying guest I'll have to ask you to leave the premises," she said curtly.

"And go where?" Faye asked.

The receptionist shrugged. "Go wherever you like, it's not my problem."

"Bit heartless," Faye said.

"I'm a night manager, madam, not a social worker. Now, if you could just make your way over to the main door, I'll buzz you out."

"Kicked out into the cold, dark night," Faye wailed, vaguely imagining lying down on the marble floor in the foyer and going back to sleep as a protest against their appalling customer service. They'd have to carry her out, or drag her out by her feet – she was glad she was wearing her best knickers.

She was just starting to sag on her feet when Brian pulled her up and moved away from the reception desk. She shuffled along with him like a monkey clinging to its mother.

"Thank you," Brian snapped at the night manager, "You've been most helpful."

"You're welcome, sir."

"Where am I?" the lycra-clad man asked.

"You're still at the hotel, lad."

"What hotel?"

"The hotel near Epsom."

"Epsom?" The man managed to focus his eyes on Brian's face and looked alarmed for a brief moment. "What am I doing in Epsom?"

"You brought the food."

"Oh."

Behind him, the young girl, standing crooked with her head almost touching her left shoulder, whimpered, "Can you help me?"

"Broken neck?" Brian asked.

"I'm lost," she said.

"Do either of you have a room?" snapped the woman at reception.

"No," said the girl.

Lycra-man shook his head, then raised a hand to his pounding skull.

"You'll have to leave," snapped the woman, "If you're not guests you're trespassing on private property."

Brian forced his fuzzy brain to function. With Faye still hanging off his arm, possibly asleep judging from the weight of her, he moved towards the front door. He heard a buzz as the night manager unlocked it. He started to open it, peering over his shoulder, until he saw the night manager walk briskly into the back office.

"Quick!" he breathed, pushing Faye sideways.

She gave a tiny shriek of alarm as he dragged her back into the lounge. She let go of his arm and, smiling, went to lie back down on the sofa.

"We can't stay here," he hissed, "Grab a cushion and a blanket."

"Ooh," Faye said, brushing a soft, comfortable cushion across her face and doing the same with the blanket she'd so recently been sleeping under. "Can we just stay here for five minutes?"

"That's how we got into this mess in the first place."

Brian was tugging at her again, a blanket and cushion under his arm, and she gave a half cry as the soft, comfortable sofa was taken from her; so close and now so far. Not fully understanding what was going on, she fell against Brian as he halted by the lounge door and looked out. The girl and lycra-clad man were still standing like statues in the foyer. The night manager was still in the back office. He pulled a stumbling Faye across the foyer and into the reception room. It was filled with hotel staff, all cheerily clearing away the debris of the wedding, shouting orders at each other and clattering plates and glasses and cutlery onto metal trolleys. The noise cut through Brian's head like a bevy of knives. Nobody seemed to notice them and nobody challenged their presence.

He hurried over to the buffet table and snatched up a bottle of water, handing it to Faye. He grabbed another, unscrewed it and poured it down his throat in one go. He went to pick up another, but had to help Faye open her bottle. She sipped at it delicately, while Brian, parched beyond comprehension, tipped another bottle into his mouth. He snatched up two more bottles and hurried towards the open patio doors. It was cold outside and very, very dark. Stars twinkled in a clear night sky.

"Where are we going, Bri?"

"You'll see."

"Do you have a cunning plan?"

"No plan, just an irresistible urge to lie down somewhere."

Back in the foyer, lycra-man and the girl slowly turned their faces towards each other. The girl's eyes were bloodshot. Before they could muster up the energy to speak through the cotton wool in their mouths, the night manager reappeared behind the reception desk.

"Do you want to book a room?" she snapped.

"No," said lycra-man, forcing his feet to move towards the front door. "We were just leaving."

The night manager humphed, buzzed the front door again, then marched back into the office.

The girl shuffled over to the man and held his hand. Having watched the old people, he pulled her into the lounge and grabbed two cushions, but couldn't find any blankets. Checking the coast was clear from the doorway, he rushed across the foyer into the wedding room, with the woman hot on his Max Air heels.

"Here," he said, passing bottles of water to her and watching the chattering night staff in case they were spotted, "Take these."

The girl struggled to hold them and dropped one on the floor. A couple of the staff glanced over but didn't seem overly concerned, assuming they were guests who'd come downstairs for a drink.

Lycra-man turned and pulled a slightly stained tablecloth off a cleared table and handed it to the girl, who gripped it between her teeth as she balanced cushions and bottles in her arms, swaying slightly. The other tables still had piles of plates and cutlery and glasses on them. He gripped the edge of one tablecloth and quickly yanked it, hoping the magic trick would work. It didn't. Plates and cutlery and glasses crashed to the floor.

One of the night staff cried, "Oi!"

Lycra man, tucking the tablecloth under his arm, ran

through the doors and onto the patio beyond, with the girl stumbling behind him. She took one breath of fresh air and flung her head over the concrete balustrade. She heaved once, twice, then straightened up and opened a bottle to rinse her mouth out.

"I feel better now," she said.

Lycra-man wrinkled his nose in disgust and ran down the steps. The girl stumbled after him.

* * *

Around the fountain in the garden, on one of the many wooden benches circling it, Brian and Faye tried to share a bench by spooning, but Faye was crushed lying behind him and flung off onto the gravel when she perched precariously in front.

"You could lie on top?" Brian suggested, winking.

"Well, that's just asking for trouble, isn't it," she grinned.

"Nobody can see us."

Faye was just about to crawl on top of Brian when the young woman and lycra-man shuffled into the fountain area. The man nodded at them, the woman wiggled her fingers. They both lay, side-by-side, on the wooden bench next to them, covering themselves with dirty tablecloths and resting their heads on cushions. The girl immediately started giggling.

"Hey!" Brian shouted, "No funny stuff over there."

Faye stood looking down at their bench for a moment, Brian filling all of it with his legs hanging off the end. She grabbed a blanket and a cushion and moved to another bench.

"But we wanna be together," Brian wailed, holding out a hand.

"Not unless they do king-size benches," Faye huffed, lying down and pushing the cushion under her head, before wrapping the blanket tight around her.

"Sleeping under the stars," Brian sighed, "It's almost romantic."

"Romantic apart from the plummeting temperature.

We're going to freeze to death, all because you didn't want to pay for a room."

"I could buy a fortnight's holiday in Lanzarote for that kind of money."

Faye didn't answer. Into the ensuing silence came the small sound of one of them gently breaking wind. The young woman giggled.

"Call that passing gas?" Brian said, raising his head and letting loose a loud ejection of air. "Now *that's* how you break wind."

"Brian!"

"I'm bored and lonely," he huffed, "So lonely."

"Just go to sleep."

"G'night, John-boy," he called out.

"G'night, giant," said lycra-man.

The girl giggled. The white tablecloths rose and fell.

Brian rolled over, the wooden slats beneath him creaking, and went to sleep.

* * *

"Brian! Brian!"

"Huh?"

"I'm cold."

Brian sleepily lifted up his blanket without opening his eyes.

"I don't fit, remember?"

"What do you want me to do?"

"Let's lie on the grass and snuggle up for warmth."

His eyes still closed, Brian grunted to his feet, peered beneath a half-open eyelid and followed Faye onto the lawn behind the bench. Faye put her blanket on the ground and lay down, tucking the cushion under her head. Brian crumpled next to her like a felled tree and threw his blanket over them both. Faye fidgeted. Brian prayed for sleep. Faye fidgeted some more.

"Keep still," he hissed.

"I can't get comfy, the ground's too hard."

Brian rolled onto his back and enfolded Faye with one giant arm. She snuggled up to his chest, threw a leg over his, and continued fidgeting.

"Are you getting frisky?" Brian asked, "Only I should warn you, I'm very, very tired."

"And I'm not?"

"Stop wriggling then."

"I'm trying to get comfortable."

He pulled her closer. She rested her head on his shoulder, brushing her hair away from her face and flopping an arm across his chest. She moved her leg, moved her head, coughed and fiddled with her hair.

"For the love of God, woman, keep still!"

"I'm just getting comfortable."

"Can you two keep it down over there!" cried lycra-man from the bench, "Some of us are trying to sleep!"

"All the grunts and groans I've been hearing all night say otherwise."

Brian started praying again as Faye continued to squirm and rearrange her limbs. *"Keep still!"*

She fell still, for a good ten seconds, then started fidgeting. She rolled over, sighed, adjusted her cushion, then said, "Spoon me."

He turned with effort and cuddled up to her back. She fidgeted with the blanket, the cushion, her hair. "Can you come and lie on this side, Bri?"

"No."

"Please?"

Brian started making crying sounds, not sure if they were real or simply an expression of his exhaustion. He briefly wondered if sleep deprivation could be fatal and thought it might be. Brian rolled onto his back again. His patted the grass beside him until he found a bottle. He took off the top and, in one quick movement, upended the bottle into his mouth to assuage his screaming thirst.

"Pass me one," Faye said, extending a hand. He did. She took the top off and slowly tipped it towards her upturned face. A waterfall cascaded down on her and she gasped for air.

"*Bo-locks!*" she cried.

Brian tried mopping up the water with the sleeve of his jacket and discovered that polyester isn't particularly absorbent. Her makeup smeared across her face and her hair was drenched. Growling, she turned onto her side again, damply snuggling up to him and pulling the blanket tight around them both.

"Stars look nice," she said.

"Don't care."

"It is a bit romantic, isn't it."

"No."

"Apart from the cold, hard ground, and whatever it is that's sticking into my–"

"Be quiet!"

"Sorry, Bri."

"Be quiet!" lycra-man snapped.

The girl giggled.

Lycra-man started giggling too.

Brian sighed into the darkness as Faye gently started snoring.

CHAPTER FIFTEEN

The Morning After

Annie, curled up under the duvet, reluctantly prised open her eyes and was shocked to find a madly grinning face staring at her from the other bed.

"Oh no," she groaned. "We didn't. Tell me we didn't."

"Morning, gorgeous," Lucas said brightly. "I've been watching you sleep."

"How very creepy of you." She rolled onto her back and pulled away the duvet, relieved to see she was still fully dressed. "Ugh, kill me now," she said, as her brain shifted inside her skull.

She risked turning her head to see if Lucas was real or a figment of her drunken imagination. He was still there, still staring, still grinning madly. She watched his eyes move from her eyes, to her lips, to her eyes again.

"You want to kiss me, don't you," she said.

"No."

"No?"

"No, I can smell your breath from here, it's *rank*."

Groaning, Annie hauled herself off the bed and into the bathroom.

"Where's my stuff?" she cried.

"In your room."

"So whose room is this?"

"Mine."

She tried to remember what had happened last night, but her memory banks were empty, or submerged under a sea of gently sloshing alcohol.

"Use my toothbrush," Lucas said, "And the mouthwash, and the breath freshener."

"Jeez, how to make a girl feel attractive!"

"You are attractive. Your breath, not so much."

She cupped her hands and drank profusely from the tap. She'd never been so thirsty. How much had she had to drink, and what exactly happened last night that ended up with her in Lucas's room? She stood up straight and looked at herself in the mirror. Expensive makeup was so worth it, she thought, inspecting her almost immaculate face. She primped her hair and snatched up Lucas's toothbrush from the glass shelf above the sink.

"I need coffee," she cried.

"I've ordered breakfast from room service."

"How long ago?"

"It should be here any–"

There was a knock at the door. She could sense his excited vibes, like electricity surging into the bathroom, and was pretty certain they weren't directed at breakfast. She heard the rattling of trolley wheels and the door closing again. She stepped back into the bedroom, plonking herself on the edge of the bed, and reached for a tiny cup of coffee.

Lucas was still grinning.

"Stop it," she reprimanded.

"I can't."

She drank her coffee. Coffee had never tasted more delicious.

"More," she said, holding out her now empty cup.

Lucas emptied the small coffee pot and she drank it down.

"Better?" he asked.

"Marginally. Can you please stop grinning at me like that."

"I can't help it, I'm happy."

"Good for you."

"*Really* happy."

She eyed him suspiciously as she raised a glass of orange

juice to her mouth. "Are you sure we didn't–"

He shook his head. "I am the perfect gentlemen. I'd never take advantage of an intoxicated, vulnerable, impossibly sexy woman."

"I'm not vulnerable," she said, reaching for the other glass of orange juice.

"Aren't you?" he said, tilting his head.

"No, I'm not."

"Are you sure?"

"Quit teasing me, Lucas, it's far too early."

"Sorry." His grin didn't dim. It was driving her nuts.

She picked up a piece of toast and, without buttering it, nibbled on a corner to calm her rolling stomach. She tilted her head and, through the fog of memories, said, "There was kissing."

"There was."

"Why was there kissing?"

"It was a mutual activity."

"Was there much of it?"

"A little."

"And then what?"

"You fell asleep."

"Before, during or after?"

"There was no during or after." The light from the window reflected in his eyes. They really were incredibly blue.

"You're not eating," she said, to break the silence.

"I couldn't sleep, so I went down to the dining room earlier and had a full English."

"You do seem inordinately pleased with yourself."

"I am."

"May I ask why?"

"I'm in love."

"Poor woman. Instant attraction over the buffet table, was it?"

"Desperate yearning over a long period of time, actually."

"It's me, isn't it." He nodded. "You think you're in love

with me." He nodded again. "You're not, you just think you are."

"I most certainly am." Impossible as it seemed, his smile went up another notch. She briefly wondered if the top of his head would fall back if he smiled any wider.

She threw down her toast and stood up. "I need to change," she said. "Direct me to my room."

"Out the door, turn right, go all the way down the corridor, last door on the left."

She marched off without saying another word.

Funny how she was smiling though.

***

"Morning, Mr Husband."

"Morning, Mrs Wife."

They snuggled under the duvet, staring at each other.

"On a scale of one to ten," said Sophie, "How happy are you right now?"

"One hundred and eighty-five."

"That's not on a scale of one to ten."

"There's no scale big enough to measure my happiness." He planted a kiss on her nose.

"My happiness is currently oozing across the whole universe," she said. "Life forms from other planets can feel it."

"Oh, good one."

"I thought so." She snuggled closer to him. "Fancy christening our marital status?"

"Again?"

"Is there a limit? You never mentioned there'd be a limit. There's never been a limit before."

"A limit to my stamina," Tel laughed. "We'll never reach our first anniversary at this rate."

Sophie sighed. "It was a good wedding, wasn't it."

"The best. Well, apart from the fighting and the bloodshed and all the relatives falling out."

"Hardly anybody saw that, and you can't have a wedding

without at least one drunken punch-up."

"It was all bark and no bite."

"I'm already planning to renew our vows in the future so we can do it all again."

"At the pub, with a pint and a packet of crisps?"

"And an appalling pot of plastic flowers on the table. They weren't that bad actually, people commented on them. They weren't favourable comments," she laughed, "But they did add a touch of–"

"Vulgarity?"

"I was going to say creativity. They were a talking point. I particularly liked how your mum had glued diamantes onto them that made the petals droop, they looked like shiny dead things."

"What about Beth though!" Tel gasped.

"The boob or the baby?"

"The baby."

"I know! Pregnant!"

"With Jim as a dad!"

"I think he'll make a very good father."

"Me too. You looked beyond beautiful, by the way, did I tell you that?"

"About a million times." She kissed him gently.

"That dress was stunning."

"It was. I felt like a princess in it. I might wear it around the apartment from time to time."

"I look forward to removing it again and–"

There was a firm knock on the door and a voice cried, "SOPHIE! TEL! ARE YOU UP?"

"NO, MUM, WE'RE STILL FAST ASLEEP!"

"Some of the guests are leaving."

"That's what they supposed to do after a wedding, mum."

"Do you want to say goodbye to them?"

"Not particularly."

"It's de rigueur to say goodbye to your guests, darling."

"I'm not feeling very de rigueur at the moment, mum."

She couldn't hear it but she could sense her mum sighing.
"WE'LL BE DOWN IN A BIT, CAMILLE."
"A bit?" Sophie grinned, wrapping a leg around his.
"HOW LONG IS 'A BIT'?"
"That's what I'd like to know."
"FIFTEEN MINUTES," he yelled.
"What can we do in fifteen minutes?" Sophie pouted.
"Quite a lot," he said, diving under the duvet.

* * *

"*BRIAN!*"
Brian was awake in an instant, looking around, wondering where Faye was and what was happening. He spotted her jumping up and down a short distance away, furiously ruffling her upside-down head and screaming, "*BRIAN! BRIAN!*"
"WHAT?"
"*Squirrel!*"
"Where?"
"*In my hair!*"
Brian couldn't believe how difficult it was to get up from the ground and hurry over to his wife; his bones and his flesh felt like lead, his eyes like burning orbs, his brain pounding with a heavy, throbbing heartbeat. He grabbed Faye's violently bouncing head and peered down at it, running his fingers through her hair.
"It's gone," he said.
"Are you sure? Are you sure, Bri?"
"I think, even in my delicate condition, I'd notice a squirrel clutching at your head."
"It was in my hair, Bri!"
"It's probably back in its tree, traumatised and coughing up hair balls."
Faye straightened up. Brian took one look at her and couldn't, if his very life depended on it, stop himself from laughing. His howls echoed across the garden.
"What?" she snapped. "WHAT?"

There was his normally pretty wife, standing before him, the very epitome of a woman who'd been dragged through a hedge backwards; hair like an exploded haystack, makeup smeared across her face, her dress wrinkled and dirt-stained and hanging off one shoulder.

"You look lovely in the morning light," he said.

"I look terrible, don't I."

Brian, not trusting himself to speak, just shook his head.

"Be honest, I'm a mess, aren't I."

Brian sucked in his dry, cracked lips and nodded.

Faye turned her mouth upside-down in a frown and slumped on her feet.

"You may look like the scribbled drawing of a five-year-old, but I still love you." He kissed the top of her damp head and she flopped against his chest.

Behind them, the giggling that had been going on for most of the night started up again. Brian rolled his eyes, instantly regretting it as pain shot into his head.

And then he sniffed the air. "Coffee," he said, "I smell coffee."

"Coffee?" cried a voice from the wooden bench next to the fountain.

"Lead the way, husband," Faye said, patting down her hair and running her fingers under her black-smudged eyes.

A yellow and orange cyclist wriggled off the bench, followed by a very tousled young woman. They both came shuffling over towards them.

"Coffee?" the man said. "Where's the coffee?"

"Well," Brian drawled, already regretting his poor attempt at humour so early in the morning, "I don't know if you've noticed but there's a bloody great house over there and nothing else for miles around, so I'm guessing–"

The young couple took off at a brisk pace, holding hands as they crossed the lawn.

"Quick," Faye said, hurrying after them, "They might drink it all."

Brian lumbered along. The young couple in front kept glancing at each other and giggling, swinging their hands between them.

"Have you known each other long?" he asked.

"No," the girl giggled, "But we sure know each other now." To lycra-man she said, "I'm Etta, by the way."

Lycra-man nodded and said, "I'm Paul."

"Nice to meet you, Paul."

"Very nice to meet you, Etta."

"Hurry up, Bri!"

"Coming, my love."

* * *

Annie opened the door to her room and was alarmed to find that Fi wasn't in her bed. She pushed open the door to the shower room. It was empty. With growing concern, she stared down the corridor outside. Lucas was standing outside his door at the far end, leaning against the wall. When he saw her, he waved. She tutted, then noticed the door opposite was slightly ajar; from it came the familiar sound of Fi sleeping, like a tiny asthmatic hamster. She pushed it gingerly with one finger and peered inside. A man was lying face down on the first single bed, snoring heavily. She pushed the door wider. On the second bed lay Fi, fully clothed on top of the duvet, legs and arms akimbo. She was surrounded by cans of energy drinks.

"Fi," she hissed. "Fi!"

Nothing.

She stepped into the room. A man lay on the floor in front of her with a woman cuddled up to his back. In between the single beds lay what looked like a woman, her legs and head under the beds with just her torso showing.

Orgy? she thought. Fi? Surely not.

"Fi!"

"Hmm?"

"Fi, wake up."

"I dowanna." She rolled over, hugging the duvet. The empty cans clattered together.

"Wake up!"

Fi opened an eye. The eyeball wobbled, then settled on Annie. "Morning," she mumbled.

"Good night, was it?"

"No idea."

"Who's this man on the bed?" For clarity, Annie pointed at the man on the bed.

Fi slowly raised herself into a sitting position, brushed back her hair, and glanced at the man. "He was there when I arrived," she said.

"And these people?" She made a general motion with a hand to indicate the people on the floor.

"Dunno."

"Have you been orgying?"

Fi dropped her head to look down at herself, fully clothed. "No," she said, disappointed, "As if my life could be that exciting."

"Come on," said Annie.

"Where are we going?"

"To our room."

"I thought this was our room."

"No, it isn't."

"Oh."

Fi stood up and started picking up cans, shaking and dropping them one by one.

"You don't have to clear up," Annie said impatiently, "They have cleaners for that."

"I'm trying to find a full one."

Huffing, Annie turned and left the room, to the sound of a hissing can tab. Fi walked across the corridor with the can upended to her mouth. She saw Lucas out of the corner of her eye and waved at him, still drinking, and he waved back.

"Energy drinks are clearly the way to go," she said, as she closed the door behind her. "Just add alcohol as required. Oh!"

she cried, staring at the single beds and noticing they were both still made up, "Where did you sleep then?"

"Somewhere else."

"With Lucas?"

"What makes you think that?"

"Because he's a gorgeous hunk of a man who clearly adores you. I wish you'd put him out of his misery. Or maybe you have?" she grinned.

Annie was in the middle of the room, struggling to pull her bridesmaid dress up over her head. Fi wandered over and pulled down the zip on the back before settling on the end of a bed and sipping at her can.

"Have you?" Fi asked.

"Have I what?"

"Put Lucas out of his misery?"

Annie glared at her, then stomped into the bathroom.

"Ooh," heckled Fi, "I think you have."

* * *

"Look casual," Brian whispered, as he and Faye and the young couple sloped through the patio doors into the dining room, where they were serving breakfast. Brian breathed in the delicious smell of bacon and sausages and his stomach cried out like a growling dog.

Several people in the room stopped eating and stared at them. Faye, wobbling her wild hair and jauntily swinging her arms, strutted as casually as she could to the buffet table, where an espresso machine gently hissed. She poured a cup and turned to drink it. The entire room was staring at her in silence.

Brian quickly poured orange juice from a jug into what looked like a shot glass. He poured and drank, poured and drank. Behind him, the room became loud again. The aroma of fried breakfasts tormented him.

"If anyone asks," he whispered to Faye, "Tell them you've been in a car crash."

"Why?"

"Because you look like you've been in a car crash."

She patted her hair, making no difference. "Shall we just sit down and order breakfast?"

Brian made a crying noise at the back of his throat, rolling his yearning eyes over the steaming plates on the tables, before saying, "They'll want our room number."

Faye sighed, then turned back to the buffet breakfast. "Grab some boxes of cereal and some mini cartons of milk and let's go. Oh, spoons, don't forget the spoons! And some Danish pastries."

Brian was just hurrying from the room behind Faye when someone on a table near the door pushed away their plate. There was a full sausage left on it. Balancing boxes and cartons and Danish pastries, Brian whipped it up as he passed and popped it into his mouth. It was the most delicious thing he'd ever tasted.

Behind them, Etta and Paul were gulping at mugs of coffee and tipping glasses of orange juice into their mouths. When they saw the older couple moving away with their arms full of boxes they did the same.

They all hurried across the foyer with their stashes and out the front door.

* * *

After Annie had showered, changed, packed her things into a suitcase and opened the door to her room, she found Lucas standing in the corridor outside.

"Help with your suitcase. madam?" he grinned.

"Stop smirking, Lucas."

"I am here to pander to your every need."

Annie rolled her eyes. Lucas stopped grinning. "Are we going back to the way we were before?" he asked, "With me chasing after you and you cutting me down all the time?"

She didn't answer.

"Because," said Lucas, taking her suitcase from her, "If

we are I'd like to know now and conserve my adoration for someone who might actually appreciate it."

Annie, not really sure what to do or say for possibly the first time in her life, called back into the room, "Do you want to follow me back to London, Fi?"

"No, London's quite big, I think I'll be able to find it on my own."

"Are you sure?"

"Yes. Let's catch up next week sometime."

"Assuming you're home by then and not infinitely traversing up and down the M1."

"Bye, Annie."

"Bye, Fi."

Annie strode off down the corridor. Lucas paused for a moment, then huffed and followed her, rolling her suitcase behind him. "I'm not up for any more games, Annie. I think we had a moment, I think it was an important change in our relationship."

"We don't have a relationship, Lucas."

"Well, not yet, but maybe...?" He let his words drift away in the hope that she'd fill the void. She didn't.

Annie stepped delicately down the stairs. Lucas humped the suitcase after him. "What have you got in here?" he gasped, "Bricks?"

"Shoes, mostly."

"Wow, the honour of carrying your shoes!"

"I know. Don't drop them."

Annie made her way to the reception desk. Not once had she looked back at him. He was starting to feel annoyed and more than a little frustrated. She was giving him the cold shoulder again. He really didn't want to do this anymore, not after what had happened last night.

As Annie handed her key card to the receptionist, he slammed the suitcase down next to her and stomped off.

"Lucas!" she called after him.

"What?"

"Would you mind carrying it to my car?"

Lucas stopped stomping and sighed. The audacity of the woman! He was starting to wonder why he'd ever liked her in the first place; apart from the fact that she was everything that he wanted from a woman; intelligent, charismatic, and utterly bloody gorgeous.

"Please?" she said sweetly.

He stomped back, snatched the suitcase up and held out his hand. "Keys to the car?" She handed them over and he stomped out of the front door.

On the steps he found four rather scruffy people pouring tiny cartons of milk into tiny boxes of cereal and digging in with spoons. Danish pastries sat on napkins beside them.

"Morning," he said, "Excuse me."

The four parted, creating a gap for him to carry down the suitcase. He searched the driveway for Annie's car and saw it, right at the end. He threw the suitcase down and started dragging it, muttering furiously to himself.

"Oh, good morning," Annie said, spotting four vagrant people sitting on the steps and eating from cereal boxes.

As she moved down the stairway she overheard the big man with a beard say, "I'll call a taxi."

She glanced over her shoulder as she reached the bottom. Only then did she recognise that they were the people from the campsite; the big, hairy man with the loud voice, his little wife, now wearing what could only be described as an electric hairstyle, and wasn't that the orange and yellow clad cyclist who'd brought a takeaway all the way from London? Next to him, underneath a pile of messy hair and wearing a ridiculously creased dress, she vaguely identified Sophie's secretary.

"Rough night, was it?" she asked.

"You could say that," said the big man. Bernard, was that his name?

"Are you heading home?"

"Back to the campsite."

"Oh yes, of course."

Annie glanced over at Lucas, furiously hauling her bouncing suitcase across the gravel. She wasn't looking forward to a final farewell since she wasn't quite sure how she felt yet. Subconsciously, she raised a hand to her mouth and touched her lips. She turned back to the group on the steps.

"I can give you a lift, if you like?" she said.

"Could you?" gasped the wife – Franny, was it? "It's just us two. Paul has a bike and Etta is driving back."

"Just as soon as she's sobered up enough," Brian said firmly.

"After your hospitality the other night it's the least I can do."

Lucas drove up to the steps in her small, red sports car. The roof was up.

"I'll never get in that," Brian said.

"Scrunch," said Faye, "I just want to go back to the caravan."

Lucas pressed a button in the car and the roof started to fold back. He got out and gave Annie the keys. His face was expressionless. She still didn't know how she felt, but there seemed to be some heaviness inside her. Was that regret? Loss? Yearning?

Brian and Faye shuffled over. Faye got in the tiny back seat. Brian eased himself, inch by inch, into the front passenger seat, grunting and huffing and struggling to close the tiny door next to him. His head stuck up above the windscreen. He looked like a giant wedged into a plastic children's car with his knees under his chin. The car creaked and sunk closer to the ground, tilting gently. He felt if he breathed in too hard the car would explode into pieces around him.

"Well," Lucas said curtly to them all, raising a hand. "Bye. Safe journey back."

He turned to walk away.

"Lucas."

"Yes?"

Annie stared at him, fiddling with the keys in her hands

before walking towards him. She stopped and looked up. He looked down. And then she raised herself up on her toes, put a hand around the back of his neck, and kissed him, softly and slowly. His arm wrapped gently around her waist as he kissed her back. She lowered herself down again, staring into his bright blue eyes.

"Can I … can I call you?" he breathed thickly.

"You'd better," she said.

She strutted back to the car with a huge smile on her face. Opening the door, she bent into the tiny space that the big man's shoulders would allow and sat in an awkward position behind the steering wheel.

"Ready?" she cried.

"Yes."

As the car slowly and laboriously pulled away, they didn't see Lucas fist-pumping the air as he strutted back into the house.

***

Mark, Olivia, Beth and Jim sat quietly on the grass between Brian and Faye's caravan and their motorhome. Mark looked at his watch.

"How long have they been asleep now?"

"Four hours."

"I think they had a rough night," said Olivia.

"Wonder where they slept."

"Outdoors, by the look of Faye."

"Shh, they're coming."

There was a pounding of footsteps in the caravan. The door swung open and Brian, wearing a dressing gown, stepped down. He held up a hand to help Faye navigate her way down the steps. They both had bags under their eyes and looked dreadful.

"The creatures emerge from the pit," Mark laughed. "Morning. Or should I say, good afternoon?"

"I'll get you both a coffee."

"Thanks, Liv."

"So, come on, spill the beans," Jim said. "Where were you all night?"

"In the garden."

Mark reached into his jeans pocket and handed Jim a five-pound note. "I bet you'd slept in the lounge," he explained. "I knew I'd lost the minute you extricated yourselves from that posh bird's car and staggered into camp looking like you'd both crawled out of ditches."

"Thanks!" Faye said. "Thanks," she said again, as Olivia handed them both a steaming cup of coffee. She sipped it gratefully.

"I've never seen a car door ping open like that before," Mark said. "That's going to need some serious bodywork."

"I offered to pay," Brian muttered.

"She said she'd just buy a new one," Faye gasped.

Jim stared unnervingly at her. "Is this going to be your new hairstyle from now on, Faye? Blow-dried in a hurricane?"

"Truck just sped past doing ninety," Mark added.

"Leave 'er alone," Beth said. "She's clearly 'ad an 'ard night fighting off bushes and werewolves."

Faye huffed, put down her coffee and stormed off into the caravan. Brian, exhausted, hungover and hungry, decided not to follow her and was relieved when she came storming back out with a large, floppy hat on her head.

"Why did you sleep in the garden?" Jim asked.

"Because we missed all the buses back to the campsite," Brian said, "Thanks for noticing."

"We thought you'd caught an earlier one."

"No, slept through them all, and then we were catapulted from the hotel by the Wicked Witch of the West."

"South," said Faye, "We're south, aren't we?"

"South-east, I think," said Olivia.

"There's no Wicked Witch of the South-East," Mark laughed.

"There is, and she works as a night manager in a hotel near

Epsom."

Beth shifted in her seat and Jim suddenly said, "You okay, babes? Is there anything you need? Are you comfortable," he mouthed the words 'up here' whilst circling his chest with a hand.

"Stop fussing, Jim, I'm fine. And I'm firmly encased inside an industrial strength bra, just so you all know."

Brian looked at Faye. Faye looked quizzically at Brian.

"Oh!" Olivia cried, "They don't know!"

"Don't know what?"

"Oh, you missed a lot while you were sleeping in the lounge," Mark grinned. "A *lot*."

"What? What did we miss?"

"About Beth's ..." Olivia grimaced, trying to figure out how to word it without sounding sordid.

"Her boob fell out," Jim said.

"Fell out?"

"It did," Beth said. "Of its own accord, of course, I didn't just whip it out on a whim and start swinging it round or anything like that. I had a Janet Jackson wardrobe malfunction when the strap on my dress finally gave up under the weight and *oops*," she cried, flopping the palm of her hand in front of her, "Out it popped."

"Because," Jim said, holding Beth's hand and grinning, "She's pregnant. Beth's pregnant."

Faye's eyes widened to twice their normal size. She slammed the coffee mug on the table and jumped up, hurrying over to Beth and screeching. *"You're pregnant?"*

"I am."

"Oh, that's brilliant! Congratulations!"

"Ta."

Brian heaved himself over and planted a kiss on her cheek. "Well done, girl!"

"Er," said Jim, pointing at himself with both hands.

"Well done, Jim."

"I thank you."

"Yeah, well done for doing the easy bit," Mark laughed.

"That's so exciting!" Faye cried, bending to hug Beth again.

"Isn't it!" cried Olivia. "I already know what I'm getting for the baby shower."

"Going 'ome in a bit to tell the mothers," said Beth. "I wanna see their face. They're gonna go *wild*."

"Yeah, we'd better be off too," Mark said, stretching. "Can't sit around here all day enjoying ourselves, we've got a campsite and a garden centre to run."

"We might hang around until the alcohol in our blood lowers to legal limits," Brian said, "Maybe have lunch at the pub to soak it up."

"Ooh, lovely," said Faye.

"Come on then, babes." Beth stood up. "Let's go and give our parents the good news."

Olivia stood up too and said, "I'll start packing things away."

"We'll just sit back and watch," Brian sighed. "Wife, fetch my breakfast, or lunch, whichever."

"Cheese on toast?"

"Excellent."

It took Beth and Jim ten minutes to pack up their motorhome. "Just threw everything back into the boxes," Beth said.

With no awning, just a canopy to wind back, Mark and Olivia took just fifteen minutes.

"Impressed," Brian nodded, chomping on his toast. "Takes us nearly an hour to get ready for take-off. Stowing the multitude of cushions takes the longest."

"No it doesn't!"

"I'm not looking forward to taking the awning down with a hangover and a hefty lunch inside me."

Mark looked at Jim, who nodded. They both dashed into the awning and started emptying the tables of books and bottles and miscellaneous paraphernalia, carrying it all inside. Giggling, Olivia dashed into the caravan to stow it all away.

The men folded the tables and chairs and stacked them at the back of the caravan before rolling up the groundsheet. They pulled out poles and canvas and, with Brian instructing them from his comfort of his chair, they rolled it up and returned everything to its bag. Mark went round raising the stabiliser legs with Brian's battery drill.

"That saves a few arguments," Brian said when they'd finished. "Cheers, lads."

"No problem," said Mark, revving the drill next to his head, "It's the least we can do for you old lushes."

"Hey," Faye grinned.

"I've stowed everything in drawers and cupboards," Olivia said, sitting down again, "You can sort it out later."

"Thanks, Liv."

A Range Rover crunched down the driveway and pulled up next to them. Tel and Sophie got out and, with everyone screaming and talking at once, they merged into a mass hug.

"Rough night, was it?" Sophie laughed, looking at Brian and Faye.

"You could say that."

"We're running a bit late," Tel said, "We, er, slept in." The men made suitably lewd noises. "We're just going to hook up, put the van back in storage, and then go home to pack for the honeymoon."

"We haven't even started yet," Sophie gasped.

"Where are you going again?"

"Mauritius, a beach house with its own swimming pool and room service for fourteen fabulous days. I can't wait!" She stepped forward and gave Beth another hug. "Fantastic news about the baby, you take care of yourself."

"I will."

"And you," she added, looking firmly at Jim, "You look after her."

"Oh, I will, believe me."

"What time's your flight?" Brian asked.

"Ten o'clock tomorrow morning."

"We've got so much to do! We're going to have to love and leave you."

"Need your stabilisers lifting," Mark asked, revving the battery drill again.

"Cheers, Mark."

"Well, this is it," Sophie shrugged, "Thank you so much for coming, and you, Beth, for singing so beautifully."

They all hugged again, saying what a great wedding it had been and how much they'd enjoyed it, and how they would have to get together again soon, probably at Olivia's campsite again. Tel reversed his car up to the tow ball and Mark and Jim helped manoeuvre the caravan into place.

"Have a lovely honeymoon," Olivia cried, waving as they pulled away from the pitch.

"Don't do anything I wouldn't do," Beth laughed, patting her abdomen.

"Love you both."

"See ya, plebs."

"See ya, posh gits."

Jim and Beth left soon after, followed by Mark and Olivia. Brian and Faye sat alone outside their caravan.

"Oh," Faye puffed, "I'm all hugged out."

"I'm all partied out. We're getting old, lass."

"Speak for yourself!"

"Fancy some pub lunch."

"Love some."

"Going to do something with your hair first?"

Faye pulled the floppy hat down tight on her head and said, "Nah, bugger it."

CHAPTER SIXTEEN

Two weeks later

There was so much mail behind the door of their flat they had to push it open. Sophie picked it up and flipped through it as Tel and John, who, along with Camille, had picked them up from the airport, dragged the suitcases and bags in. In the lounge sat their huge pile of wedding presents, still unopened.

"Now, darling, make a note of which gift came from whom as you're opening them," Camille said, taking off her coat and hanging it on the coat stand. Tel glanced at her, grimacing. "And you should start the thank you cards straight away. I'll write the addresses on the envelopes."

Sophie took down her mother's coat and handed it back to her. "Thank you so much for everything, mum," she said, kissing her cheek before guiding her back down the hallway, her dad following. "I appreciate all your help with the wedding, but," she said, opening the front door, "I think I can take it from here."

"Oh?"

"Come on, Camille," John said, gently urging her out and winking back at Sophie, "Let's leave the lovebirds in peace."

They both breathed a sigh of relief.

"Should we unpack now?" Tel sighed, staring at their luggage.

"You're going to have to drag me kicking and screaming back into the real world. Let's snuggle up on the sofa watching TV instead, I have the perfect viewing material." She waved a padded envelope at him. "DVD of all the messages from the wedding reception. The photographer left a video camera in the lounge. It'll be the perfect antidote for impending post-honeymoon blues."

"I'll get the wine and nibbles."

The DVD started off quite well, with sober, nervous guests sitting on the sofa, staring wide-eyed into the camera and wishing them all the best, saying what a lovely wedding it was, what a lovely couple they made, and sending lots of love.

Several messages later, Cousin Charlotte's face appeared on the TV, standing so close to the camera they could see the pores of her skin. She sat down on the sofa and noisily slurped from a glass of champagne.

"I hope you do better than I did," she started, pausing to let out a burp. "I made a terrible mistake with Ike, should never have married him, but since you've now done the dreaded deed I wish you lots of luck." She crossed her fingers in front of her.

They heard a door opening and music coming from another room before it was muted by the door closing again. Ike came and sat down next to her, not noticing the camera.

"What do you want?" Charlotte snapped.

"What are you doing?"

"I'm doing a video message for Tel and Sophie! Can't you see I'm busy?"

"I just wondered where you were."

"I'm here!"

Charlotte tutted and turned back to the camera. "You see what I mean? Can't get a minute's peace. He can't think for himself, he's–"

"Wind it forward a bit," Tel said.

"Yes, it is a bit depressing."

"Hope we don't turn out like that."

"We won't."

Charlotte and Ike fast-forwarded through a lot of finger pointing and what looked like an argument. Eventually, Charlotte stood up and turned the camera off.

Aunt Mildred and Uncle Carl were next, sitting side by side.

"What should we say?" Mildred whispered.

Carl, who seemed almost hypnotised by the camera, said, "I don't know."

"Probably should have thought this through before we hit the record button."

"Yes."

Mildred put on her biggest smile and said, "Congratulations to you both, you make a–"

"I was going to say that," said Carl.

"I've said it now. Say something else."

"I can't think of anything else."

"Carl and I wish you every happiness in your glorious future together," Mildred said.

"Oh that's good, 'glorious future.'"

"Yes, it just popped into my head. It's very upbeat and optimistic, isn't it. We love you, you're both beautiful people, and ..."

They looked at each other.

"And?" said Carl.

"And ... we wish you every happiness."

"You've already said that."

"I can't think of anything else to say. I think the champagne's gone to my head and dissolved my brain."

"Let's turn it off and go."

"Do I just touch this button?"

"Just press it once and see what–"

Pam, Sam and Tam, Sophie's old friends, appeared next, all giggly and squiffy on the sofa.

"We love you both," Pam squealed.

"And you're going to be stonkingly happy together."

"Kia ora, mates. Be healthy and happy." Tam stuck two fingers up in front of the camera.

"Other way," Sam hissed, "V for Victory."

Still smiling at the camera, Tam turned her fingers round, while the other two made heart shapes with theirs.

Giggling, they stood up and turned the camera off.

Charlotte and Ike's very nervous son, Pete, appeared next.

"Congratulations," he said, sitting down. They watched his Adam's apple bobbing up and down like a piston in his neck. "Erm," he said, looking down before bringing the front of his phone up to the camera, "If Beth wants my phone number, this is it, please pass it on. Tell her to call me whenever she wants. Tell her I love her, I'll always love her, and I'll wait for her." His Adam's apple bobbed again before he said, "I guess that's it."

A plethora of other guests at increasing levels of intoxication sat on the sofa, sending love and best wishes. Rupert, of the magnificent moustache, and his prim wife, Penelope, said the usual things and then forgot to turn the camera off. They bickered their way out of the room, with Penelope hissing, "Will you *stop* flirting with women!"

"I'll flirt with the men then."

"Have you no control? It's *so* embarrassing!"

Immediately after they left, Sue, Camille's cleaner, and an associate from their law firm, a woman called Angela, rushed into the room and started passionately snogging on the sofa.

"Oh," Sophie gasped, "That's interesting."

Tel leaned forward in his seat.

"Did the photographer not edit this?" Sophie asked, winding it forward until the couple disappeared.

"Seems not. Makes it more interesting though. How long is it on for?"

Sophie checked the screen. "Six hours!"

"Blimey, I'd better get another bottle of wine."

On screen, the sofa stayed empty for a while. Sophie sped it forward until an unknown couple came into view, walking behind the sofa and disappearing onto the floor. There were giggles and a bit of grunting, before the couple stood up again and left.

"What was in those mini meals?" Tel said, "Viagra?"

The parents arrived, two at a time, gushing love and pride and blowing lots of kisses – except for Henry, a man of few words, who simply said, "Good luck," as he stood up.

"Shall I turn it off?" Jacquie asked him.

"It was on when we ... came in. I'd leave it ... on."

The room got a little darker. Instead of turning on a lamp, some guests sat in the semi-darkness like talking ghosts, whilst others used their phone torches to eerily light up their faces.

"It'll have night vision," David told Travis as they arranged themselves on the sofa. "We've got our own lighting anyway." They turned to the camera, smiling insanely, and switched on their suits, illuminating their faces with multi-coloured patterns. "*Fabulous* wedding," David squealed, "We've loved every minute, and you, Sophie, looked beyond gorgeous, I've never seen such a beautiful bride." He waved jazz hands, adding, "Welcome to the family, sis. We love and adore you."

"Wishin' you folks a heck load of happiness," Travis drawled.

"Hurry up and make babies so we can spoil them." Sophie and Tel laughed. "And call me, we'll go shopping, or drinking, or both, drunken shopping is the best, you never remember what you bought so you get double the joy when you open the bags."

"Short, sweet, and very camp," Tel said, as they minced out of view.

"I love them." Sophie paused the DVD. "You know, I've never heard your dad mention anything about David being gay, did your parents just accept it?"

"My mum did, she always knew."

"And how did your dad react when he 'came out'?"

"Oh, David never 'came out', he was born that way and never tried to hide who he was."

"Good for him. So your dad's okay with it?"

"I don't think he's noticed."

"Not noticed?"

"No, to dad David is just David."

"That's lovely." Smiling, Sophie pressed the Play button on the control.

The campers were next.

"Bit dark in here," Brian said, "Where's the light switch?"

"Best not to touch anything," said Mark, "You might set off the security alarm or something."

Faye and Olivia sat down first, scooting along to make room for Beth on the end. The men stood behind for a moment before realising the camera angle would only show their torsos. Brian stuck his stomach out and rubbed at it profusely. Faye told him to stop it. With much oomphing and grunting, the men kneeled down.

"Who's going to start?" Jim asked.

"Brian, say something."

"Why me?"

"Because you always know what to say."

Brian cleared his throat and, looking straight to camera, said, "Erm."

"Congratulations, after three," Mark said. "One, two ..."

"CONGRATULATIONS!" they all cried.

They enthused about the wedding, the dress, the reception, the lovely day they'd had, what a lovely couple they were, and sent 'oodles and poodles' of love and best wishes as they all blew kisses. Brian had to be hoisted to his feet by Jim and Mark. Nobody turned the camera off.

Sophie fast-forwarded through the empty sofa part, which was slowly disappearing into darkness. Other people came and went, some turning a light on, some not.

Annie threw herself onto the sofa with a champagne glass and slurred, "Brilliant wedding, madly jealous of your love and happiness, long may it continue. Don't forget about me now you're married, I'm available for dinner parties, nights out, barbecues and christenings. Live long and prosper."

Fi arrived and said, "Tel and Sophie, I love you both to pieces, you make a remarkable couple and I'm very proud to have you as my friends. I hope ... oh, this sofa's quite comfortable, isn't it." She leaned back and rested her head, her eyes flickering. Sally and Harry burst into the room at that moment, waking her up. Fi staggered to her feet, blew a kiss at the camera and disappeared. Sally and Harry took up residence and left their message, which, because they were both drunk, didn't really make much sense.

More people, more messages, mostly about how dark it was, their slurred words a testament to how successful the free bar had been.

"Should we turn on a light?" someone they couldn't see asked.

"I can't find the switch."

"Is this it?"

"Looks more like a mains switch."

"What about these lamps."

"We might break them."

"By turning them on?"

"By knocking them over in the dark, they could be valuable antiques."

"I don't see a camera, are you sure we're in the right place?"

"It's too dark anyway. We sent them a card, that'll be enough."

They left.

Tel and Sophie leaned forward in their seats as the TV screen was lit up by the light from the foyer, and two shadows disappeared into the darkness at the back of the room. Another couple entered.

"Isn't that Michael?" Sophie asked, as they disappeared into the darkness on the other side of the room.

"So it is. Who's that with him?"

"His wife, I assume."

"I don't think that's his wife."

"Oh. Probably shouldn't show this to anyone then."

On the TV screen they heard the door open and close, but nobody sat on the sofa. There were footsteps, followed by giggling.

"I'd know that giggle anywhere," Sophie grinned. "It's Olivia and Mark. At least, I hope it's Mark."

Mark's voice growled, "You gorgeous creature."

"Maybe we shouldn't watch this," Sophie said.

"No, leave it on. I want to see who else is enticed by a dark room."

"If my parents arrive I'm turning it off."

They heard heavy breathing, some sighing, and the occasional gasp.

"It's like a badly produced porn film," Tel laughed

"How would you know?"

"I came across some when I was Googling," he winked.

"What did you Google?"

"*Pawn Stars*, that TV programme."

"A likely story."

A beam of light across the screen drew their attention back. Brian and Faye slumped onto the sofa.

"Oh, I'm definitely not watching this," Sophie cried.

"That's four couples in one dark room!" Tel laughed. "Leave it on, let's see what happens."

They listened to Brian and Faye talking about water pipes and ghosts, and then what appeared to be a clown emerged from the shadows and quickly left the room, followed by a woman, who asked Brian and Faye not to not tell her boss.

"Etta and Charlie the clown!" Sophie cried, "I knew it! I'll be having words with her first thing on Monday morning."

"Oh, don't mention Monday morning!"

Huffing and puffing came from the TV as Brian and Faye sat wide-eyed on the sofa. Bickering, another couple emerged from the darkness and left the room. Now Brian and Faye were talking to someone behind the camera, before the door was opened and closed again. Brian did a bit of yelling, Faye did a bit of arm punching, and then they both fell asleep.

The sound of Brian's snoring took them back to the campsite, to happy times and happy memories. It was rhythmic and comforting, soothing and familiar.

They both drifted off.

Three weeks later

When they got home from the wedding, Brian reversed the caravan onto the driveway and Faye unlocked the door. When she peered inside she cried, "Oh no!"

Brian lumbered over to have a look. The whole blind structure at the front of the caravan had fallen off and was lying, broken, in the middle of the caravan. Mould and soft wood and copious dollops of glue were now exposed around the windows, which seemed about ready to give up and fall out too.

"I think it might be nearing its end-of-life," Faye sighed.

"I think you might be right."

"Really?"

"Yes." He looked at her and held her shoulders. "I think it's time, lass."

"Oh. It'll be sad to see it go. I'll just check what's available on eBay." She hurried into the house, tapping on her phone.

It had taken three weeks of searching, bidding, losing, and watching caravans inexplicably disappear from the listings before, one night, while he was having yet another browse, Brian cried, "Got one!"

Faye hurried over to the computer and peered over his shoulder. "That looks nice."

"Just been listed. Quite close, reasonable price. This could be the one."

"Fingers crossed."

Having emptied their savings accounts and their piggy banks, they went to view it the next day. They liked it, paid for it, took it home and managed to squeeze it onto the driveway next to the old one, which now seemed very small and more than a little scruffy by comparison. They sat in the new one, marvelling and admiring, touching and opening.

"Is this really ours?" Faye kept gasping.

"It's like an upgrade from a damp basement flat to the penthouse," Brian said, staring at the smoothness and uncrackedness of it.

Bursting with excitement, Brian immediately started a WhatsApp video call with the camping gang.

"Look at the size of the cupboards!" he boomed, giving them a tour of the caravan wearing a smile so big all they could see was teeth behind the beard.

They oohed and aahed and said 'lovely' a lot. Sophie, eventually tiring of oohing and aahing as the video tour dragged on and on, leaned away from her office desk and pulled a Thesaurus from a shelf. "Fabulous," she said when Brian showed them the oven. "Lovely. Charming. Delightful. *Gorgeous.*"

Tel, in his office down the corridor, caught on to Sophie's downward glances and brought up the Thesaurus website on his computer. "Splendid," he said, when Brian showed them the bathroom and shower. "Exquisite. Beautiful."

"Charming," Sophie countered.

"Enchanting."

"Magnificent."

"Marvellous!"

They suddenly realised that everyone else had gone quiet.

"Competitive much?" Brian laughed.

"It's lovely, Bri," said Sophie.

"Superb," said Tel.

"Bet that cost you a pretty penny," Jim whistled.

"Several pretty pennies. We're now officially broke, but *look at our caravan!*"

"Bring it to our campsite any time to test it out," Olivia offered.

"We'll give you mates rates," said Mark.

When the video tour finally ended, Mark immediately called everyone back on WhatsApp.

Everyone except for Olivia.

***

After driving around endlessly and eventually finding the

only parking space left in London on a Saturday night, three streets away from his destination, Lucas hurried down the road towards Tel and Sophie's flat. He glanced frequently at his watch. He was going to be late. He was always late and it usually didn't matter, but this was Tel and Sophie's first dinner party as a couple and they were relying on him for moral support. He quickened his pace.

As he turned into their road, half walking and half running, he collided with a man on a bicycle who was cycling on the footpath. As body and bike clashed, Lucas glimpsed the cyclist's face beneath his helmet and squinted; he looked vaguely familiar in his yellow and orange lycra outfit. Behind the cyclist a woman on a bicycle cried, "Are you alright, Paul?"

"Sorry, mate," the cyclist said, "My girlfriend doesn't like riding on the road."

"No problem," Lucas said.

Glancing at the woman, now screeching to a halt in front of him, Lucas squinted and got the same sense of knowing her from somewhere too.

"We should ride on the road, Etta," said the cyclist, manoeuvring his bike off the footpath.

The woman followed and they rode off.

* * *

"You're late," Sophie cried, when she opened the door to him. "You're forgiven."

"Pretty sure I've just seen your temp secretary on a bicycle," he said.

"She's not my temp anymore."

"Oh?"

"I offered her a permanent job as my PA. She's excellent, we just can't invite her to any company events where alcohol is being served, it's written into her contract."

"Lucas, my man!" Tel cried, coming over to shake his hand. "Come and cast an eye over our efforts."

In the living room, next to the window, a table had been set out with shining crystal and the best bone china.

"What do you think?" Sophie asked nervously.

"It's lovely, but it's only set for four people."

"You're our test subject before we move on to important people."

Lucas laughed. "So I'm nobody then?"

"I didn't mean it like that." She stood on tiptoe to kiss his cheek. "I'm just nervous. I've never had to entertain clients at home before, I normally take them out."

"She's cooked," Tel said.

"Oh." There was a prolonged pause. "Has your cooking improved since last time?"

"Let's hope so," Tel said, crossing his fingers.

"Who else is coming?"

"Guess."

Lucas shrugged.

Sophie handed him a glass of wine. "You know that secret you've been keeping since our wedding?" she said.

"No."

"Oh, come on, Lucas, you're a terrible liar."

"No idea what you're talking about, Sophs."

"The 'secret' everyone knows about," said Tel.

Lucas shook his head.

"We know you've been trying to keep it under wraps and failing miserably," Sophie said. "We thought it was time you put us all out of our misery.'"

The doorbell rang. Sophie went to answer it and came back with Annie.

"Oh, hi Lucas," she said, seemingly surprised to see him.

"Hello, Annie, lovely to see you again."

Tel and Sophie burst out laughing. "You know we know, don't you?"

"Know what?" they both said in unison.

"That you two are an item. You're together. You're a couple. We know. *Everybody* knows. It's the worst kept secret in our social circle, you've been spotted literally *everywhere* together."

"I don't know what you're–" Lucas caught Annie's eye, and suddenly they flew towards each other and embraced passionately in the middle of the room.

"Thank goodness for that," Annie gasped, "I couldn't have kept that up all night, it was killing me."

"Me too," he said, lifting her off her feet for another good snog.

"We have buckets of ice-cold water on standby," Sophie said. "Now, come eat, tell me if my cooking is likely to kill any clients."

Four weeks later

"That was lovely," Olivia said, as she and Mark got out of the car and walked towards the Woodsman Pub.

Mark had taken her to lunch in a fancy restaurant in Oxford; "No special reason," he'd said, "Just a treat."

He'd planned to propose, but the 'right time' never seemed to present itself; too many people, too many waiters asking if they were enjoying their food, too much background music, and too much anxiety. Mark could barely swallow his food his mouth was so dry, and his hands shook the entire time. He thought he was ready, had mustered up enough courage, but obviously he wasn't, and hadn't.

"You okay?" Olivia had asked, as he raised a trembling wine glass to his lips.

"I think I might be coming down with something," he said.

"Oh, poor you."

"I'll be fine."

The couple at the next table started indulging in a hissing argument about who did what at home. "I'm not your mother!" the woman snarled, "Why do I always have to tidy up after you?"

"Liv," Mark began.

Olivia raised a finger and leaned an ear towards the hissing couple.

"Do you mind?" snapped the woman, turning to her, "This is a *private* conversation."

"Probably shouldn't do it in public then," Olivia snapped back, and the moment was gone.

By the time the bill came he thought he might be able to do it. He was wrong. Asking the question over an unpaid bill just seemed to be tempting fate. In the car outside it didn't feel like the right setting. He practised the words in his head as he drove home, thinking that if he posed the question now and Olivia said no he might crash the car. Outside the Woodsman Pub seemed like a bit of an anti-climax.

When they walked into the pub Olivia exclaimed, "Gosh, it's quiet in here tonight!" The tables, normally filled with chatty diners, were empty, as were the bar stools. "Has there been a bad review or something?" she asked Melissa behind the bar.

"Not that I'm aware of."

"Why is there nobody here?"

Melissa shrugged, then turned to Mark and raised her eyebrows.

"I'll just check the kitchen," he said, hurrying off.

In the kitchen stood a crowd of silent, restless people. More silent, restless people were waiting at the back of the lounge near the patio doors, crouched down and hidden from sight.

Mark went up to one of them in the kitchen and whispered, "I couldn't do it, Bri."

"You couldn't do it?"

Mark shook his head.

"Why not?"

"Too scared she'd say no."

"She won't say no," Faye said quietly.

"She might."

"Do it now," Tel whispered. "It seems scary, but once you've done the deed you'll feel great, trust me. Just don't lose the ring."

Mark thrust a hand into his jacket pocket. Horror wafted across his face and his jaw fell. He thrust his hand into the other pocket and sighed in relief when he felt the box.

"Have you changed your mind?" Jim whispered.

"No, of course not!"

"Then what are you waiting for, divine intervention?"

"Ooh," Tel said softly, "Listen to you with your fancy words!"

Jim preened and said, "I heard it on the telly."

"Good for you."

"Come on, babes," Beth said to Mark, "It ain't 'ard, it's just four little words. Say the words."

"Will you marry me?" He shook his head again. "I can say it to you, but my throat closes up just thinking about saying it to Liv."

"Do it now, before Dick turns up like the proverbial bad penny," Jim whispered

"Heaven forbid!" Sophie breathed.

"And hurry up about it," hissed Brian, "I'm gasping for a drink."

"You're always gasping for something," Faye said.

"Love and affection, mostly."

Faye prodded him.

Mark rubbed his trembling hands together. "I can do this."

"You can."

"It's just a question," Tel said.

"If she answers no my life is over." Mark slumped on his feet.

Brian put a hand on his shoulder. "You can do this, lad."

"I can."

Brian put his other hand on the other shoulder. "Get out there and make us proud."

"I w-will."

He was suddenly spun around by Brian's giant hands and pushed towards the door. "Get on with it then!"

Mark took one look back at them all, then straightened

himself and strode into the lounge. They all quietly shuffled to the kitchen door, cracked it open an inch, and peered through the gap.

Olivia was seated at the bar, sipping orange juice. "I just can't understand it," she was saying to Melissa. "We normally do a roaring trade on a Friday night."

Mark slid onto a stool next to her. Melissa glared at him with wide, impatient eyes. Mark was about to put his hand on Olivia's, resting on the counter, then saw that his hands were trembling, as were his stomach and all his internal organs. Melissa subtly nodded her head toward Olivia.

"Liv," Mark said.

"Yes, darling? Oh, you're very pale! Are you feeling alright?"

"Y-yes, y-yes, I'm fine. I just wanted to–"

"Get him a glass of water, Mel." Olivia placed a hand on his forehead. "You're a bit warm, perhaps you are coming down with something."

"Will you–?"

Melissa placed a pint of iced water in front of him and he stalled as he gulped at it.

"Come on, lad," Brian breathed from the doorway.

"You can do this," Sophie breathed.

"I need a pee," Tel said, wriggling uncomfortably.

Mark took another gulp. It caught in his throat and he started coughing. Olivia patted him heartily on the back.

"Come *on!*" Tel gasped.

"Better?" Olivia asked.

He nodded. As if sensing the mounting tension coming from the kitchen and the back of the lounge, Mark took a deep breath. Before the words could come out Olivia said, "Maybe you should lie down for a bit."

Mark grabbed her hand. "Olivia."

"Ooh," she giggled, "You sound very firm and formal, are you going to tell me off for something?"

"I love you," he gasped.

"I love you, too." She leaned forward to plant a soft kiss on his mouth.

"Olivia," he said again, and she suddenly looked anxious.

"Are you okay, darling?"

"Come on, lad."

"Hurry up!" hissed Tel, bouncing from one foot to the other.

"Just ask her!"

"Olivia, will you …?"

"Come with you?" she giggled, sliding off the stool. "Of course, darling. It's not like we're busy or anything."

As she stood, Mark crashed down onto one knee, fiddling in his pocket for the box containing the ring. He hoped she'd like it, he'd searched through her jewellery box like a thief trying to figure out what type she preferred.

"Do it, Mark!"

"Say the words!" Beth hissed.

Olivia looked down at Mark with her mouth open. "Have you lost the use of your legs, darling?"

"Now!" Jim hissed, "Do it *now*!"

"W-will you m-marry me?" Mark said, trying to open the box but failing because his fingers were shaking too much. He finally prised the top back with his palm and presented the white gold and diamond ring to her.

Olivia gasped out loud, her hands flying up to her face. Behind the bar, Melissa held her breath, as did the group behind the kitchen door and all the people with dead limbs crouching in the back.

"*Yes!*" Olivia squealed, jumping up and down. "Yes, yes, I'll marry you, of course I'll marry you!"

There was a collective sigh of relief as people poured through the kitchen door and struggled to their feet at the back, including Sue and the good-looking barman. Olivia screamed in surprise as they clapped and cheered, one making a dash for the toilets shouting, "Congratulations!"

Music started playing over the speakers as Mark, still on

his knees, slipped the ring onto her finger. "Do you like it?" he asked.

"It's beautiful, Mark, *beautiful*." She pulled him up and kissed him, then turned to the crowd gathering all around them. "Sophie! Faye!" she cried. "Mum! Where have you all come from?"

"We've been hiding," her mother said, giving her a tight hug.

"For a very long time," said Brian, kissing Olivia's cheek and saying, "Congratulations," before leaning towards Melissa behind the bar and saying, "Pint please, love."

"We've got champagne," she said, nodding at Sue at the end of the counter, who was handing out flutes of champagne.

"None of that frothy, sweet stuff, just a pint."

"Me too," Jim said, sidling up.

"He's paying," Brian said.

"Hey, I've got a family to take care of now!"

"It's all on the house," Mark said, coming over.

"Well done, lad, you got there in the end."

"Hardest thing I've ever had to do."

"Getting married is harder," Sophie said.

"Nothing compared to having a baby," said Beth, rubbing her emerging bulge.

"Gosh, it's getting big, isn't it!"

"Yeah, it's gonna be big-boned, like me."

"It's going to be gorgeous," Tel said, returning to the throng and kissing her cheek, "Just like its mother."

"Hopefully not much like its father," Mark laughed.

"Shut up."

"Do you sing to it every day?" Sophie asked.

"I do," Beth laughed, "Until the neighbours start banging on the wall telling me to turn the radio down." She looked down at her lump. "Having my first scan next week."

"How exciting!"

"Send us pics," Faye said.

"We're gonna do better than that, Jim's gonna do a video

call so you can watch."

"Nothing too gory, is it?" Tel asked.

"It's just a scan, Tel, not the actual birth."

"Oh," Jim said, turning from the bar with his pint, "That's a thought."

"I ain't giving birth in front of a camera, babes."

"How's married life?" Brian asked the glowing couple.

"Fabulous," they both said in unison, grinning broadly.

"Incredible," Sophie said.

"Outstanding," said Tel.

"It matures like a fine wine." Brian hugged Faye against him and she smiled up at him. "Love and a solid sense of humour will get you through most things. And beer."

"To love," Mark said, raising his glass.

"To beer," Jim said.

"To friends," said Sophie.

Behind them, on the back wall, hung the framed black and white photograph Sophie had sent to them all, of them standing on the back patio at the wedding, leaning into one another and laughing. It captured their friendships perfectly.

"Can I have your attention please!" Sue yelled from behind the bar, and everyone quietened down. Sue raised a glass and said, "A toast to the newly engaged couple."

"Hip, hip!" Jim yelled.

The sound of everyone yelling "*HURRAY!*" nearly brought the ceiling down.

"Happy?" Mark asked, snuggling up to Olivia.

"Always," she said, "With you."

"Right," Brian boomed, "Pour out the pints, turn up the music, and let's get this party started!"

Five weeks later

The camera was wobbly but they managed to see Beth, lying on a bed in a hospital room, with a woman in a midwife's uniform moving an object over her tummy.

"And here we have the mother," Jim narrated in a deep

voice, "Lying in repose for her first baby scan."

The camera did a close-up of her face. Beth smiled, then turned her head to the monitor next to the bed. Jim focused on the black-and-white screen.

"Here is the baby, looking all snug and cosy inside mummy."

"Is that…?" Sophie to say, then stopped.

"Ooh," said Faye.

Mark, peering closer at his screen, said, "Isn't there…?"

"Shh," said Olivia.

"I don't see anything," Tel said.

"Just checking baby's heartbeat," said the midwife. "Oh."

"What?" gasped Beth. "Is there anything wrong?"

The midwife smiled as she turned to look at them both. Jim did a quick close-up on her face, then focused back on the black and white screen.

"It is," Sophie gasped.

"I'm very pleased to tell you," said the midwife, "You're expecting twins."

Beth immediately burst into tears of happiness and joy. Everyone watching went, "Ahh."

Jim said, "What?"

"Twins," the midwife repeated. "You're having twins. Congratulations."

"Twins?"

"Buy one, get one free," Beth laughed, staring at the screen in awe.

"Get one free?"

"Two babies, babes."

"Two?"

"There are two little people in there," Brian boomed into his phone.

"No wonder the bump's so big," said Faye.

"Ahh," Sophie cooed, "You can see their little heartbeats."

"I can't make anything out," said Tel.

The camera wavered from side to side, before swinging up

to the ceiling. There was the sound of a heavy body hitting the floor.

"Babes?" Beth cried. "Jim?"

Six weeks later

An email arrived. Tel and Sophie, sat behind their desks, opened them straight away.

Tel immediately raced down the corridor and burst into her office. "Have you read it?"

"Read it and just about to confirm it," she said, picking up the phone.

He sat on the edge of her desk as she spoke. When she eventually put the phone down and just sat looking at him, he said, "Well?"

"It's legit," she grinned. "It all checks out. They said it's an unusual request but not unprecedented. Do you think the others have read it?"

"Have we been inundated with excited phonecalls and text messages?"

"No."

"We should let them know."

He sent a group text: 'Read your emails. WhatsApp video call in ten minutes.'

Faye was the first to appear on Sophie's computer screen. "Is it real?" she shrieked.

"It's real, I've checked."

Faye's mouth dropped open.

"This can't be genuine," Mark said, popping up.

"It is."

"It's real?" Olivia cried from her video box.

"It is."

Faye's face blurred as she started jumping up and down; images of old, startled faces flashed by.

Brian's first words when he appeared were, "Blimey! All expenses paid?"

"That's what it says."

Mark was whooping now. Olivia started giggling. Faye was still jumping up and down.

"*Iain Flemmingway, writer,*" Brian read out.

"That's the man in black from the campsite a couple of years ago, remember?" Mark said. "Creepy guy in a tent who kept scaring the women."

"*Cordially invites you to a screening of the first rushes of the camping film, as yet untitled.*"

"A two-night stopover!" Sophie cried, adding, "We could easily extend that if we make our own arrangements, turn it into a celebratory holiday."

"Oh, it's *so* exciting!" Olivia breathed.

"They finally did it," Tel said, "I didn't think it was ever going to happen."

"I told you, making a film can take *years*."

"I'll need new clothes," said Faye.

"You won't," Brian said.

"I will."

Mark punched the air and cried, "America, here we come!"

OTHER BOOKS BY DEBORAH AUBREY

If you enjoyed this book please leave a rating or, better still, an actual review (I *love* those), on Amazon and/or Goodreads. I thank you.

You might also like my other books:

Pitching Up!: Book 1 in the much-acclaimed Pitching Up! series. A thoroughly entertaining read with a wonderful cast of charismatic characters in caravans in the Cotswolds, who romp from one catastrophe to another. Touching, captivating, and very, very funny.

Pitching Up Again!: Book 2 in the Pitching Up! series. The Woodsman campsite is under new management, with new staff and improved facilities. The old gang, plus some additional characters, return by invitation to 'check it out', and the chaos begins.

Tipping Point: The struggles of marriage, family life and work. It'll make you laugh (a lot). It'll make you cry (a bit). It'll make you go "Ooh" and "Ahh" and "Oh my God!" Emotional drama blitzed with huge dollops of humour. You'll love it.

My Mom's a Witch (writing as Debbie Aubrey): Funny, magical, fantasy fiction for younger readers that's ever so slightly bonkers.

SHORT STUFF

Oobe Doobie Doo: A short story. A man, a suspected heart attack, and a close encounter of the heavenly kind. Unbelievably funny.

How NOT to Kill Your Teenager: A thoroughly tongue-in-cheek approach to surviving the angst and agony of adolescents.

Contact Details

I'd be thrilled to hear from you about anything!
Email: deborahaubrey01@gmail.com
Facebook: AuthorDebbieAubrey

Printed in Great Britain
by Amazon